BOOK OF THE MONTH

D0505276

Months after t... international commu... is still ... its f... ...rs c... ...ined in c... ...ng th... ...undreds of westerners who tr... ...ke ... or marry jihadists – people like Shamima Beg... ...vay from the UK in 2015 and is now awaiting a decision on her fate while living at the al-Hol facility.

On one side of the debate are those who argue these bleak features create a fertile environment for further radicalisation, on the other are the voices warning of more terrorist attacks if she and others like her are allowed to return home.

Army veteran John Carney has been closer to the controversy than most. Beginning in 2016 he launched a series of raids behind enemy lines to extract women who wanted to escape Daesh, the full story of which he tells in this book. It was through his work on the security circuit that he found himself being asked to help by the women's desperate families back home in Europe.

The account of the action unfolds like a Le Carre novel, as co-author Clifford Thurlow brings Carney and a cast of colourful accomplices to life. All of this comes across in gripping style in Operation Jihadi Bride. The issues around foreign jihadists remains highly complex, but the book largely steers clear of politics, opting instead to tell a straightforward story of one man's efforts to help in the only way he knew how, even if his decisions often blurred the lines between bravery and insanity.

It also offers a stark warning - the "Islamic State" may have collapsed as a geographical entity, but its ideas live on in its surviving members.

SOLDIER MAGAZINE
AUGUST 2019

JOHN CARNEY is 42, served six years in the Yorkshire Regiment and did two tours in Northern Ireland. He was a team leader in Iraq with Aegis Defence Services, the multi-million-pound private security firm set up by Colonel Tim Spicer. He has operated a close protection service in Iraq since 2011 and currently organizes deradicalization programmes on the Syrian/Turkish border. To protect his family, the name John Carney is a pseudonym. Names of his family and colleagues have been changed.

CLIFFORD THURLOW has lived all over the world and has worked as a gem stone dealer and a foreign correspondent for the *Observer* in Athens. The winner of the London Arts Board New Millennium Prize for short fiction, he is best known as a ghostwriter. His recent books include: *Making A Killing*, the inside story of a hired gun in Iraq, and *Escape from Baghdad* with Captain James Ashcroft; *Fatwa, Living with a Death Threat*, for Jacky Trevane, and *Today I'm Alice* for Alice Jamieson.

OPERATION
JIHADI BRIDE

OPERATION
JIHADI BRIDE

MY COVERT MISSION TO RESCUE
YOUNG WOMEN FROM ISIS

JOHN CARNEY
with CLIFFORD THURLOW

monoray

An Hachette UK Company
www.hachette.co.uk

First published in Great Britain in 2019 by Monoray, an imprint of
Octopus Publishing Group Ltd
Carmelite House, 50 Victoria Embankment, London EC4Y 0DZ
www.octopusbooks.co.uk

This edition published in 2020

Distributed in the US by Hachette Book Group
1290 Avenue of the Americas 4th and 5th Floors
New York, NY 10104

Distributed in Canada by Canadian Manda Group
664 Annette St. Toronto, Ontario, Canada M6S 2C8

ISBN 978-1-913-18305-9

A CIP catalogue record for this book is available from the British Library.
Printed and bound in the UK.
10 9 8 7 6 5 4 3 2 1

AUTHOR NOTE

The vast majority of names and physical descriptions of individuals have been changed in order to protect the identities of people often in extreme and life-endangering situations. Exact descriptions of many of the locations featured have also been altered for the same reasons.

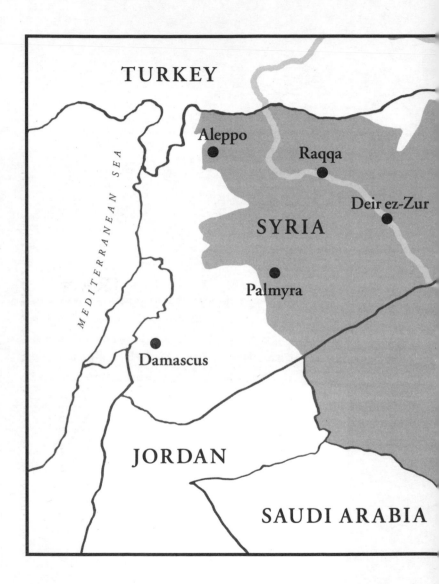

If goods don't cross borders, armies will.
—Frederic Bastiat

The man who never alters his opinions is like standing water,
and breeds reptiles of the mind.
—William Blake

Trust in Allah and tether your camel.
—Arab proverb

Preface

Shamima Begum was 15 years old when she left her London home in March 2015 to travel to Syria. Within a few weeks, she became the jihadi bride of a Dutch convert to Islam. They had two children. Both died. One of her babies from malnutrition.

She came to public attention again in February 2019 after fleeing from the Islamic Caliphate's last stronghold in Baghuz. She was eight months pregnant. From a tent in the al-Roj refugee camp, she appealed through British newspapers to be allowed to return to England to have her baby. She showed no remorse for having run away to join ISIS.

In response, Home Secretary Sajid Javid revoked her British citizenship. He argued that she was the responsibility of Bangladesh, the birthplace of her parents. Geoffrey Robertson QC, a former United Nations judge, told the BBC that the United Kingdom was duty-bound to bring Shamima home and face charges of aiding terrorism. It was up to a judge – not a politician – to decide whether she deserved mercy or a prison term of up to ten years.

Shamima Begum, now aged 19, gave birth in mid-February. She

named her little boy Jarrah. He was three weeks old when he died of breathing difficulties on 8 March. He was buried with two other children who had perished in a fire at the camp.

Even before the horror show of jihadi barbarism entered our living rooms on the evening news, disenchanted girls who had travelled to the Caliphate to marry jihadi killers were begging their families in Europe to bring them home. Many, perhaps the majority, knew they had made a mistake on the very day they arrived.

John Carney, a British ex-soldier with a close protection (CP) business in Iraq, was contacted through the security network in June 2016 with a request to smuggle a woman and her two children across the minefields surrounding the Caliphate to the safety of Kurdistan.

Against his better judgement, the assignment Carney took on became an unrelenting mission that continued for the next two years. With three Kurds, ex-soldiers like himself, he led perilous raids behind enemy lines to save the lives of hundreds of women and children: British, European, Syrian and Iraqi.

I was introduced to John Carney by a contact who said he had a unique story to tell. We met in a pub. We had sandwiches. John ordered a pint of cider and studied me across the table. He is a big man, modest to the core, with the soft voice of those who have seen the butchery and carnage of terrorism close up. Prodded by my questions, he talked about his role in the struggle against ISIS and it struck me that John Carney is a remarkably brave individual, a born soldier with a big heart bursting from his chest.

Are the young women who went to join ISIS and now have children of their own naïve girls who deserve a second chance? Or terrorists who should be locked up? This is the moral crisis facing Europe and the entire western world. Carney's response was to put the politics to one side and act. As he said that day over our second round of drinks, every jihadi bride who wants to come home is proof that Islamic State is a failure.

John Carney's story is moving, personable, heroic, an adrenaline-fuelled account of front-line combat against the death cult of Islamic State, the most terrifying army of modern times – a fallen army he predicts will rise again.

Clifford Thurlow
London, March 2019

CHAPTER 1
Rebel Bride

It was a perfect day on the Med, sea calm as a mirror. I could hear the kick and slap of flippers as my daughter dived down to the seabed to search for shells. Two fishing lines stretched from the back of the boat and the music played softly, eighties new wave, my wife's choice. Kali was wearing a white bathing costume and a straw hat. Her bare feet tapped along to the music.

I snapped open a can of Mythos. This is what life's all about. This is what I've worked for.

That's what I was thinking when the phone rang.

'Is that John Carney?' Male, hesitant, non-English.

'Who's asking?'

'I was given your number by Matthew Lambert,' he replied, and my ears pricked up. 'There's a girl stuck in Mosul, a jihadi bride. He reckons you'd be able to get her out.'

'From Mosul? You having a laugh?'

'It's desperate, Mr Carney. They're being bombed for one thing, and she's being beaten every day by her husband…'

'The military can't get into Mosul. I certainly can't…'

'It's a matter of life and death…'

'For about two million people.'

'I'm only concerned with this one. Her name's Laura…'

'I'm sorry, mate. I can't help you…'

The line went dead. It happens with satellite phones, especially on the water.

'Everything all right?' Kali asked, sitting up, and I nodded.

'Just some chancer. Nothing's going to come of it.'

A nervous look had entered her brown eyes. She knew what I did for a living, I'd been doing it long enough, but hearing the word 'Mosul' had put her on edge. It was June 2016, two years after Abu Bakr al-Baghdadi had stepped into the pulpit of the Great Mosque of al-Nuri in Mosul to deliver a Ramadan sermon declaring himself the new Caliph. The jihadis had by then overrun vast stretches of Iraq and Syria, planting their black flags over the Islamic State and bringing beheadings to the evening news.

It seemed unlikely that anything was going to come of the call, except the contact was Matt Lambert, a Brit I had never met, but was considered reliable. On the security circuit in the Middle East, reputation is everything. If you don't know someone, they're probably not worth knowing.

I took a swig from the can of Mythos. I had grown to like Greek beer. It was one of the perks, but it wasn't why I had chosen to make Crete my base. I had spent more than a decade working in and out of Iraq, and Baghdad as the crow flies is close without being too close. Ntileini surfaced with a cone-shaped shell. My daughter was 12 and in serious danger of turning into a fish. She handed me the shell, took a deep breath and I watched as she dived again.

A breeze had blown up. Clouds drifted along the horizon. The man who'd called was frightened. Genuine. Sure it was a matter of life and death. Every day in the territories held by ISIS was a matter of life and death. The jihadis caned women's feet if they saw a glimpse of their faces and stoned girls to death if they were caught with a mobile phone. The Islamists had turned Iraq into a wasteland.

I had first arrived in Baghdad in 2003 after the overthrow of Saddam Hussein and blagged my way into a job as a bodyguard with CRG Security Solutions. I was 28 years old, a hard bastard with a lack of self-confidence and a chip on my shoulder. I was the bloke at the bar who asks: Are you looking at me? And when there was no action, I would stand on street corners taking on all-comers – something I wouldn't advise on the streets of Doncaster. I was a fighting machine. From the age of eight, when my dad broke my front teeth with a back-hander, I had spent my entire life fighting myself.

After two years with CRG and some leave in the land of the living dead – Wiltshire – I returned to Iraq as a PSD (Protective Services Detail) with Aegis Defence Services, the controversial outfit run by Tim Spicer, a veteran of South Armagh like myself. I had never taken to military discipline, but six years in the Yorkshire Regiment had taught me everything I knew, and the moment I landed back at the shell-pocked airport in Baghdad, it felt as if I had arrived home.

When Aegis made me a team leader, it seemed incredible at first. Then it felt as if destiny was at work. I had always thought deep down that you could do and be anything you wanted. In a sand-coloured shirt and cargo pants, with Ray-Bans and a 9mm Glock in a thigh rig, I was in my own skin. Once I was given responsibility for the lives of others, I stopped looking for slights and started to get the best out of people. In private security, there are no ranks. You climb the pay scale, not by who you know, but by what you can do. It was an opportunity for ordinary squaddies to make a name for themselves and bank what they were worth – up to a $1,000 a day in the good times.

There is a misconception that military contractors are violent misfits who swagger about with a cocked machine gun and bandoleers of shells across their tattooed chests. For the cameras, maybe. In reality, the work requires patience, sensitivity and knowledge of the local culture. You drag a man from a car in front of his family at a road block and spreadeagle him in the dust for a body search, and you've just scored a new recruit for jihad.

In the Green Zone one day, I was lining up with my team at a pizza bar set up in one of Saddam's old palaces. I heard marching boots in the corridor and a swarm of Americans from the Private Military Company Blackwater appeared. I was just about to order my pepperoni with black olives when a guy, broad as a boat with a red bandana, barged in front of me.

'Shift your ass, buddy, captain on deck.'

He stared into my eyes. I stared back. This is how it starts. Your ego kicks in and you let fly. We had just escorted an American general down the BIAP – the Baghdad International Airport Highway, also known as Route Irish – a nerve-jangling experience with civilian vehicles changing lanes at speed, often on the wrong side of the road. I was thirsty, hungry, and it was my turn to order. I so wanted to floor Johnny Rambo in front of his squad, and I think this was the first time in my life that I backed down.

'You want to go next?' I said.

'Damn right.' He glanced back at an older man in civvies. 'After you, sir, best pizza outside Chicago.'

The entire entourage followed while I took slow breaths through my nose. To use an apposite phrase, this was a Road to Damascus moment. I saw the light. I was taking to my new role as a team leader like an F-35 taking off from the tarmac. I had picked up some Arabic and had started to feel an affection for Iraq and its people.

After her successful day harvesting the seabed, Ntileini wanted to guide us back into port. The boat was a 31ft Sealine power cruiser with two big diesel engines, a lot of oomph for a 12-year-old, but she had learned how to handle it and I made an effort not to interfere.

I wanted my daughter to have the emotional support I'd never had. I ended up spending a year in reform school. Ntileini was at private school, where courtesy and confidence came naturally, and she had developed a firm sense of self. I was learning from her. Kali and I agreed on most things concerning our daughter. We only disagreed if she thought I was taking needless risks when my business was at a stage when it was no longer necessary.

After climbing the greasy pole at Aegis, I looked at myself in the mirror as I shaved every morning and said: John Boy, you're not such a wanker after all. I had stopped clenching my fist except to hold a pen and my main concern was the lip of fat that had slipped over my belt. I had learned the security game from the bottom up, from boots on the ground to my arse in a chair.

American forces began to stand down in 2011 and executives from the oil companies began to arrive big time. Was the second war in Iraq about finding Saddam's WMD – weapons of mass destruction – or the usual cause behind conflict: economics? It didn't matter to me. The troop withdrawal left a gap in the security market and I opened shop providing CP, close protection, for the new breed of adventurers and entrepreneurs. With more luck than ability, in 12 months I had a turnover of £1 million with 100 expats and local Iraqis on the books.

Now I had some money for the first time in my life, I bought a pink villa on the edge of a conservation area outside Heraklion. It had three floors, a flat roof, a view across open country to the sea and an orchard of oranges, lemons, olives and avocados with the strangely magical taste that comes from fruit you pick from your own trees. The dogs patrolled the chain-link fence and every stray cat in Crete found its way into our compound.

It was a 20-minute drive from the port to the villa. As the building came into view, the lowering sun turned the plaster the colour of red coral and my heart beat faster. It was a reminder of how lucky we were and how perilous life was for people in Iraq and Syria.

Ntileini opened the gates. I drove in slowly, parked under the bamboo shade and stepped out into a welcoming committee, about 20 cats meowing and chasing their tails. They seemed pleased to see us and I was always pleased to see them. Animals are good for the spirit and the cats did a good job keeping the rodent population under control.

Several times I had been outside having breakfast – a bowl of fresh fruit with yoghurt – and my wife and daughter had run off screaming as Nikko, the big tabby, strolled up with a three-foot snake in his mouth, head bitten off, the wriggling remains between his teeth. Nikko was a fighter with a scarred right eye. He reminded me of me, but I don't think Nikko had seen the light.

I went straight upstairs to the office. A barrel-load of emails pinged into the inbox when I opened the laptop. Inevitably, there was a message from the man who had called on the satphone. The girl he wanted me to rescue was named Laura Angela Hansen, aged 21, from Holland. She had married a Palestinian with Dutch papers she'd met on a Muslim dating site. They had left Amsterdam the previous year, in September 2015, and travelled through Turkey and Syria to get to Iraq. Laura wanted out and was bringing her two children aged four and one with her.

…Please, Mr Carney, they have no one else to turn to. This young mother and her children will die unless you help them…

I thought he'd told me he wanted to bring out one person. Now it was a package.

It was a joke. It was impossible. It couldn't be done. ISIS didn't arrest *kaffirs* – white faces, infidels. They cut off their heads. I sat back and stared at the big map of Iraq on the wall. Turkey shared 500 miles of frontier with the Caliphate and people-smugglers were making fortunes worming their human cargo through the leaky border. If you could get people in, there was some logic in the notion that you could get them out again.

Eight million people lived in the Islamic State, two million in Mosul. It was a stronghold of tunnels and narrow streets where the Assyrian masons had laid the first mud bricks 2,000 years before Christ. The Coalition bombing campaign had turned the city to rubble, but land forces had been unable to penetrate its defences.

My palms had become clammy. Fuck it, I said. Impossible.

On the desk was a photograph of Ntileini in her school uniform holding the certificate for her bronze Duke of Edinburgh Award. I picked up the frame and looked at my daughter. Kali and Natty were my life. I didn't start out with ambitions. I didn't know what I wanted. But I knew what I had. There was going to be a lot of slaughtered jihadi brides, a lot of dead children. You do what you can, but you can't save the world. I glanced back at the map and shook my head. No. No way. Not interested. No can do.

That's what was running through my mind and that was how I intended to respond to the email. I reached for the laptop. I pressed reply and as my big fingers tapped away on the tiny keys, I could barely believe that what came out was a delaying strategy, a request for further information and how this proposed task was going to be financed.

I hit send, then searched in my contact book for Matt Lambert. I left a message on his service, flicked through the pages and stopped at the name Hassan Ghazi, a Kurd as reliable as the sun shining on the desert, hard as nails with piercing grey eyes and a warrior moustache like Genghis Khan. I had no intention of trying to get into Mosul. That would have been suicide. I didn't call Hassan. But the puzzle was intriguing and I had started to put the pieces together in my head. I was about to go down to the kitchen and grab another Mythos when the phone rang. It was Matt Lambert.

'John, I got your call. You must have heard from the Dutch family?'

'I did, mate. They want me to pop into Mosul and grab a girl and her kids when no one's looking.'

'Impossible, I imagine?'

'You said it.'

'It came up through some people I know. I thought I'd pass it on.'

'I appreciate it.'

'This is the first girl who wants to get out, as far as I know. There's going to be a lot more.'

'They were bloody idiots for going in the first place.'

'Their families are aware of that, John.' He paused. 'Laura's people have raised ten thousand dollars to bring her home.'

'Ten thousand dollars,' I repeated, and laughed. 'Put another zero on that and they might get some mad bugger to do it.'

'They're modest people. They'll never find that kind of money.'

I thought for a moment. 'So, what's in it for you?'

'I know you've got the contacts. There's not much chance, I know. The least I could do was put you in the picture.'

'Who's your contact in Holland, if that's not classified?'

'Thomas Kuntze. He's a German academic. Works with the Muslim community, integration, that sort of thing. A decent chap.'

He sounded sincere. The bastard. I was being drawn in. I took a breath through my teeth.

'So, this is the deal. These people want some nutter to plan, prepare and organise an escape from the most dangerous place in the world and they're putting ten thousand dollars on the table?'

'Like I said, John, I just wanted to put you in the picture.'

'I'll tell you what I'm going to do. I'm going to make one phone call.'

'That's good of you. I don't want to give you any hassle.'

'What's life without a bit of hassle?'

As we clicked off, an email pinged with an attachment.

It was a reply from Holland containing two images, a girl with big dark eyes who looked about 16, and two children standing in a cot, a small boy and a lively little girl with lots of curly dark hair and the biggest smile I had ever seen. She looked like Ntileini when she was that age.

The German doing the liaison confirmed that they had $10,000 that would be made available to a middleman in Erbil, the capital of Iraqi Kurdistan. The families of jihadi recruits in Europe were being monitored and could not make regular money transfers – it would be considered as aiding terrorists. They used instead what's called the Arab bank – which is not a bank, but a system of trust among the *ummah*, fellow Muslims. How it works is that the family in Europe would give the cash to a cousin or close friend of the middleman in Iraq, who would in turn produce the equivalent sum or provide the necessary kit or service. The Arab bank was convenient to avoid taxes, buy property and finance holy war – jihad.

Everything was moving quickly. It usually does, and you get whirled along in the slipstream.

My address book was still open. I made the call I'd promised and Hassan gave a sinister laugh when I told him I wanted to get a girl and two children out of Mosul.

'Mosul is an ants' nest. You go in there and poke it with a stick and the whole Middle East could explode.' I heard a hiss as he sucked breath through his teeth. 'It is impossible, my friend.'

'Nothing's impossible.'

He laughed again and I pictured him rubbing his thumb and first finger together. 'You are becoming more Arab than the Arabs,' he said, and paused, a reminder that he was a Kurd. 'There is no help for these people. You know what your governments say? Leave them there. Let them die.'

'Yeah, but you don't believe that.'

'What I believe is of no matter.' Again a long pause. 'John, you are a very funny fellow. I always say that.'

'I'm going to send you some pictures…'

'Never mind pictures. You find a way to get the family to the border, I will find a way to bring them across.'

'You're a bloody star, you know that? What are we looking at?'

'One vehicle, renting a house, some equipment…fifteen hundred dollars.'

That was cheap. He knew that. I knew that. I'd done him favours. Kurds have long memories.

'I'll be in touch. Thanks, mate.'

'You are welcome, *mate*.'

I stood. The sun was going down over the sea and a pale silvery stripe lit the horizon. Hassan spoke good English, a bit old-fashioned. I wasn't *a funny fellow*. I was a bloody idiot. There was no way I could get into Mosul. I was six inches taller than most Iraqis, with pale skin that turned pink after ten minutes in the sun. My family came originally from Donegal, though I grew up in Warminster, and the only thing I knew about Ireland was patrolling the streets of Crossmaglen with an assault rifle under a sign that read: 'Snipers At Work'.

When you love someone and they love you, they read you like a book. They know your body language. They note your silences. They look into your eyes and see into your heart. Before Kali, my life had been aimless. She had given me direction as well as focus. After dinner, when Ntileini had left to go to her room, Kali stretched her arms across the table and we joined fingers.

'Don't go to Mosul, John.'

'I'm not, darling, no way.'

'Remember your promise.'

'I'll never lie to you, Kali. I'm not lying to you now.' I stood. 'I want to show you something.'

I took her hand as we climbed the stairs to my office. I brought the images of Laura and her children up on the computer screen.

'There are bombs falling on their heads and the mother's getting beaten up by her so-called husband.'

Tears welled into her eyes. 'You've got a daughter as well. You've got us to worry about.'

'I'm not going to Mosul. The family's got ten grand to get them out. I'm going to make a few calls, that's all. Get the girl and her kids down to the border. Safe as houses.'

She stared back into my eyes. 'Don't do anything stupid.'

'What, me?' I replied, and there was laughter in her tears.

'You're just a big softie,' she said, and I held her tight as she laid her head against my shoulder.

It was game on. The German handed over 10K and I was informed that the funds would be released to me by the middleman. I was given the name Zabeer, an address in Erbil, a phone number and the code word INGLISCHE.

I spent three days emailing and phoning everyone I knew in Mosul. Matt Lambert and Hassan Ghazi did the same. Calls came back at all hours, when I was in the supermarket, waiting in the car outside my daughter's school – the flood of girls spilling out at two o'clock a reminder, if it were needed, that we were playing for the lives of two little kids and their idiot of a mother.

The ten years I had spent networking had produced an extensive web of contacts: drivers, linguists, politicians, border guards, sheikhs, Iraqi staff in foreign embassies. Everyone is for sale and nothing is done in Iraq without baksheesh, a backhander. To pass an exam you pay the examiner. To post a package you tip the mailman. It is how it works, and understanding the intricacies of the bribe culture was crucial if you wanted to stay alive.

Islamic State ruled with a bloody fist, but there were a lot of people who had welcomed the sense of order the Islamists had brought when they first arrived, only to grow horrified by their perverse reading of the Quran. Women vanished from the streets. Men got 80 lashes if they were caught drinking a beer. I had seen footage of school teachers and doctors being crucified by jihadis draped in black and wearing gold death masks.

Journalists I had escorted around Iraq wrote about the Caliphate as being backward and the European-born recruits as ill-educated psychopaths from disaffected communities. What they failed to grasp was that ISIS is a death cult literally craving its own annihilation. The followers believe in a prophecy from the *hadiths*, or sayings, attributed to the Prophet that when Muslims across the world suffer injustice, first the apocalypse will come, then a Messiah will appear to usher in an Islamic utopia. Whether Muslims had faith in the prophecy or not, it is a lucid analysis of the scriptures and explains why those who felt oppressed or alienated were charging headlong into the abyss. Western intervention in Afghanistan and Iraq, torture, rendition and Guantánamo were all fuel to the flame of holy war.

It was useful having some context, not that it helped trace Laura. After dozens of calls that led nowhere, it occurred to me that finding one fully veiled girl in a teeming city of bombed houses and identically covered girls was impossible. Luckily, Laura must have reached the same conclusion. On the fourth day of our search, she made a 30-second phone call to her father and told him exactly where she was.

There was no mystery as to how she had managed to get her hands on a mobile phone. Laura's husband had clearly had his fill of life in paradise and was fleeing with her.

This changed everything. Rescuing Laura from ISIS could result in legal complications – MI6 was aware of my activities; one operative often called me for intel – but at least in saving babies I would have one foot on the moral high ground. Not so extracting the Palestinian. He was an enemy of the state and my role in getting him out would be a clear case of facilitating terrorism.

When Laura's location came through with a photo of her husband, I had a better idea why, on a grey day in rainy Amsterdam, she had fallen for him. He was a latter-day Che Guevara with a straggly beard and a dreamy look in his dark eyes. Bringing him out was a complication we didn't need, but there was some consolation in the upside. Now he had joined the escape, we wouldn't have to find and pay for a driver.

Earlier in the day, Kali had taken a long look over the tops of her eyes as I heaved several six-packs of Mythos into the supermarket trolley. She didn't say anything, but I knew that look and felt guilty as I went to get another beer. I returned to the office, can in hand, and looked again at the picture of the two little kids in the cot. The girl with the curly hair had so much life in her face, how could I leave her in Mosul among those maniacs? Get them out first, worry about the law later, I said to myself.

I had done everything I could do from my desk in Crete and booked a flight to Erbil, leaving later that same day. I then Skyped Hassan to arrange a pick-up.

*

Customs waved me through at Erbil airport, a lucky call seeing how I carried a webbing holster in my luggage. You can get any weapon you want in Iraq – they sell old AK-47s at the market alongside lettuces and bags of onions – but a snug sheath for a 9mm is hard to find.

The immigration officer opened my passport, looked at my head shot, then back at me.

'What is the purpose of your visit?'

'Pleasure,' I said.

He nodded his head as he glanced through the glass partition at Hassan, unmissable in his red and white checked *shemagh*, shades and impressive facial hair. He then stamped my passport. Was I expected? Had everything been arranged? I had no idea, but everyone in Erbil seemed to be related and every Kurd was linked by a common cause: the dream of an independent Kurdistan.

Hassan turned as I exited immigration and I followed him out to a white Toyota Land Cruiser. The driver fired the engine. I stepped into the front passenger seat. Hassan sat in the rear looking out of the back window as we pulled away.

As soon as we were on the open road, Hassan asked after my family. I did the same. All was well. We were lucky men. Praise be to Allah. The driver was Hassan's nephew, Elind. It means dawn, he said. Elind grinned, teeth as shiny as the automobile. He was young and fit, muscles bursting from a black T-shirt with a Rolling Stones tongue on the front. He loved his music and bobbed up and down to the ouds and tablas pouring from the speakers.

I gave Elind the address as we hit the ring road and followed the signs to Ankawa, an upmarket suburb north of the city where the spires of Christian churches rose into the sky alongside the domes and minarets of the mosques.

While Hassan fingered his amber prayer beads, I telephoned Zabeer, the middleman holding the money. The German had scanned my photograph to him and had confirmed before I left Heraklion that Zabeer expected to hand the $10,000 in Iraqi dinars to me that day.

The line was dead. I tried again. Nothing. Even the clacking behind me had stopped.

'We are nearly there,' Hassan said.

I tried calling Zabeer again, several times, and all I got was the dead tone of disconnection. I stared out the window at the mountains rising in jagged slopes. We followed the GPS along a wide sweeping road lined with mature trees and pulled up at a villa with bougainvillea climbing the walls. I hit recall for Zabeer one last time. No reply. I didn't expect one.

We debussed and spread out as we approached the building. Weeds seeped from under the high gates. We scaled the wall. The windows were shuttered. The garden was overrun and hummed with insects. There was nobody home. Nobody had been home for a long time. It could have been an address pulled from a hat as far as I knew. The German had been conned and I had blundered on, forgetting the cardinal rule in the Middle East: only trust the people you know personally.

Elind lit a cigarette. 'No one here,' he said.

'I can see that, mate.'

Hassan picked a bloom from a pink tiger lily and stuck it behind his ear, a gesture that was enchanting and absurd. There were a lot of bad people in Iraq. I was lucky to know some of the good ones.

Now what?

I glanced up at the western hills. If you took the back roads and put your foot down, you'd hit Mosul in two hours. Was I going to leave Laura and her kids there to die? The girl had made a mistake. Everyone deserves a second chance. The wheels were in motion. Promises had been made. I would just have to suck it up and finance the escape myself.

CHAPTER 2
Bonding

I woke in a rusty metal-frame bed on a sunken mattress with a pain behind my eyes and drums pounding in my head. A chute of dazzling light pierced the barred window and I was already sweating.

It was a few moments before I remembered that I was in a safe house in Erbil.

I'd been screwed.

I swung my feet to the floor and stood up slowly like Lazarus rising from the dead. The room smelled of dust and dead insects. The solitary, high-set window needed glass and the walls were mottled with water stains. I glanced at my watch and couldn't see the time.

'Never again,' I said. Of course, I'd said that before.

After failing to collect the money to finance the op, I had decided it was better to cover our arses and go first class rather than economy. I didn't get the 10K so, fuck it, I thought, I'll seek out every ATM in the city and spend whatever it costs. There was a girl and two children out there. If I didn't bring them in, I'd never be able to live with myself.

I had asked Hassan to find two more men. He made a few calls and, later that evening, we'd met up with Dozan and Cano Ali in a *kafenion* in the old town. A folk band played the same jangly music that had accompanied our journey to Ankawa and Elind sat opposite me snapping his fingers.

'You like this music, do you?' I asked, and he punched the air.

'I love it,' he replied. 'You like?'

'Well, it's not Fleetwood Mac, is it?'

Cano lit a fag from the dog end of the one he was smoking. I studied the grainy black and white photographs on the green-tiled walls – scenes of Erbil in the 1950s. Every table was occupied, mainly by men, but with a smattering of women with their faces uncovered and the confidence to look you in the eye. As I glanced around, it occurred to me that it must have been hard for the police to write up descriptions of suspects. Every man at the long trestle tables was swarthy, with wide shoulders, watchful dark eyes and moustaches like beloved pets they were fond of stroking.

Dozan Rostami was a former pilot who had trained with the Royal Air Force and spoke English with the clipped accent of old war movies. He had lived well under Saddam. Like many Sunni officers, he had lost everything when the Shias came to power in Baghdad. Cano Ali was a big bull of a man with a shiny bald head and a smile that could light up a room. These guys were as solid as blocks of granite, I expected no less from Hassan, and could put the drink away like there was no tomorrow, a sad reality for the people in Mosul.

The music droned on, every tune the same as the last one. A girl in red with a gold chainmail waistcoat appeared with a tray containing plates of *dolma*, vegetables wrapped in vine leaves, lamb baked in tomato and yogurt sauce, yellow rice and crispy naan, flatbreads good for wiping the bowls clean. It was similar to Greek food, but Erbil is 1,000 miles east of Athens and the dishes were more spicy.

Hassan poured shots of arak, a clear, aniseed-flavoured liquid that turns cloudy when you add water.

'The milk of lions,' he boomed, slapping the table.

We threw back the fiery liquid and refilled the glasses. Arak doesn't taste like milk, it doesn't even look like milk, but it made us roar like lions as we drank toasts to each other, our families and the Queen – for some reason, Kurds love the royal family. Finally, Cano added double hits to our glasses and tears came to his eyes as we drank to independence.

Everyone in the café stood for the toast. They raised clenched fists and the band broke into 'Loy Loy Kurdistan', a popular song belted out on ouds, tablas and a zurna, the whining wind instrument that tempts cobras from baskets and hums in your head like a dentist drill the following day.

In a way, every Kurd was a freedom fighter and, unlike in the rest of Iraq, or the rest of the Middle East, the fact that women were treated as equals here had created a society more at ease with itself. The Peshmerga – the army – had female regiments with 10,000 volunteers on the frontline. It was said the jihadis were terrified fighting girls because death at their hands meant there would be no place for them in heaven.

Twenty million Kurds live in an area that spans south-east Turkey, north-west Iran, and northern regions of Syria and Iraq. Their dream of a free Kurdistan is resisted by those countries and the closest they have come to their own state is the autonomous region of Iraq – with Erbil the capital and the Peshmerga an independent military – that had, to my mind, done more to combat Islamic State than any player in the conflict.

*

It was the day after the night before. I took a shower in cold water that dribbled out from a cistern fed by a hand pump. I drank eight cups of strong bitter coffee. Cano Ali chain smoked and Dozan twirled one side of his handlebar moustache as he jabbered into a mobile phone. He stabbed the off key and threw up his arms.

'Women,' he said, without explaining. We'd all been there.

Hassan appeared. I slipped on my Ray-Bans and we followed him out into a courtyard with a row of dusty palm trees and two Toyotas parked behind tall metal gates. Hassan had rented the house at 'mate's prices', $25 a night. The building was boxy, with small windows and grey walls criss-crossed with cracks. It was tucked away in the back streets and had everything we needed except fast Wi-Fi, vital in modern warfare. Elind stayed behind to wait for the internet guy. When everything was up and running, he'd be going back to college, his part in the mission over. He closed the gates behind us and we set off in one vehicle on a shopping trip.

Between knocking back shots of arak at dinner, we had chatted about the operation and reached a decision regarding Laura's husband. To avoid legal complications, if we managed to grab him, we would hand him straight to the Kurdish border officials. If we were able to separate him from Laura and the children, our plan was to take them to the safe house. This would serve two purposes: to acquire intel, but also to assure Laura before escorting her to the authorities that whatever she had to face, there were people on her side. She was the first jihadi bride trying to escape from ISIS and, as yet, we had no idea if she was going to be treated as a terrorist or a victim of terrorism.

Missions are like jigsaw puzzles. This one had so many missing parts there was no clear picture. Self-financing the show was the least of my worries. I didn't like to admit it, but I was superstitious. I saw the

German's mishandling of the cash as a sign: when things go wrong, they don't get better – they tend to get worse. My part was a balancing act along the high wire of international law – a Brit in Kurdistan with dubious authorization trying to bring a Dutch girl back to Europe. There were no precedents, no agreements, no protocols.

I was no stranger to bending the rules; it is the nature of security work. But attitudes had hardened. Six months before, on Friday 13 November 2015, ISIS-inspired terrorists had killed 130 people at the Bataclan concert hall, the Stade de France and on the streets of Paris. If I was suspected of facilitating terrorism, they'd lock me up and throw away the key.

Dozan, the pilot, was at the wheel. He turned right out of the compound and we bounced over a rutted track with loops of overhanging cables, evading the mangy dogs I would have fed if there were more time. I gazed out at the waking day unsure if the haze belonged to the city or my morning hangover. I sent a text to Kali: *All OK. Kisses.* We had a rule when I was away. She didn't text or call me, but I checked in regularly.

Yellow taxis buzzed in and out of the traffic stream. Old men in baggy trousers stood on street corners chatting as they ran prayer beads through their fingers. It's called *komboloi* in Greece, where the custom is dying out. Not so among the Kurds, where conversation is regularly punctuated by the clacking of beads.

Glass and marble high-rises were shooting up like new teeth among the ruins of adobe houses, and there were new mansions built by rich Kurds who had made money abroad and returned to invest in their homeland. Unlike Baghdad, or any large town in Iraq, I didn't see policemen in body armour or security guards cradling assault rifles. There was an air of optimism and, for all its noise and chaos, Erbil was the calm heart of the Iraqi tempest.

The traffic clogged up as we skirted the Citadel, a towering jumble of ancient towers and turrets that look down from a steep-sided hilltop. It is a World Heritage site, apparently inhabited for the last 7,000 years, the longest continuously occupied settlement on the planet. I had always meant to climb the hill to visit but had never found the time.

We reached the Qaysari Bazaar, on the south side of the Citadel. Girls in short skirts from Mango wandered alongside by side with women head to toe in black niqabs. I saw tribal chiefs in intricate turbans and lads in skinny jeans and T-shirts. It wasn't so different from many English cities, except for the donkey carts clattering along among the polished BMWs with tinted windows. Honking and leaning out of the car to wave his fist, the pilot snaked through the pedestrians and halted in a narrow lane beside a store displaying the sort of muskets and bolt-action rifles you might find in a museum.

A bell tinkled as if we were entering an old strawberries-and-cream tea shop in Cornwall, although, once inside, my eyes popped as I gazed upon shelf after shelf of modern, sophisticated weaponry. The owner took Hassan in an embrace and kissed his cheeks. You never see a man kiss a woman in the Middle East, but men do show affection to each other. He did the same with Dozan and Cano, then shook my hand.

There was no question of talking business. We removed our boots and sat cross-legged on low leather stools around a red and green carpet. A boy of about ten in a white *dishdasha* brought a plate of baklava and served chai in glasses that burned your fingertips. There were two rules for these occasions: never stretch out your legs towards another person, and don't use your left hand to put food in your mouth.

They lit cigarettes and stroked their moustaches. Everyone's family was well. Praise be to Allah. Aras, the shopkeeper, had twin daughters who were about to get married in a joint ceremony. It was going to cost him every penny he had and he looked to the heavens to thank Allah for the recent upsurge in trade.

'I love my daughters. What can I do?' he asked hopelessly.

Cano held up four fingers. 'Four!' he exclaimed. 'I have four. Now they want to go to university.'

'You must have a clever wife to have such clever daughters,' Hassan said, and we laughed.

'Pity the man cursed with a clever wife,' Dozan said seriously, and Hassan took a grip on his shoulder.

'Only if she is cleverer than you,' he remarked.

They laughed again and I thought, it's the same the world over: put five blokes together and, if it's not football, they'll be talking about their wives, the children, the bills.

The glasses were refilled. We drank more tea. Then Hassan put his beads away, came to his feet and produced a file of dog-eared forms from his inside pocket. Aras pulled at his beard as he glanced at the paperwork. Gun laws were pretty lax in Iraq – at the end of the war in 2003, the Coalition in an act of sheer lunacy disbanded the army and sent a million men home with their rifles. Times had changed. Kurdistan was modernizing, but the old baksheesh culture was alive and well. Someone in Erbil with a government contract was growing rich printing documents and pocketing a few dinars to stamp them.

I gazed around the walls. It was like being in a sweet shop, except the goodies were rocket launchers, machine guns, American M-16 rifles.

There was a variety of submachine guns: German MP5s, British Sterlings; Skorpion machine pistols and a selection of handguns, shotguns and hunting rifles. I noticed a matt-black Glock 17 and turned to Aras.

'May I?'

'Of course. You are my guest.'

The Glock 17 semi-automatic is known as the 'plastic pistol', first choice among cops in the United States. The polymer hilt slips into your palm like holding a child's hand and your finger curls around the trigger like a key sliding into a lock. It felt good.

Hassan's grey eyes were sparkling. 'You like?' he said.

'It'll do the job.'

'First time today I see you smile.'

'Not that much to smile about, is there?'

Cano mimed drinking shots, tilting his hand back and forth. He said something in Kurdish I didn't understand.

'He says you are a lightweight, John. You need more practice.'

I stared back at Cano. 'I imagine everyone's a lightweight compared to you, mate,' I said.

As they fell about with laughter, I realized how stupid I must have sounded and laughed at myself.

The documents were in order. I turned back to the display of weapons and asked Aras the prices. A decent Kalashnikov had cost $300 two years ago. Now the price had doubled. An American M-16A2 assault rifle fetched $1,700; an M-4 carbine $2,000. American 5.56mm rounds cost 10 cents a hit, the Russian 7.62mm were 5 cents. Aras said a lot of civilians were now buying weapons, but he also had clients in Asayish, Kurdish intelligence, the military and policemen who needed better equipment than they were officially issued.

'Before ISIS, business was slow. Now people are afraid.' Aras pulled at his beard and lowered his voice. 'I only like to sell to people I know. No Arabs.'

Learning the prices was useful, not that we planned to buy anything. As with the vehicles and safe house, we rented what we needed: four Serbian AK-47s with folding stocks for CQB – close-quarter battle – and rails for a dot sight, scope and flashlight. Magazines hold 30 rounds, but we would load up 28. The mags were notoriously unreliable when filled to capacity, the main reason for stoppages. We took eight spare mags, four Motorola mobile radios, low-profile body armour and the Glock with six 17-round magazines. The others already had handguns discreetly under their jackets.

We shook hands, thanked Allah for our health and well-being, and left with the kit without so much as a deposit. Trust among the Kurds created a bond. Not that it was wise to betray that trust. If you did, every time you turned the lights out to go to bed, you'd wonder if someone was going to slit your throat in the middle of the night. That's probably why all the houses had bars on the windows.

We locked the guns in the car and crossed the street to a stall where a peddler in a white turban served soft cheese and honey on naan heated on a metal plate, the typical breakfast. We scoffed the naan and I began to feel better. Cano opened his second fag packet of the day, lit up and let out a long stream of smoke. Kurdish cigarettes are an inch or so longer than most, with a pungent smell that makes your head spin after a few hours locked in a car with the windows up.

Luckily, it was hot and the windows remained down as we drove out of the city towards the Zagros Mountains. There was snow on the high peaks. The foothills were lush, with winding rivers and plantations of olives, walnuts, figs and pomegranates. The sky was cloudless, deep blue and pricked by the spires of minarets rising over villages of adobe houses. Outside these small settlements, flocks of sheep with brown faces and curled horns were watched over by shepherds in traditional clothes in scenes little changed since the time of the Bible.

The music on the radio broke up as we climbed into the hills. It was a relief when Dozan turned it off. I leaned my head into the wind flow. The air was dry and sweet. Every day with Kali and Ntileini was a precious gift and I wasn't sure why I felt so at home crossing strange roads with the reassuring weight of a 9mm on my hip. I had spent a lot of time those last six months in the office and wondered for a moment if my impulse to rush to the rescue of an unknown girl had obscured the risk. Civilians under fire run the wrong way at the wrong time. They panic. Laura and her babies could easily get killed. I could wind up in prison. Or worse. I had stopped beating myself up with self-doubt a long time ago, but one way to ruin your life is to have dreams bigger than your abilities.

We had put another ten miles on the clock since passing the last village. The landscape was dramatic, primeval. Dozan turned into a ravine between walls of slate-grey rock. He curved in a half-circle to park in the shade facing the exit and this one action, swift, automatic, a show of expertise and forward planning, was all it took to wipe the moment of uncertainty from my mind.

We stepped out of the vehicle and stretched. Hassan pointed up and I watched an eagle pass over the narrow strip of sky above our heads.

'Very good,' he said.

I wasn't sure of the significance, but if this was a good sign, I'd take it.

Cano popped the boot. We needed to zero and test-fire the weapons. The walls of the ravine would at least muffle the sound. He slotted a mag in the first AK and turned the selector dial to single shot. A thorn tree stood in the distance. He shouldered the rifle and fired three shots into the trunk.

'Not bad,' I said.

Cano turned with a wide grin. 'Practice,' he replied in English.

We went to inspect the tree and Cano adjusted the rifle sights. We took turns testing and zeroing each weapon. We checked the spare mags. The springs were clean, the cartridges without damp stains. It looks phoney in a movie when the baddie's gun jams and the hero is saved at the last moment, but it happens. Rounds may have been in a mag for a long time, or the spring is faulty. The round fires but goes anywhere but the target. Other times, the firing pin strikes the primer and all you get is a dull thud. Or, worse, a bullet is pushed halfway up the barrel. When the next round goes off, it's best if you've already written your music list for the funeral.

Cano produced a pack of paper targets from the car. He stuck four in a row on the far wall of the ravine with tape and stamped back with a jaunty grin. We fired in turn and went to inspect the results. We'd all done well enough, keeping the shells in the three rings around the bull, but I was astounded by Cano's target. He'd let off eight rounds that drew a perfect smiley face, two wide-set eyes, a bull's-eye nose and a curving smile to match his own. He looked at my target, his large head bobbing up and down.

'Practice,' he said, his favourite word, and they all had a good laugh.

Men whose job is to put their lives on the line bond through rivalry, mock hostility, by taking the piss. This way, you learn each other's strengths. Cano Ali could take off a fly's bollocks mid-flight. Hassan was an organizer, a natural leader. Dozan was a born getaway driver. In contact, or in a fast exit from contact, the tail driver in the package will remain six inches from the lead vehicle's rear bumper. This needs great skill, but it is the lead driver who sets the pace, decides on the escape route and must calculate when he crosses a flaming bridge or skirts an exploding land mine that there is space and time for the following vehicle.

As we climbed in the car, I glanced up just as the eagle settled on a high crag, his kingdom at peace again.

We headed back towards Erbil and turned off for the frontier to recce border routes, checkpoints and crossings. There were few private cars on the roads, but a steady stream of new oil tankers. Since gaining autonomy, the Kurds had managed their own oil income and turned Erbil into a boom town.

We stopped the car at the foot of a steep hill and climbed up to scope out the lay of the land in ISIS territory. As we neared the peak, the walk turned into a race and I thought my heart was going to burst out of my chest making sure I kept up. It was 32 degrees, with soaring humidity. I must have dropped a couple of kilos on the run.

Before returning to the safe house, we toured the ATMs. There was a little over 10,000 Iraqi dinars to the dollar and the wedge of red 25,000-dinar notes I handed to Hassan made him an instant millionaire.

CHAPTER 3

Plan for the Worst

The internet guy had done the job. Emails rolled into the inbox. I Skyped Kali, then spoke to Ntileini. She wanted to take the boat out with some friends and stamped off in a huff when I said no. 'She's just like you,' Kali remarked, and I took that as a compliment.

I called Thomas, the German. I told him the 10K had gone walkabout and he was at a loss for words when I explained that we were still going through with the rescue.

'I am not sure what you are saying?'

'I'm not leaving the girl there. If we can get her out, we'll get her out.'

'What about the cost? The family have spent everything they have.'

'Let me worry about that.'

'This is…this is so very kind of you. It is a very Christian thing to do. You are a good man, Mr Carney.'

'Nice of you to say, but you don't know me.'

'Perhaps you don't know yourself,' he replied and I thought, that's a bit cheeky. 'If you can do this, especially now, you will be compensated in other ways.'

'I don't believe in karma, mate. I believe in a bird in the hand.'

'I'm sorry…'

'Never mind. What else have you got?'

'I have a map of the route they will be taking and a photo of the vehicle. I am sending them to you now.'

Skype whooshed and I opened the images.

'Got it,' I said.

'They plan to leave in three days' time, on Wednesday 12 July at 0530, at daybreak. They estimate a journey time of between two and three hours.'

'Where do they plan to cross?'

'I do not have this information. I will ask Laura's father. I assure you, he passed over the money in good faith.'

'Looks like the Arab bank's no better than ours,' I said. 'Now, let me take a look at what we've got. We'll speak tomorrow.'

'Mr Carney, again, I thank you.'

We hung up and I looked at the map. It is just over 50 miles, an hour's drive on Route 2 from Mosul to Aski Kalak, the first town over the border in Kurdistan. Laura's husband had charted a winding course over the old camel tracks that skirted the towns of Ali Rashsh, Bakhdida and Kabarli. He would cross the Great Zab River and arrive at one of the two or three small frontier posts between Aski Kalak and Al Kuwayr. I had no idea why he had chosen this particular route, bearing in mind that the desert was littered with IEDs (improvised explosive devices), and there was always the danger of bumping into an ISIS patrol, even bandits.

At least they had picked a good time. Leaving in darkness would have aroused suspicions. In the early morning, they would have light without heat and the Islamists would be at *Salat al-fajr*, the dawn prayers.

I sat down with the guys to share the intel. Cano spoke little English and Dozan quietly translated as we worked out a plan. Hassan produced a large map of the area and traced the course the family would be taking with a yellow marker pen.

'Do you think this route's going to be safe?' I asked. Hassan shrugged his big shoulders.

'Only Allah knows,' he replied.

'You'd think if Allah knows everything he'd know how to stop the bloody carnage in Mosul.'

There was silence for several seconds. I'd obviously put my foot in it. Hassan drew breath and his wide thumb flicked at his beads.

'Allah gives us free will,' he explained. 'He points the way, but each man must choose his own direction.'

'Let's hope our driver's chosen the right one.'

He touched his palm to his chest. '*Inshallah*,' he said.

We looked back at the map. Deserts the size of Britain stretch from the cities in Iraq and Syria into unpopulated areas of Turkey and Iran. Borders drawn up by cartographers following French and British interests a century ago were ignored by the camel trains and nomadic tribes. The 500 miles of razor wire erected in recent times to mark the frontier between Kurdistan and the regions of Iraq seized by Islamic State were impossible to patrol, easy to cut through, and unfinished in the mountainous areas that lacked passes or roads.

On the journey from Mosul, Laura would be carrying a mobile phone. She would call when they were close to the border. We still did not know if they would exit at an immigration post or illicitly, with our assistance, through the fence. Our two vehicles would be 20 miles apart patrolling the area, waiting for the call.

If the driver did avoid the official crossing, we would instruct him to stop and kill the motor at an unobstructed standoff point with good sight lines 300 metres from the border, then complete the journey on foot. We would tell Laura to bring the children one at a time to the fence and carry nothing more than a small bag with water and essentials for the children. Once we had one child, we would be more secure.

Secure from what?

However unlikely, we had to consider the possibility that the flight from Mosul was an elaborate ISIS trick and Laura was a martyr bringing a suicide bomb to remind the West that there was no escape from the Caliphate. This was an extreme scenario, but you learn in the army to hope for the best and plan for the worst.

We studied the shot of the vehicle on my laptop. It was a white Toyota Hi-Lux with Arabic writing scrawled along the sides and a flatbed useful for bolting down a rocket launcher. After we had Laura and her kids, assuming they were clean, we wanted her Palestinian husband to approach with his hands in the air, carrying nothing at all. Once he was secure in plasticuffs, I intended to cross those 300 metres into ISIS territory with a five-gallon jerry can and torch the vehicle, one less battle bus for US drones to knock out.

While Hassan and Cano took Laura and the children back to the safe house, I wanted some time to debrief the husband with Dozan before we handed him over at the nearest border station.

'All good,' Cano said and mimed shoving a spoon in his mouth. 'We eat.'

He cooked some beans and rice in the filthy kitchen. Dozan whispered irritably down his mobile phone. I watched Hassan counting his amber beads and suddenly understood that the ritual had no spiritual significance. It was a form of meditation and he was thinking through everything we had discussed.

We drank water with our modest meal. Kurds have a different relationship with alcohol. I had a few beers and opened a bottle of wine with Kali every night. Muslims who follow the rules don't touch alcohol. These guys drank like drains on festive occasions – my arrival in Erbil, the end of Ramadan – but didn't appear to suffer from the after-effects and didn't crave it the following day.

It was early to bed and out at daybreak in two vehicles. Dozan drove me in Team 1. Cano was at the wheel with Hassan in Team 2. Kalashnikovs run on a battery, as do the radios. They had all been charged overnight and tested first thing. When you buy property it's about location, location, location. In the military, it's preparation, preparation, preparation.

My rifle was within easy reach, tucked down between the seat and the door. We carried field glasses, wire cutters, full jerry cans, spare mags and the medical supplies I had brought with me from Greece. Nine out of ten fighters wounded in action and who don't reach medical facilities in time, die from one of three causes: blood loss, collapsed lungs or obstructed airways. To counter those risks, my kit included iodine solution, painkillers, antibiotic ointment, trauma bandages, a one-handed tourniquet for self-application, 'quikclot' packets, and a nasopharyngeal airway tube.

We had gone through the kit. Everyone knew how to use the supplies. The first loyalty of soldiers in the field isn't to something grand and abstract like patriotism, it is to each other. When they say 'no man left behind', though, it doesn't guarantee that your mates are going to rush into enemy fire to get you out. It means if you are likely to be taken prisoner, one of the team will have the courage to put a bullet in your skull.

We headed towards Aski Kalak. Parts of Kurdistan are as picturesque as rural Wiltshire. This part of the country was a wilderness of gritty sand below a sky that was oven hot at midday, void of vegetation and empty except for the unexpected appearance of rows of white tents turning brown from the dust that blows continuously over the desert. Grit gets into your eyes and teeth, no matter how tightly you fold your *shemagh,* the headscarf used by men and women alike for sun and sand. Beside the camp was the biggest car park I had ever seen, the cars like ghost vehicles sinking into the sand.

In June 2014, when ISIS seized Mosul, 500,000 people jumped into their automobiles and fled down Route 2 to the frontier. The UN set up camps for IDPs (internally displaced persons) outside Aski Kalak and the people were still there. There were no fences. They were not imprisoned. But there was nowhere to go unless they had funds to pay people smugglers and set out on the journey to Europe.

Dozan slowed so as not to kick up the dust. Passing cars were the only entertainment and a crowd had gathered to watch as we drove by. I saw a group of women in black with pink headscarves, the flash of colour like a sign of hope in the muted greys and yellows of the desert. Some children waved. I waved back. I felt totally useless that we could do nothing to help them.

'Not much of a life, is it?' I said.

'Better than where they came from,' Dozan replied, and he was right about that.

He swerved to face the exit at the border post. Cano slid to a halt beside us. I followed Hassan into the office and remained silent while he outlined our activities. The immigration officials nodded, pulled on their cigarettes and smoothed down their moustaches. They glanced at me and back at Hassan Ghazi. He was a big man with the presence of a politician, a patriot, one of them. They had no love for ISIS – an Arab entity, the enemy – and agreed to accommodate our plans. No money changed hands. It would have been inappropriate.

We drove to the next frontier post and went through the same procedure. We wanted to ensure that all the officials along the line knew that our main focus was to extract a young Dutch woman and her children. Her husband would be handed over immediately – a deserter from inside Islamic State with useful information, a prize worth having.

The heat stoked up and we kept the air-con on full. I had not bothered to shave that morning. My nerves were taut. My brain raced. We were not in danger. I was getting into character. Battle is performance art. Soldiering is about patience, awareness and drills. You stand about on street corners in Northern Ireland for six hours at a time, eyes peeled, trigger finger tense just on the off chance that a Provo pops up with an Armalite. You drive through the hell of the BIAP to Baghdad Airport to collect a client and the plane is delayed by eight hours.

When you are not hanging about doing sod all, you run up and down hills, lift weights, shoot targets. You may not fire a shot in anger for two years, but, as Cano would say, you have to keep in practice. The work is so intense, so demanding, it explains why soldiers rarely settle as civilians and half the street beggars are ex-servicemen.

After all the drills, plans, schedules and orders, most important is you have to be flexible.

*

We drove back into Erbil to collect some provisions. I wanted to buy some treats and Team 2 followed us through the afternoon traffic to Ghazi Antab Sweets, where the proprietor was another distant cousin of Hassan. I filled 50 small bags with selections of bonbons, guava candy, caramels shaped as teddy bears and wafers dipped in ice sugar. At 50 cents a bag, it was the best $25 I had ever spent.

'For your daughter?' Hassan asked, but Dozan was already ahead of him.

'For the children at Aski Kalak,' he replied, and Hassan shook his head.

'And next week, you must send a dentist.'

'I'll leave that to you, mate. I'm not planning to be here next week.'

We collected some groceries. I bought some bleach to clean the kitchen. It had been a good day. Everyone was on side. I was happy. And that's always a bad sign.

By the time we got back to the house, the jungle drums had echoed up and down the lines of Kurdish security. Hassan received a call from a friend in Asayish: Laura and her children would be accepted once they crossed the border. Her husband would be turned back.

This was short-sighted, in my opinion, but there was nothing I could do about it. The decision was going to make the extraction more tricky. The guy would be assisting his family and deserting ISIS. This wasn't the Boy Scouts when you tie the wrong knot. One wrong move in Mosul and you were the star of a decapitation movie.

I spoke to Kali – Natty wasn't talking to me – and then took a call from Matt Lambert. He was upset about the missing money, he was the contact with Thomas Kuntze, and he made an offer I didn't take too seriously at the time: to contribute to the cost of the mission.

'Keep an account of everything, I'll see what I can work out,' he said, and I wondered if this was a touch of *noblesse oblige*, Matt being an officer and all that.

'I'm not proud, mate, I'll take anything that comes my way.'

'The extraction's on course?'

'Not really. Usual fuck-ups. The Kurds won't let Laura's husband in the country. Now we've got to lift out the girl with her kids and send him back.'

'A couple of warning shots will sort that out, John.'

'Problem is, I've never done any warning shots. I'm just as likely to take out his kneecaps.'

'Whatever works. Don't tell Thomas Laura's husband won't be able to gain entry.'

Here we go, I thought, top-down officer think.

'I wasn't planning to,' I replied.

The German was next on my call list. After giving me the spiel about what a great bloke I was, he informed me that Laura would text when they left the city, and call when they were close to the border. They had still not decided whether to use a frontier crossing, or take their chances along the perimeter fence. That would become clearer on the day.

I hung up and scrolled through my contacts. They were listed in code with notes giving their preferred methods of communication. Expats use encrypted applications such as WhatsApp, Telegram and Skype, useful systems to share images. The best platforms for encrypted emails are Proton and Tutunota. Security operators mirror the methods of the terrorists in order to take advantage of the same positives and understand the restrictions. To defeat an enemy, you must think like the enemy.

I stopped at jackrabbit, aka Jack Fieldhouse, a former British Para who had worked in Iraq since 2003 and had hooked up with an Iraqi nurse named Tamara in Mosul. Jack was a fixer. Literally. He could make anything, repair anything, and drink a pub dry in his spare time. He had learned Arabic and the last I'd heard, he had got out with his girl and was somewhere in Erbil. I gave him a call on WhatsApp. He answered immediately.

'Fuck me, you in Erbil?' he began.

'How do you know?'

'Sixth sense, mate. What's up?'

'I've got a jihadi bride and her kids coming out from Mosul tomorrow in a pickup. We're going to scoop them up at the border somewhere.'

'Need any help?'

'That's good of you, but I've got Hassan Ghazi and a couple of his people with me. It's a delicate situation with the Kurds.'

'I can imagine. What can I do?'

'You can buy me a pint when it's over,' I said, and he laughed. 'They'll be taking the desert roads. Any danger areas? Any tips?'

'It's all a danger area. There's mines everywhere. She travelling alone?'

'With her husband. He wants out as well,' I said without elaborating.

'You know as well as me, John. Low profile, easy on the gas till they're well out of the city, then put your foot down. The less time they're exposed, the better.'

'ISIS patrols?'

'There are, but I don't have any intel on times or routes.' He paused. 'A lot of the Europeans who go out there to volunteer believe all the rubbish they read online. They think this is what God wants, all that bollocks. They can't believe it when they meet the locals. A lot of them are fucking animals. It's not a holy war, it's a holy fuck-up. And I'll tell you something else: it's going to get worse before it gets better.'

'My thoughts exactly.'

44

'Where are the people from?'

'They're Dutch, at least the girl and her kids are.'

'You got a safe route back to Europe for them?'

'No, Jack, we're winging it.'

'Aren't we always.' He laughed. 'Sorry I haven't got anything more useful for you.'

'Every little bit helps,' I said.

'Let's speak. Good luck, mate.'

That's something we did need. We hung up and I stretched out on the narrow bed with my legs dangling over the end.

One thing I was sure of, we were not going to have a Hollywood ending with this one. If they got through the minefields and avoided the patrols, we were still going to have problems at the border. When we grabbed Laura and the children, her husband, after risking his life, was going to be furious. He would be armed and might well try to impede our exit. We could incinerate the vehicle, as I'd planned, and hand him over to the authorities. But that was the very thing we had been warned not to do. They were hard choices. The Palestinian was probably terrified, not exactly blameless, but he had made one stupid mistake that would almost certainly ruin his life, if not end it.

My mind spun with different scenarios, and it was a relief when Cano appeared at the door with a bottle in his hand and a fag dangling from the corner of his mouth.

'Beer?' he said.

'You're a bloody star, you know that, mate.'

He removed the cigarette and grinned. 'Practice,' he replied.

*

45

Next day, we went back over the same roads. It was great to see the children grinning as they dipped into the bags of sweets in Aski Kalak. I noticed some smiles among the women in pink scarves and was moved by the sheer power of the human spirit. It was the women more often than the men who kept families and communities together. Given the chance, they would rebuild their lives and start again.

'I hate to say it, but they don't look unhappy,' I said as Dozan moved through the gears and pulled away.

'I wish I could say the same about my wife,' he replied.

'I had been wondering...'

He threw up his hands, then dropped them back down on the steering wheel. 'She is not Kurd. She is Iraqi. In Baghdad, we had everything, big house, picnics, good schools. She cannot understand why we can never go back.'

'Never's a long time.'

He shook his head. 'The past is dust. It disappears behind us. There is no way back,' he said earnestly. 'We are Sunni, like Saddam. My uncle was one of his colonels. We were what you call upper class.'

'That lot,' I said, and he shrugged.

'The Americans do not understand how democracy works. They assumed they would bring the Sunni exiles back to Baghdad and everyone would fall to their knees in thanks. They did not realize sixty per cent of the population are Shia. They had an election and were surprised when the Shias voted for Shia candidates. You know the rest...'

Nouri al-Maliki was elected president and Shia death squads unleashed a wave of revenge killings on the Sunni minority. Thousands of ex-soldiers joined ISIS, not because they had heard the call to jihad, but because it was the one area where they could use their skills and earn a living.

The differences between Sunni and Shia were key to understanding the Middle East and operating between the two communities. The schism had begun immediately after Muhammad died in 632. Those who became known as Sunni believed the new leader – or caliph – should be chosen by vote or consensus. The rival clique wanted to select a new caliph from among the Prophet's descendants. They promoted his cousin Ali, and became known as Shiites, or Shia, a contraction of Shiat Ali, followers of Ali. The rival groups have been at each other's throats ever since.

Not everyone who took up arms in the Caliphate was a religious zealot. There were just as many guns for hire who switched allegiance depending on the financial package. War zones are magnets that attract our best and basest instincts: on one side, charities and volunteers; on the other, psychos and war profiteers who provide every manner of vice and decadence the human mind can conceive.

Hassan had not been correct in his assessment: the ants' nest had been poked with a stick on 1 May 2003, when President Bush stood on the decks of the aircraft carrier USS *Abraham Lincoln* and gave his 'Mission Accomplished' speech declaring the war over.

That was the day ISIS began its rise to power.

CHAPTER 4
Flight from Mosul

Wednesday 12 July 2016.

I had set my alarm for 4am. After a shower, I dressed and sorted out my accessories: *shemagh*, sunglasses, passport, iPhone with ear buds, thermal mug filled with hot coffee, Glock oiled, loaded, good to go. After the liberation from Saddam, private security operatives working in Iraq were sanctioned to bear arms – literally licensed to kill – by the US State Department. If the rules had changed, no one had told me about it.

While I flicked through my emails, I ate a couple of wedges of what I call toenail bread – denoting width, texture and colour – with cheese and a brew. Cano removed the batteries from the chargers and loaded the weaponry, rope, wire cutters, meds, water and food. There were no Starbucks along the border. He came back inside and collected a carton of cigarettes, a sure sign that it was going to be a long day.

'You're going to kill yourself, all that bloody smoking,' I remarked.

He grinned and lit up. Hassan opened the gates and we were on the road at 5am.

Erbil was a noisy, energetic city with blasting horns and blaring music. In the hour before dawn, it was quiet except for the whisper of the wind and the clatter of donkey carts rattling along with fresh produce for the markets. The Citadel surfaced from the mist like a city floating in clouds and a hazy green light seeped along the horizon. We drove at a leisurely pace around the ring road into open country and passed a group of tribesmen leading a herd of camels.

'Muzuri, from the north,' Dozan said. 'They cling on to the old ways.'

'Perhaps the old ways were the best ways.'

He made a tutting noise as he shook his head. 'Time is like an aeroplane after takeoff. It is always moving and only goes in one direction. That's what I keep telling my wife.'

That reminded me. I sent the usual text to Kali with a row of kisses.

By the time the sun lifted above the hills, it was already hot. Dogs doing their job barked half-heartedly as we passed through villages where flapping chickens and stray goats with devil faces skittered away from the approaching vehicle. Sandals made from car tyres stood in rows outside a mosque where the faithful were still at morning prayer. I kept the window down and enjoyed the smell of the air.

Fleetwood Mac paused mid-beat. I had received the text.

I took the buds from my ears. 'The family has left Mosul,' I said.

'They should be here in three hours.'

'Home for some dinner and a pint,' I suggested, and he laughed.

'I learned to drink pints of Guinness when I was in Cranwell. It is a very pleasant vocation.'

'You're not wrong there.'

'They drink two pints, then they sing rude songs.'

'That's the English for you.'

'I like the English. They are reserved, like us, like the Kurds, but they have hearts of gold.'

I didn't want to disillusion Dozan, he had a wife to do that. I grabbed the radio and passed on Laura's message to Hassan. We closed the windows and put on the air-con. When we reached our destination halfway between Aski Kalak and Al Kuwayr, Team 2 remained static while Dozan drove on. There were no trees, no focal points, just a featureless plain that shimmered in the heat haze. The fence was new in places, broken-down in others. I was unsure if it had been built by the Iraqis to keep the Kurds out, or the Kurds to keep the Iraqis out. Not that a 500-mile fence was going to keep anyone from crossing if they had a mind to.

We made regular comms checks and watched the sun climb over a blue sky that reminded me of days on the Mediterranean with Kali and Ntileini. I felt mean not allowing her to take the boat out. My daughter was perfectly capable, but what if the motor failed, or a storm blew up? She needed more drills. She needed to learn that if something goes wrong, there's not always going to be someone standing behind her to put it right.

Once when I was away, Kali was woken at night by the sound of a vehicle as it came to a halt outside the villa. The road leading to the property ran between empty fields and no one had cause to use it unless they were visiting or making a delivery. From the window, she saw two men in a Toyota Land Cruiser who were waving their hands about and appeared to be arguing. Kali went to the cupboard, grabbed my shotgun, inserted a cartridge and returned to the bedroom. A few minutes later, the car pulled away.

'They were probably just lost,' I said.

She shrugged. 'The thing is, there's something wrong with that gun,' she replied. 'When I lowered the barrel, the cartridge fell out.'

We went to have a look. What she had done was insert a 410 cartridge in a 12-bore shotgun. I held the brass-capped case in my palm. It was about the size and colour of a tube of lipstick.

'Of course it fell out. It's the wrong cartridge.'

Her dark hair swirled about her face as she shook her head. 'Well, how was I to know?'

She was right. I was like the shoemaker who makes shoes for everyone while my children go barefoot. That same day, I brought my guns down to the orchard and taught the girls how to use them. Kali and Ntileini quickly progressed from picking off oranges from the trees to shooting people-targets with the 410. I now had guns and ammo stashed on every floor and felt a lot happier when I was out of the country knowing my girls were able to use them.

The view was unchanging. Flat, dry, hilly along the horizon. I watched a man wandering along in the middle of nowhere and wondered where he had come from and where he could possibly be going. There may have been a village hidden in the haze, not that I saw one. Perhaps he was a holy man, or a madman lost in his own world. When I first arrived in Iraq, I'd often spotted animals, the small Arabian wolf, sand cats, hares, gazelles in the mountains. Now there were less. The wars were destroying everything, even the wildlife.

I pointed. 'Maybe he needs some water?' I said, and Dozan shook his head.

'He is going about his own business. He is probably looking for hand-grenades to sell.'

He dropped a gear as he swerved around a stretch of rocks.

We were now heading for Al Kuwayr and knew it was close by the glimmer of shell cases strewn across the desert. Kurdish volunteers had fought street battles to drive out jihadi militias and the town as we approached looked like an open mouth full of broken teeth. Burnt-out vehicles littered the landscape, cenotaphs to the hundreds who had died. The survivors had buried their dead and started again. They lived in the ruins of their houses while they rebuilt them and farmers had set up stalls beneath ragged strips of canvas. It was desolate, desperate, but the people hadn't given up. Before driving back, we bought some bananas and a watermelon from a silent old woman with empty eyes and a blue tattoo fading on her lined face.

I checked in with Hassan. No movement. No gunfire. No message from his contact in Asayish. Three hours had passed. A Sunday driver would have reached the border in that time. I ran all the scenarios through my mind: breakdown, ISIS patrol, roadside bomb. Most likely of all, they were lost in the desert beneath a ruthless sun that forms mirages in the vivid light and turns the road beneath your tyres into a mirror.

We stopped on an incline overlooking the badlands of what the BBC always describes in broadcasts as the 'so-called' Islamic State, and what IS simply call the State – al-Dawla. We label them as ISIS or ISIL or IS or Daesh but, whatever monikers we use, they're the same murdering zealots winding the clock back to the Middle Ages.

There was nothing to be seen from the crest of the hill. No roads, no traffic, no buildings, no telegraph poles or radio towers. I glimpsed a dark streak like a shadow in the sky. I thought for a second it was the black flag of al-Dawla, but it was only a bird, perhaps the same eagle I had seen the other day watching over us. When I exited the vehicle to relieve myself, it was like stepping into a sauna. Sweat dripped into my eyes and my piss dried as it hit the rocks.

I called Hassan again and asked him to check in at the crossing points to see if they had any new information for us. He radioed back three times in the next two hours. Nothing.

We ate our lunch parked beneath the sparse shade of some palms. The wind had dropped and the Health app on my phone read 40 degrees. I checked the weather in Heraklion. It was 32, a perfect day. The watermelon was delicious, like eating some unknown fruit from a different planet.

I kept looking at my phone. I was tempted to send a text, but if Laura and the Palestinian were in the hands of a patrol, my message would be the end for them. Then again, if they had broken down, they wouldn't get far before the heat killed them. If we knew their location, we could cut through the fence and take a chance driving full pelt into the Caliphate. I glanced at Dozan. He had closed his eyes, resting them from the glare. It's another trick you learn in the military. It doesn't matter how tense the situation, if you can get some shuteye, you grab it. Before I gave in to temptation and made that call, the radio buzzed. It was Hassan, speaking slowly and without emotion.

'I have received a communication from the border crossing at Aski Kalak. There has been an exchange of gunfire at an ISIS checkpoint close to the frontier. Civilians were involved.'

'Is it the girl?'

'They do not have that information. The army has taken control. What they have said is that the ISIS checkpoint is heavily guarded and we must in no circumstances enter the area.'

'I wouldn't dream of it, mate,' I said. 'Can you find out more?'

'I will make some calls. For the moment, we must hold our positions.'

'Roger that.'

Dozan had opened his eyes. 'Gunfire is not unusual. It doesn't tell us anything.'

'Except we haven't heard a dicky bird all day and what we do know is there's a girl and her kids just over there,' I said, waving at the fence.

'You do not play chess, John?'

'No, not as it happens.'

'It is a game that requires a lot of patience.'

'I know, that's why I don't play it.'

'One day, I will teach you.'

We swigged back the last of our water and sat there for another hour. I did not receive a call from Laura and didn't call her. They had put their lives on the line to escape, land mines on the ground, drones and Coalition fast air – what the Americans call close air support (CAS) – above, the bandits who came out like zombies at night. Everyone was a commodity. Girls were sold into slavery and prostitution. Infants were supposedly smuggled over the leaky borders into Europe where Muslim families were said to pay $5,000 to buy babies, more for boys.

The photograph of Laura's little girl with wayward hair and lively eyes was so like Ntileini, I couldn't help imagining that it was my daughter we had set out to rescue. I had told Laura's parents that I would bring Laura out and had just sat on my backside eating watermelon. Patrolling the border had seemed like a good tactic. It wasn't. I should have been more proactive and would be if similar circumstances came up again.

The sun had passed its highest point when I finally got another call from Hassan.

'We have information,' he said slowly.

'Yeah, yeah?'

'A young foreign woman and two children have been taken to safety at the border by the Peshmerga after an exchange of gunfire with ISIS.'

I gulped down the dead air. 'Must be Laura?' I said.

'It is very likely, John. It is good. The job is done.'

'What about the Palestinian?'

'There was no mention of him.'

'That's a bit of luck, I suppose.'

'It is. She is safe. We are safe. We are making our way back to Erbil.'

'Roger that, mate.'

Dozan started the car.

'Good job,' he said.

'Looks like it.'

After all the anxiety, it was a relief that Laura had made it – if it was Laura – but I couldn't help feeling frustrated that we had played no active part except to have warned the border guards that a family would be attempting to cross that day.

We arrived at the safe house 90 minutes later and locked ourselves in behind the metal gates. We were tired, thirsty, weary from doing nothing. We sat around drinking chai. Cano cooked bean stew with rice. I should have Skyped Kali but had lost the will to do anything except watch Cano as he moved around the kitchen. For such a big man, he had long fine hands and diced the vegetables as if he were playing the piano. Herbs in jars were lined up on a narrow shelf. He took a pinch from one, a pinch from another, adding them like an alchemist brewing a magic potion.

It was coming up to six o'clock when Hassan's mobile finally rang. It was his contact in Asayish. He told Hassan to tune in to Kurdistan24, the local TV station. Dozan got it up on his laptop and we gathered around as a burst of shrill brass gave way to a fading drum roll. There was a voiceover and the camera shifted straight to a close-up of Laura – a news clip that would be repeated in Holland and by the news agencies across the world in the coming days.

It struck me immediately that she did not look brutalized or oppressed. On the contrary, she had self-confidence, dark intelligent eyes; her face, framed in a black headscarf, reminded me of a painting of the Virgin Mary in the church I'd been dragged off to as a child. She seemed more relieved than nervous and didn't falter as she answered the newscaster's questions through a Dutch interpreter. Dozan translated for me and I learned more about the girl in the next five minutes than I had known from speaking with Thomas Kuntze during the last two weeks.

Laura Angela Hansen was born to a conventional Dutch family in 1995 in The Hague. She dropped out of school at 17 and met her Palestinian 'loverboy', as they were called, through a Muslim dating site. 'We had a lot of problems. He was very aggressive and the neighbours called the police a lot of times. But I was already pregnant, so I didn't want to divorce,' she said.

After she'd given birth to her daughter, Iman, the family lived in different parts of the Netherlands during the next three years. In September 2015, as ISIS was marching across Iraq and Syria, Laura's husband announced that they were going on holiday to Turkey and would be delivering donations to Muslim refugees. She had no idea where the money had come from, or if it ever existed. She stared into the camera.

'He pushed me into it. I didn't want to go,' she said. 'We arrived in Turkey and the next thing I knew, we had crossed the border into Syria. They put me in a house guarded by men with beards and guns. I was frightened all of the time.'

They lived for several months in Raqqa, in northern Syria, where she gave birth to her son, Abdullah. They were then transferred to Mosul.

'Life was horrible in Raqqa and Mosul under ISIS rule. I was trying all the time to flee from the hell in which I was living,' she said. 'I am very grateful to the Peshmerga. They helped my children. They took my hand and helped me with everything.'

When asked why she had wanted to leave Mosul, she said the children had been hurt in the American bombardments and she had changed her mind 'about everything'.

'I called my father and he paid a man ten thousand euros to organize the escape,' she said. Dozan glanced at me as he translated.

'Dollars,' I corrected.

'When we find him, we will kill him, John.'

'Right. Just get the money first.'

Kurdistan24 gave the story ten minutes and the newscaster turned away with that seen-it-all expression I'd witnessed on just about every journalist I had ever met. In this particular case, I could understand why he had an air of cynicism. There was something about Laura Hansen that didn't add up. She looked angelic and was either an innocent babe in the woods, or a smart girl who knew how to play the media. The broadcast had left a lot of unanswered questions. There had been no mention of the firefight. What had happened to Laura's husband? How had she been able to reach the Peshmerga, while he had not?

'What do you think?' I asked Dozan.

'About the girl?'

'Yeah. Is she a good girl? Is she being honest?'

He twirled his pilot's moustache as he thought about that. 'She is just a girl. We won't know the truth until she is debriefed.'

'She is out. That is the important thing,' Hassan remarked, and we agreed on that.

I thought it was deplorable that the Peshmerga had taken her directly to the TV station, not to a medical facility. Laura certainly didn't appear to be suffering from shock, but in the euphoria of being freed, trauma is often delayed and will be more severe without immediate treatment.

There was a time when I would have blamed myself for our failure to extract Laura; working blokes with a lack of confidence have that tendency. But I had got over that and learned to turn every failure into a learning process and move on.

'Hassan, can you call the television station for me? See if I can talk to someone about Laura or, better still, Laura herself?'

He found the number, spoke at length – I didn't understand a word – then passed me the phone. 'Here, someone who speaks English.'

I explained that I was the representative of Laura's family and wanted to see her.

'I am very sorry, sir, she is not here now. She has been taken by the military to be with her children.'

'Do you know where?'

'I am very sorry, sir, they did not inform us.'

'Is there anyone there who can help me at all?'

'I am very sorry, sir...'

'Yeah, I know, thanks anyway.' I shook my head. 'Fuck it, now what?'

Cano did his drinking mime. 'Drink?' he suggested.

'What a bloody good idea.'

I took a shower – I'd sweated like a pig for 12 hours – and called Kali. She was thrilled that Laura was out and I was all in one piece.

'When are you coming home? We miss you.'

'Soon. Just got to tidy up some loose ends.'

'It's beautiful here. The sea's gorgeous.'

'How's Natty?'

'Dying to take her friends out on the boat.'

'That's what I thought. Couple of days should do it. Give her my love.'

I spoke to Thomas Kuntze. News travels fast. They already knew Laura was out. Like me, he had no idea what was going to happen next. I told him I would try to get more info and he reminded me what a great chap I was.

Matt Lambert was next. The news was news to him and he quoted what I thought was a bit of Shakespeare: 'All's well that ends well,' he said.

'It hasn't ended yet. She isn't home, and who knows what the Dutch are going to do with her if she gets home.'

'We're certainly breaking new ground,' he said. His tone changed, and I sensed he was looking into the future again. 'This is going to swamp the news media in the next twenty-four hours. I've got a feeling we're at the start of something. It's going to be big.'

'I guess we'll see in the next twenty-four hours.'

We hung up, and I heard Cano shouting up the stairs.

'What the fuck?' I shouted back. Hassan translated.

'He says have you finished putting on your lipstick? There is dinner.'

'Ask the bastard if I can borrow his high heels.'

On the table stood big terracotta plates piled with rice and stew. Cano added shots of arak to the water glasses. I dug a teaspoon into the red chilli pepper and sprinkled it over my food.

Dozan blew out his cheeks. 'Your head will explode if you are not careful,' he said.

'Don't you worry about me, mate, my guts are lined with asbestos. Hotter the better.'

I added water to the arak and told the guys a joke popular with 12-year-olds. I'd heard it from my daughter.

A man is eating in a restaurant and is unhappy with his meal. He calls the waiter.

'What's this?' he demands, pointing at his plate.

The waiter leans closer. 'It's bean stew,' he says.

'I want to know what it is, not what it's been.'

Hassan nodded sagaciously. Dozan chuckled as he translated the joke for Cano, and Cano wore a severe expression as he looked back at me across the table.

'That is because it is not Kurdish bean stew,' he said.

Laura was safe. We all had daughters. We drank to that and I went to bed revved up and exhausted. I slept through the muezzin calling the faithful to prayer. The grating cry from the mosques at sunrise wakes people from their sleep and puts them on edge for the rest of the day. After the muezzin, you've got the cock crowing and the chorus of starving dogs, which reminded me, there were strays at the gate that needed to be fed.

It was almost 9am by the time I'd shaved and showered. I turned on my laptop and it pinged like a pinball machine on speed. There were dozens of emails on the same subject: bringing jihadi brides out of Iraq, Syria, Jordan and Turkey. Some of the emails had been sent directly to me. Most had been forwarded from Matt Lambert and others like him on the circuit. I read them all.

One was critical.

Dear Mister, please help my daughter. Her name Diana Abbasi. She 22. She in Mosul. She want to come home. She shamed. They hit her with stick. They rape her. Many rape. They kill her. Please Mister. She make big mistake. I pray to God you get her.

The writer explained in poor English that her daughter had lived at home with her family in London. She did not want to marry the 'good' man chosen for her. She was not a jihadi, but had run away to join ISIS. She had crossed the border to Syria, then Iraq. There was no mention of money. I read the email again.

Beaten. Gang-raped. The world had gone mad.

I made coffee. I burned my fingers nursing the hot glass and wondered why the hell they didn't use china cups. At home, at times like these, I would stand at the window in my office and stare out at the horizon. When you have space and distance, the clutter clears from your mind. You don't always make decisions. Sometimes, they make themselves. I swigged down the coffee. I was pouring another when the door slammed.

Hassan appeared. His sleeves were rolled up and he carried a bucket.

'Good morning,' he said.

'*Sabah alkhyr*,' I replied.

'Very good accent, John. You are getting better.'

'*Inshallah.*' I touched my chest. 'Come and take a look at this.'

I turned the laptop towards him and tapped the screen. He sat and dried his hands. After reading the email, he drew out his amber prayer beads.

'Big problem,' he said.

I sipped my coffee. 'Looks like it.'

The beads reverberated along the string. 'What is it you want to do?' he asked.

'I want to go home, mate. That's what I want to do.'

He nodded slowly, then waved his hand through the air. 'It is not possible to just go into the city and get her.'

'I know.'

The beads stopped and I felt the full force of his grey eyes boring into me. 'You know something, John, you are a fucking madman.'

'Course I am.' I leaned forward. 'You coming?'

He shrugged and didn't answer. I followed him out into the yard. Dozan and Cano Ali were cleaning the Toyotas we had hired. Hassan spoke to them in their own language. I only understood two words, 'fucking madman'.

Dozan wrung out the sponge he was holding and extended a wet hand. 'When we get back, I am going to give you your first lesson in chess.'

'Back?' I said.

'You don't think we'd let you go on your own?'

CHAPTER 5
Brothers-in-Arms

After wearing the Glock for the last week, I felt half-naked handing it back to the arms dealer. Aras checked the AKs, body armour, radios, unused mags. As we drank the customary tea, he showed us photos of the dresses his twin daughters were going to wear for their double wedding. He lowered his voice to share a secret.

'They cost more than ten thousand camels,' he whispered, and we bobbed our heads in empathy.

We settled the bill and crossed the road, drawn by the peppery smell of halloumi melting on baked naan. Cano wolfed his down and ordered another. He was always hungry, always fidgeting, continually lighting one of his long cigarettes. By contrast, he could sustain total stillness, a sniper focus. He was an amazing cook, better than Kali, not that I was going to tell her that. Or him, for that matter.

We high-fived like young Americans and split up. While Cano and Dozan drove the vehicles back to the hire company, Hassan walked me through the Qaysari Bazaar to his tailor. Shoppers with string bags filled the passageways beneath the high vaulted roof. Kurdish music rang out from tinny speakers and Kurdish flags hung above our heads as if the revolution was about to start. I felt the spring in my step. Few women wore veils, a reaction, perhaps, to the fundamentalists across the border. Most of the men were dressed for battle as if aware, subconsciously, that the oil boom, support from the United States and autonomy within Iraq would end in another bloody conflict.

Several people nodded and touched their palms to their chests when they saw Hassan. One woman stopped with her baby. He lifted the child into the air and kissed its forehead. She smiled warmly as she took the baby back into her arms.

We marched on past the shiny pyramids of fruit and vegetables, dishes of pink and white yogurt, wheels of cheeses, sausages stuffed with turmeric. The multicoloured spices piled in baskets created a hypnotic aroma that touched some ancient sense, a reminder that for thousands of years Erbil had been a *caravanserai*, a resting place, on the Silk Road from China to the Mediterranean. This is where civilization began – and would end, if the jihadis had their way.

A man wearing a fez and curled-toed shoes stood at a table performing the three shell game for a couple of goat herders new to the mischief of the big city. There were displays of outdated rifles and curved knives with intricate handles, and a shop with posters of imams, sheikhs, Zoroastrian holy men and a blue-eyed Jesus wearing the expression of someone who has just missed the last bus. The religions were woven together like the palm fibre baskets and it was hard to identify exactly what event had caused it all to begin unravelling.

It came as no surprise that Mazar, the tailor, was a member of the Ghazi tribe. The men kissed; they kiss cheeks, hands, even noses. A boy holding a round tray suspended on three strings waited at the entrance where we left our shoes. Mazar sent him off for glasses of cardamom tea and squinted at me over the top of his spectacles. He was thin and stooped, with the pale blotchy skin of people who rarely see daylight.

AIVD, Dutch intelligence, had acquired my contact details during a visit to Laura's parents in Holland. A bloke who spoke English better than me had called and we'd arranged to meet at noon the following day at the Divan Hotel. Against my better judgement, Hassan, Dozan and Cano Ali had persuaded me that, dressed in a suit and tie, I was more likely to get to see Laura and convince the Dutch to take the family home.

The Ghazis nattered on while Mazar ran a tape measure around my waist. Hassan, legs apart, gazed up at the bolts of cloth stacked on shelves that rose to the ceiling. I had never paid much attention to the way other men dressed, so it came as a surprise to realize that Hassan was something of a dandy. He wore saffron baggy pants, tight at the bottom, and a matching shirt nipped in with a wide leather belt containing a sheath for a small dagger. His *shemagh* had red squares to match a wine-red waistcoat with gold embroidery and a concealed pocket holding a Beretta M9.

Hassan flicked his beads along the string and I only became aware of the sound when it stopped. He climbed a ladder and slid out a roll of beige linen. He stepped down, the roll over his shoulder, and placed it on a long, shiny wooden table. Mazar was listing figures on a scrap of paper with a pencil he licked, blackening his tongue. His face screwed up as he nodded thoughtfully.

'Very good,' he said in English.

'Knowing me, that'll be filthy in five minutes,' I remarked. Hassan waved away the objection.

'You will be the perfect English gentleman.'

'Not in this life.'

He turned, raising his finger, fixing me with his dark eyes. 'You must learn from the chameleon,' he said, and spread out the material.

Why, I wasn't sure, but I did have misgivings over my meeting with the Dutch official. I kept hearing his voice in my head: high-pitched, insistent, wheedling. He reminded me of a captain in the Yorks who wanted the troops to think of him as one of us, when he was definitely one of them. He was an expert at asking after your family, how leave went, as if he cared, yet would put you on a charge if your salute wasn't sharp enough.

Hassan was right. Plans were in motion to extract Diana Abbasi. Doubt was an indulgence we couldn't afford. There had been no mention of funding from the family and it was fortunate that money was not the prime motivation for any of us. We were going to bring her out because saving someone's life is always the right thing to do. We liked working as a team and, having been sidelined in the rescue of Laura Hansen, it was a chance for us to test ourselves.

The tailor started marking the material in French chalk.

'You reckon it's going to be ready on time?' I asked Hassan.

He translated for Mazar. They both laughed.

'It will be ready in four hours,' he assured me.

The boy arrived back with the tea. It was already cold. We swigged it down. Hassan and Mazar praised the Prophet for all life's gifts and we put our shoes back on. The ritual was always the same, a code of hospitality and good manners as old as the Silk Road. It was best not to admire any object – a watch, a bag, a revolver. The owner would feel obliged to give it to you. It seemed odd with such etiquette that men never opened doors for women and always walked in front of them. I asked Hassan about that.

'It is so we don't ogle their arses,' he explained.

'You can't see their arses when they're wearing niqabs.'

'But you can imagine them,' he said, and hooked his *shemagh* to cover his nose and mouth.

Hassan had agreed – under protest – to make a detour to the far corner of the bazaar where the butchers had their stalls. The meat was laid out below neon lights and boys armed with tea towels flicked away the flies. I bought a bag of offcuts and offal. Hassan said something I didn't understand and the butcher gazed at me, grinning and shaking his head. It had cost me ten years of sweat and toil to get a handle on Arabic, commonly spoken by Kurds who had grown up in Saddam's era. Kurdish was not on my to-do list.

Hassan was still smiling as we moved on.

'So, what's the big joke?' I asked.

He peeled back his *shemagh*. 'We do not feed dogs,' he answered.

'How crazy is that?'

'They are unclean. Their saliva is *haram*.'

'So it's all right feeding chickens and goats. But not dogs?'

'I don't make the rules.'

'You don't always keep them, either.'

'My friend, I say it before, you are a very funny fellow,' he said.

'Takes one to know one.'

He laughed his big baritone laugh and the crowds parted for us as we strode in step back through the bazaar to the taxi stand.

I spent two hours on emails and Google Earth. Mosul's sprawling mass of identical low-rise buildings had been turned to rubble by American

B-52 bombers. Diana lived in a house of women and children. I could locate the block, but it would have been suicide to try and reach it. She didn't have anyone, husband or otherwise, to help her escape. We didn't anticipate problems crossing the desert. What we did need was to find a driver to transport Diana to the city limits.

I opened WhatsApp and called Jack Fieldhouse.

'What about that pint?' I suggested.

'I see the girl's out.'

'Not that I had much to do with it. The Peshmerga brought her across.'

'Better out than in,' he said. 'Now what?'

'I'm looking for someone in Mosul who can drive a girl to the outskirts.'

'Another one? You're getting in deep, mate.'

'Better in than out,' I said, and he laughed.

'I'll tell you what, I'll make some calls, Johnny Boy.' He paused again. 'Six o'clock. Usual place.'

'That's a bit early,' I said.

'You know how it is. The missus has dinner at eight...'

As we hung up, a horn blasted outside. I swung the gates open and stood back as a battered 4x4 pickup rolled in. A young lad was driving. Elind, Hassan's nephew, the music lover, was in the passenger seat, the window rolled down. He grinned.

'What's this piece of shit?' I said.

'Is very good,' he answered.

The driver killed the engine and they stepped out in blue jeans, T-shirts, trainers, Chinese rip-offs of Nike. Elind introduced Usef. He looked about 15, with a round face, small dark eyes and the downy beginnings of his first moustache. 'Very good mechanic,' Elind said.

Usef popped the hood and I gazed at the motor. It was clean enough, with new hoses and wiring. Usef made some adjustments, then went to start the engine again. It farted twice, spluttered and gave up. I glanced at Elind.

'What did you say his name was, Useless?'

'No, Usef,' he replied, then grinned as the penny dropped. 'It will be good, you wait, Mister John.'

'John will do.'

Elind watched while I fed the dogs. He was a smart lad. He went back into the yard to help Usef without saying a word.

We required two low-profile vehicles and some serviceable weaponry. Snatching Diana Abbasi from ISIS was strictly off the books. No paper trail, no interaction with the Peshmerga, no pay. It was a mercy mission. At least that's how I wanted to justify it. I was fortunate to have my three musketeers watching my back. Cano Ali had reminded me that they were taking time off from other work they could have been doing; he had daughters dreaming of an education. But I knew damn well he wouldn't have missed it for the world.

Since 2011, I had made a good living escorting the media, military, NGOs (non-governmental organizations) and businessmen around Iraq. Oil men liked to say they were 'investing' in the country, the code for exploiting the resources and opportunities. I was a party to all that. Bringing out a girl who had been brutalized was a chance to put something back. I weighed this up against my responsibilities to Kali and Ntileini. I would be putting myself – and the guys – at risk. But it would have been hard to live with myself knowing I could have done something and did nothing.

There was one more factor to throw into the mix. I had turned 40, an age when every man pauses to take stock; more so when your entire life has centred on being fit for the fight. I wasn't testing myself. What I was doing, without realizing it, was starting a new chapter.

The passenger seat in the pickup slid from side to side on every corner, but Usef had done a good job on the motor. It hummed at an even tone as Hassan drove into the city. Cano had gone to see an old army buddy about some guns and Dozan was taking his wife to a club where a jazz band from Beirut was playing. I had finally called Kali to tell her I was staying on in Erbil.

'You're not going to Mosul, are you, John?'

'The thing is, I haven't been able to reach Laura yet,' I replied. 'I've got a meeting tomorrow with Dutch intelligence.'

'You're not in any trouble?'

'No, no, nothing like that. You know how it is, these things take time.'

'The summer's going to be over at this rate.'

'A few days, a week at the most,' I promised. 'How's Natty?'

'She misses you. She's knows what you're doing out there. She's proud of you, you know that?'

'Course I do.'

I thought about the conversation and felt guilty as we drove through the back streets around the Citadel. I had promised Kali that I would never lie to her, but it was only a white lie, lying by omission. On a need-to-know basis, she really didn't need to know our plans.

Hassan parked opposite the bar. It was a hole in the wall with pictures of *biryani* and *kubba* dumplings on the dusty window. White plastic tables and chairs crowded the small space. Kurdish heroes looked down from the posters on the walls and folk music played on a transistor radio. The bar was empty except for a man and a woman with a child asleep against her shoulder. They fell silent as we entered and I had a feeling they'd been arguing. We passed through a strip curtain into a narrow passageway leading to another room that gave on to a garden with dusty palms and pomegranate trees. The backroom was an oasis. It was where you went to meet expats, find guns for hire, swap intel and drink beer in pint glasses. Every city in the Middle East, in Europe for that matter, had a bar like this, a clubhouse for brothers-in-arms who don't belong in any club.

Jack Fieldhouse was waiting at his usual table at the edge of the steps leading into the garden. He looked up from his mobile phone.

'Didn't think you were coming,' he said.

I smiled as I glanced at my watch. We had arranged to meet at six. It was one minute past.

We shook hands. Jack knew Hassan. It was a small world. The bar owner shuffled up. He was an ex-soldier with a smashed right leg and burn scars on the left side of his face. Hassan had sat and came to his feet again. As the two men shook hands, the right side of the bar owner's face filled with emotion, the other remained dead.

A young guy bought three pints of Roj on a tray. The local beer, piss weak and pricy at $4 a pint. Jack had looked twitchy when we first arrived. Now he relaxed. He was what I thought of as a professional drinker. He left his beer on the table, studying it for several seconds, a display of self-control. He then picked up the glass, took a sip, like a wine taster, and placed it back on the table while he savoured the blend of hops and barley. Satisfied, he downed it in one.

He smiled, even white teeth in a tanned face with wide cheekbones and threads of grey in his dark hair. He stood six feet six in hobnails and had a faded tattoo on his left arm that must have meant something once. It would have been interesting to put him in a ring with Cano Ali. I don't mind a flutter, life's a gamble, but I wouldn't have bet on the outcome. Sergeant Fieldhouse had led company-level raids on the Taliban in Afghanistan's Helmand Province in 2010 when 1 Para jumped from RAF C-130s, the Parachute Regiment's first combat drops since the Suez crisis in 1956. He'd come out in 2011, joined an NGO clearing mines in Iraq and wound up in Erbil with Tamara, who worked for the same NGO.

'I needed that,' Jack said and hunched forward. He took a folded sheet of paper from his sun-bleached denim shirt and slid it across the table. On it was written a telephone number. 'This guy, he's calling himself Apollo for some reason, delusions of grandeur. He's looking for five thousand dollars – in Yankee currency.'

It was $5,000 I knew the family back in the UK didn't have and I was reluctant to take out of my own modest savings.

'Lot of dosh for a five-minute job,' I said, and Jack shook his head.

'Not for the risk,' he replied. 'You wouldn't think it was possible to invent a new type of torture in this day and age, but you can always rely on ISIS. Our man's got a three-month-old grandson. You step out of line, they drop the kid on the floor and pour a can of gasoline over it. You see that, you go down on your knees and beg to have your head cut off to save the child.'

I felt a chill run down my back and remembered Hassan in the bazaar that morning lifting the baby into his arms.

'So why take the risk?' I said.

'The jihadis are drafting boys into their ranks. Apollo's got a son

74

of twenty. With 5K he can get him to Istanbul and buy a European passport. They've got family in the UK.'

'It's not as easy as that, is it?'

My companions looked back at me as if I were a boy in short trousers.

'It's a cottage industry,' Jack said. 'You can get papers for anything, travel permits, doctorate, medical degree. Afghans with a thousand bucks buy fake Taliban death threats and claim asylum the moment they reach the European border.'

Hassan finished his beer and suddenly looked weary. 'There are websites on Facebook,' he explained. 'Maps, routes, telephone numbers.'

He glanced up as two men entered, a Kurd in a *shemagh* and a white guy in camouflage pants and shades. They nodded in our direction and took the corner table. The bar lad followed. Jack caught the eye and held up three fingers.

My phone buzzed with a text from Natty that read 'miss you' with a row of hearts. I sent back a row of kisses.

'My daughter,' I said, explaining myself, and slid the phone back in my pocket.

The air had cooled. The first shadows slipped across the garden. Blue and yellow parrots chattered in the pomegranate trees. They were called 'beauty birds' and were sold in bamboo cages in the bazaar. Families made a living netting them to sell on the international market. The day will come when all the parrots have gone, I thought, same as the elephants and orangutans, and we'll all ask why no one did anything about it.

The boy came back with a plate of pistachios and three pints on a tray. He wiped the table with a filthy rag before placing the glasses in front of us. As he turned to leave, Hassan slid a blue dinar note into his hand.

'Turks are foxes,' he said. 'They take billions of euros from the European

Union to keep refugees in Turkey. More than two million in camps built for two hundred thousand.' He slapped his chest. 'Only the Kurds protect refugees.'

'You just want to impress the Americans. You're playing the long game,' Jack said, and Hassan nodded.

'We play the long game for a long time. We will never stop.' He shrugged his big shoulders. 'Do not underestimate President Erdogan. He is an Islamist at heart. He went to jail for being an Islamist. His long-term policy isn't to join Europe. It is to weaken Europe. He dreams of a new Ottoman Empire.'

'He's putting more holes in the sinking ship,' Jack remarked, and Hassan smiled.

'Your people are afraid Muslims are going to swamp your country, your schools, your hospitals,' he said and shook his beads. 'And we are. You will have more crime, more drugs, more weapons, more terror attacks. This is good for Turkey. It makes Mr Erdogan seem like a rock, a solid leader. You know, they keep asylum seekers in camps being fed by your charities and let the people smugglers take the assassins and terrorists into Europe.'

'Fuck me,' I said.

We were quiet for a moment. It all seemed so hopeless. I was setting out to rescue one girl when there were millions of suffering people flooding out from war zones and nobody wanted them. Jack and Hassan lit cheroots. We talked about old comrades, the way you do; who was where, who was dead, who had vanished into thin air.

'You still in Crete?' Jack asked.

'That's home now, mate,' I said.

He nodded. 'Know what you mean. I haven't seen the white cliffs for four years. Got no plans to do so, either.'

We sipped our beer. Jack blew smoke rings. Hassan comforted his beads. Looking at my two mates across the table was like looking at a Photofit image of myself. The men who went to that bar had shared the same experiences. They had done things no man should ever be asked to do and lived with the memories. I had seen mates die at my side and felt that odd sensation of elation and guilt that it was him not me. You don't feel good when you kill another human being. If you drink, you drink too much, and when you've drunk too much, you keep on drinking until you fall over. Men who don't feel these things are psychopaths. You recognize them and you don't let them on your team.

CHAPTER 6
First Blood

Sometimes you spend a long time planning an operation, then, at the last minute, decide to abort. That's how I was feeling about our plans to rescue Diana Abbasi. We had the will. What we didn't have was the cold hard cash.

I'm not sure why when Matt Lambert Skyped me I told him we had plans to go into Mosul to grab a girl, but I'm glad I did. I mentioned that we'd come up against a hurdle and that the driver was going to cost $5,000.

'I'll take care of that,' he said.

'Do what?'

'Come on, it's the least I can do.'

I had to think for a moment. 'The driver wants cash – in dollars,' I told him.

'They always do. Be ready for a pick-up in forty-eight hours.'

'It's strictly covert. No paper trail.'

'I'm aware of that, John.'

'Listen, mate, it's appreciated. I don't mind telling you…'

'My pleasure.'

The call ended and I sat back to reassess my feelings about Captain Lambert. I had been revving myself up to tell the others that the mission was off and was bloody glad that, thanks to Matt, I would save face.

Hassan had already spoken to Apollo and put him in contact with Diana Abbasi. They had arranged the hour and location for the exchange. Daybreak in three days' time. I had no reason to feel confident that all the pieces would slot into place, not after Laura's fixer had scooted with 10K, but Matt Lambert appeared to see some future in our collaboration and his offer was a sweetener. How the girl was going to slip unseen from the women's quarters, and how Apollo was going to be able to reach her, was their business.

We sat in the kitchen drinking coffee and looking over the maps. Cano sat across the table dismantling one of the four scrappy AKs he had acquired. A Kalashnikov in use has eight moving parts: the bolt, bolt carrier, hammer, gas piston and springs. He oiled, adjusted and wiped each part, then used a long brush dipped in solvent to clean the shell case deposits inside the barrel. As he reconstructed the weapon, it was like watching a magician, the parts clicking and snapping as they passed through his hands.

Music poured in from the yard where Usef was tuning a Nissan Pathfinder that had been in a collision, shattering the two right-side windows. Elind had attached sheets of plastic over the empty spaces, vital if you didn't want to eat sand crossing the desert. Dozan had borrowed or bought the wreck from his cousin – it was unclear which – and had seemed offended when I offered to pay for it. It was the same with Cano's AKs and the suit delivered by Hassan's tailor. The guys were financing the mission for reasons that were never discussed and were undoubtedly as complicated as my own.

80

I took a shower and felt like a bride, parading around the kitchen in my new suit. The tailor had supplied a white shirt and Dozan had loaned me a red silk tie with a silver stripe. I'd even polished my boots.

Cano Ali looked up from cleaning another rifle. 'You are very beautiful,' he said.

'You are going to get a slap if you don't watch it,' I told him. He didn't understand and no one translated.

Hassan picked off a loose thread from my sleeve. 'May I give you a word of advice?' he asked, dead serious.

'Any time you like, mate.'

'You can never trust a spy.'

Dozan curled the horns of his moustache. 'Even your own,' he added.

I was aware of that, but the guys had my best interests at heart and I just nodded like I was taking it all in.

Hassan followed me out into the yard. He stood beneath the palms gazing up at the haze-layered sky, a hand shading his brow. The sun was stoking up for a noon high of 45 degrees. I could smell the dust baking in the air. There was always dust in Erbil. Strong winds sweep it up from the desert. On days when dust storms lift the tents at Aski Kalak into the air like kites, the women in pink headscarfs sit with their backs to the wind sheltering their children.

Usef opened the gates. The street dogs sheltered in patches of shade, too lethargic to chase the old 4x4 as Elind bounced over the ruts and drove into the city. He offered me a cigarette.

'Gave it up,' I said. He lit up, taking both hands off the wheel.

'Mr John, if you need a driver, you know, I strong.'

'I can see that.'

'I am good shot. I show you.'

'What about your studies. Aren't you at college?'

'I study to be architect. I am a modernist, like Frank Gehry. He's very good,' he replied. 'You know, in my spare time.'

'I'll have a word with your uncle, see what he has to say.'

'No problem. He cool.'

I looked back at Elind. He was a bundle of energy and hormones, the new generation who would rebuild Iraq.

He screeched through the traffic, showing what he could do. The sun beat down and my back was wet when we finally jerked to a halt outside the Divan Hotel, a tower block above a pool as wide as a moat. The muezzin was calling the faithful to *zuhr* prayers. Midday. I was right on time. I passed through the scanners and X-ray machine, there was more security in the hotel than the airport, and caught sight of myself in a long mirror – windblown, hair tossed, sweat patches under my arms as big as China.

A flunky led me to an air-conditioned salon at the back of the lobby where two men were waiting. The agent who had arranged the meeting rose from his seat and stepped forward to shake my hand. In his pale linen suit, he looked crisper than a winter day in Blackpool.

'Cornelius Visser. Do call me Cor,' he said.

'Pleased to meet you.'

His companion remained seated and studied me over the spire of his fingers. Visser was tall, with long black hair down to his shoulders and green eyes like dots behind round-rimmed glasses. He had the modulated tones of a newsreader on the BBC. The other man was older and looked depressed, with drawn cheeks, hair thinning, a tic in his left eye. He sat at a gilt-legged table with a yellow notepad and an iPhone, no doubt on record.

Visser and I sat facing each other, his colleague outside my line of vision. I fancied a pint of chilled cider and made do with iced water. Visser began by asking me how I knew Laura Hansen and I told him I didn't know her at all.

'Then why would you put yourself in danger trying to bring her across the border from ISIS?'

I shrugged. 'It's what you do. She's a young girl with kids who wanted to get out.'

'And for the money?'

'What money?'

'You were paid ten thousand euros.'

'Dollars, mate, not euros. I never got my hands on the money.'

'Then why would you and your associates continue the tasking?'

I refilled my water glass and thought about that for a few moments. 'I don't know. It just felt right,' I said.

'You were sent money through the jihadi network?'

'I just told you, mate, I never got the money.'

'But it was sent.'

'I imagine it was. But they're all bloody thieves. They left me in Erbil with my dick hanging out.'

Visser smiled. His eyes brightened. He was vaguely androgynous with his long hair and fine features. I imagined he was the sort of bloke who went to clubs dressed in black leather, but could probably kill you in two seconds with a paperclip.

He sat back, smile gone, and asked me about Laura's husband. I told him I knew no more than what I'd heard on Kurdistan television. He then asked me the same questions in a different way, the oldest trick in the book, and I gave him the same answers. I'd played the game before. It's called drain my brain, give nothing and make yourself look good when you write up a report for your superiors.

'You do know the Hansen family are supporting the jihadis?' he continued.

'I wouldn't know one way or the other. But I would find it unlikely.'

'You were contacted by complete strangers offering ten thousand dollars to rescue Laura Hansen?'

'As we've established.'

'The money disappeared and still you went ahead?'

I felt a sigh rising through my chest. 'That's right,' I answered.

'Why?'

'You're going round in circles, mate. Laura made a mistake going to Syria. She decided she wanted to come home.'

'A life-changing mistake.'

'We all make mistakes,' I said. 'You can't always explain what you do. Sometimes, you just do it. You see a fence and jump over it. You see a box in the street and you kick it. Laura was fed up in Holland and decided to have a look at Syria. She didn't think about the consequences. She just did it...'

'Because she believes in jihad.'

'I doubt if she even knows what it means.'

'Laura Hansen converted to Islam at seventeen.' He removed his glasses to emphasize the point. 'Converts are the most dangerous, the true believers. She could be putting the whole of Europe in jeopardy.'

'One girl! You having a laugh?'

'When ISIS plans an attack in Europe, it doesn't send encrypted emails. They send women who learn the information by heart and whisper it in the ear of commanders on the ground.'

'You think that's what she's up to?'

'I do not know. Not yet. The point is, neither do you.' His lips tightened. He put his glasses back on. 'Had it not been for the Peshmerga bringing the woman out, you would have been arrested.'

'On what charge?'

'Aiding terrorism.'

'You know that's bollocks. I decided to try and get Laura and her kids out of Mosul because I had a chance to help someone and would have felt like an arsehole if I didn't try,' I said. 'My intention was to debrief her, then hand her over to the authorities.'

'You were going to debrief Laura Hansen?'

'Look, it's obvious. Actionable intelligence from people who have come out from inside Islamic State is gold dust – ISIS strategy, ambitions, weaponry, methods of recruitment. Anything we can get. We have to profile volunteers and build a bigger picture. It will save lives in the long run.'

He took a long breath. 'God save us from the idealist,' he said, and shook his head. 'Are you working covertly for British intelligence?'

'You know I'm not.'

'So what you are doing, Mr Carney, is expanding your own network?'

'I don't have a network,' I replied.

This was largely true. I had contacts from my years in Iraq, but creating a network to smuggle jihadi brides and defectors out of the Caliphate had not been on my itinerary until that second. It was exactly what I needed. Exactly what Matt Lambert had been hinting at. I saw what was happening in Iraq and Syria as a human crisis that needed a human response, the very opposite of Cornelius Visser.

'What I was hoping…' I said, and paused before starting again. 'What

I was hoping was that I might get some money out of you people...'

'From me?' His eyebrows rose, and the way he crossed his legs it was as if the two motions were connected.

'From Dutch intelligence. There might be other young women with intel that I could bring out.'

Visser spoke to his companion in Dutch and they both laughed. He pulled his chair closer.

'There is a theory that the future determines the present. Conflict is not always initiated by today's circumstances, but with the fear of how much worse conditions could become tomorrow.' He raised a warning finger. 'If we don't hit the terrorists now, hard, without pity, we shall pay a higher price in the years ahead. We must put the fear of God into people answering the call to jihad, or ISIS will grow stronger. Governments cannot negotiate or give rights to terrorists, or we will face far greater acts of terrorism in the future.'

'I don't disagree. But you don't want to kill innocents thinking they're terrorists.'

'And we do not want to give freedom to terrorists playing innocent.'

He was right. We were both right. We fell silent until the older guy piped up for the first time.

'Every mosque is a potential centre of terrorist activity, a Trojan horse in the midst of our towns and cities,' he said. 'Last month, in Wales, in Cardiff, an imam told his gathering that war is coming and Islam allows men to rape women and keep them as slaves.'

'War is not coming. We are at war,' Cor Visser added. 'You don't want to be on the wrong side, and you don't want to be seen as being on the wrong side.'

Visser stood. The meeting was over. AIVD was not going to allow me to see Laura Hansen. I didn't ask. There was going to be no exchange of information; certainly no financial aid. Whatever I did from this day forward would be without pay and strictly below the radar.

I crossed the lobby to the bar and had a pint of cider. Then I had another pint.

The sun in August rises over Mosul a few minutes after five. We were in bed at 9pm, and up at 1am after four hours sweating restlessly in the faltering air-con. I remember an old sergeant saying once there was plenty of time to sleep when you're dead. Coffee. Cold showers. Dozan carried five-litre bottles of water out to the two vehicles. Cano, fag in his lips, loaded the batteries and attached the mags to the AKs.

On the table, incongruous among the coffee glasses, stood one hundred $50 bills in a paper sheath stamped by the bank. Matt Lambert had come through and Hassan had collected the $5,000 from a lawyer with an office close to the parliament. He shoved the wad in his tunic and pulled out a 9mm Glock. He snapped the magazine into the hand grip, pulled the slide back and snapped a shell into the chamber. He handed the gun to me butt first.

'For you,' he said.

I weighed the weapon in my palm. It was better than any Christmas present I ever got as a child.

'Fucking hell, you serious?'

'It is my pleasure. We are ready.'

I went back upstairs to collect my webbing holster and felt dressed for the part.

Cano closed the gates and stepped into the 4x4 with Dozan at the wheel. I joined Hassan in the Pathfinder. He fired the engine and our two-car package slid through the empty streets. The world was silent. People living in buildings with flat roofs slept in the cool under the stars. We turned on to the ring road and headed south towards Al Kuwayr.

Hassan switched off the lights as we crossed the frontier at a place where the fence was broken. He followed the camel tracks along the banks of the Tigris towards Hamman al-Alil. The previous month, in July, Coalition F-16 fighters had destroyed ISIS bases in the town. We had no confirmed intel, but according to the latest reports, there was little ISIS presence and few patrols.

Two winds cross the desert and whip the surface grit into dust storms: the dry southern *sharqi* and the cold *shamal* from the north. We were lucky. They were absent. The night was still, breathless. The universe was infinite, alive, a watercolour of constellations and shooting stars that made you believe in the divine.

The track Hassan followed was a line of compressed sand like a scar lit by the moon. The milky glow shaped the stumpy mounds made by killer ants, the surviving date palms, the jagged profile of the Zagros Mountains. Dotted over the landscape were the glinting husks of cars and tanks torn apart by mortars and rockets. Booby traps and IEDs lay hidden along the way, but the desert is vast and it's best to think positive. Nervous sweat had soaked my suit that day with the Dutch agents. I was relaxed now, senses honed, heart steady, the Glock snugly against my hip.

We took the long way around Hamman al-Alil and entered a valley with some plucky fields of cereals irrigated by the Tigris, a world unchanged. At least in the dark. A few goats skipped off into the night. A dog howled, and the silence followed us through the clusters of barns and mud-walled houses outside Mosul. I had Hassan's map on my knees, but he had memorized the route.

We approached the low-build apartment blocks on the outskirts, most in ruins, a thick layer of silvery-white dust coating everything as far as the eye could see. Even with the windows closed, I could smell dead smoke, burnt fuel, ammonium nitrate. There were no lights. Nothing moved except our two vehicles; four guns in the jittery heart of the Islamic State. I glanced at my watch. It was five minutes before dawn.

We pulled in to the rubble in a narrow street of bomb-scarred buildings. Hassan sent a text. A reply pinged immediately. The fixer was on his way, the girl on board. He forwarded the text to Cano and Dozan in the second vehicle. In ten minutes, we'd be heading back across the desert before the sun had time to crank up the boilers.

Hassan pointed. 'They're here,' he said. He placed the $5,000 on the dash above the steering wheel.

A black VW people carrier moved slowly towards us.

'Fuck! What's that?' I said.

A pickup with bull bars and a machine gun bolted in the flatbed appeared from the opposite direction. I watched in the side mirror. The vehicle slowed at each parked car and the passenger aimed the beam of a flashlight into the interior. I unsnapped the stud on my holster.

The people carrier and the ISIS patrol drew closer. We were in the worst possible position. Bang in the middle. I wasn't sure if Dozan and Cano were aware of the sudden threat and there was no time to text them. The fixer in the VW must have scented danger. He turned into a side street and sped away from the scene. The pickup stopped and the flashlight picked out my red English face.

The jihadi gunman lowered the light and stepped from the vehicle.

So did I, Glock in the firing position. I dropped two rounds in his chest. He went down like an empty sack. The driver threw himself into the street. He let off a stream of bullets that arced wildly across the ruined buildings. Cano Ali had exited the 4x4, weapon shouldered. He loosed two in response and strode swiftly across the space towards the pickup.

I was back in my seat beside Hassan. He held up his finger before I could speak. I watched Cano relieve the jihadis of their weapons. He then rooted around inside the cab and moved fast as a shadow back to the vehicle, rifles over his shoulder, arms laden with spare mags. Dozan fired the engine and led the way back into the desert as the first glimmer of sunrise touched the horizon.

CHAPTER 7

Butterfly Effect

Karimabad, the main city in Pakistan's Hunza Valley, is a picture postcard with narrow streets and wood-trimmed stone buildings below an unimaginably blue sky. At the end of the long Himalayan winter, the cherry trees light up with balls of pink blossom. Snow-capped mountains stretch through wreaths of purplish mist and it feels at first glance as if you have arrived in Shangri-La, somewhere secret and otherworldly.

Curiously for a region bordering Afghanistan and China, the people have European features and are thought to be descendants of Macedonian soldiers who reached the valley with Alexander the Great. Men and women dress alike in traditional *salwar kameez*, baggy trousers and long shirts, the men in plain white or shades of brown, the women in colourful patterns with white headscarves. You don't see niqabs or burqas, and the mosques in Karimabad with their bright mosaic tiling have a distinctly Oriental feel about them.

Diana Abbasi had received her degree in international relations at London South Bank University. She was thrilled to get her British passport and visit her parents' old home in the Hunza Valley for the first time. The couple had married in the 1980s and arrived in London with £50 to start a new life. Her mother still worked in the post office, weighing parcels and selling stamps. Her father, after 30 years trudging the streets as a postman by day and driving a taxi at night, had saved enough to buy a half share with his brother in a Londis convenience store.

They were doing well. The family observed Muslim customs without being strict. Diana wore jeans, tops from Gap, a headscarf when she was with her parents. She planned to continue her studies before finding work, perhaps with an NGO or the United Nations. Two women Diana admired as role models were the journalists Mishal Husain and Fatima Manji. They had shown that Muslim women could observe their religion while being in the public eye. They were authoritative, self-confident, feisty – and nothing gave Diana more pleasure than watching as they revealed shady politicians for what they were.

Mishal Husain chose not to wear a head covering. Fatima Manji was the first woman on British television to report wearing a hijab. They had made opposite decisions on how they wanted to present themselves, and that, to Diana, was how it should be in a modern, integrated society.

She had been led to believe that the family holiday with her two brothers had been arranged, in part, as a gift for her doing well in her degree. What she had not imagined, and would never have imagined, was that the principal purpose of their trip to Pakistan was to introduce her to her future husband, a distant cousin from the rural village of her grandparents. Malik was twice her age. He had dirty feet, yellow teeth and didn't speak a word of English. With a wedding to attend and a job in the convenience store guaranteed by his future father-in-law, his visa application had already been approved.

As Diana gazed at Malik across the room, her world fell apart. Her heart beat harder. The scales fell from her eyes. When she had first arrived, Karimabad had appeared quaint, picturesque. Now reality rained down on her like falling stones. What she saw was crumbling buildings with that uncertain look of being half built or half in ruins, filthy streets awash in mud, open sewers leaking the sulphurous smell of bad eggs. Malik's village was a scene from the Middle Ages, dirt poor, no running water, a hole in the ground serving as a toilet. It was little wonder her parents had left.

When they returned to London, Diana couldn't eat. She couldn't sleep. She cried bitter tears that stained her pillow. She tried to reason with her parents but a wall had grown up between them. They had allowed her the freedom to go to university. That was enough. Her father told her she 'belonged' to the extended family; the tribe. Her duty was to obey her father, and to obey Malik when they were married.

After 30 years in England her parents were outwardly liberal, assimilated, but their mentality remained in the Hunza Valley. Her brothers had not suffered the same humiliation. They were men. They were free. She was a 'possession' imprisoned in a culture from which there was no escape. She wanted to run away, but to where, with whom? Her education had all been for nothing. She would never be allowed to contribute like Mishal Husain and Fatima Manji.

Diana would look back and see how the decisions she made in the weeks following her return from Karimabad were driven by desperation and anxiety. She lost her sense of self. Her dreams lay broken. She had never given much thought to what it meant to be a Muslim and was surprised, when she went online, to find out how ill-informed and naïve she had been. Like an explorer in a new land, she followed links through the maze of endless websites. She watched documentaries made in Iraq,

Syria, Afghanistan. She wept over photographs of children with missing limbs in shattered hospitals. There had always been wars in the Middle East. But there was a philosophical war, too. A war of ideas, a battle between the greed-driven past and the vision of a new and better future. Diana had lived securely, obliviously, in London, while people like her were fleeing their homes from firebombs, shelling, drone attacks and barrel bombs.

She found her way to a chat room where she made friends with a woman her own age named Eva, a British-born Muslim with a wide smile and laughter in her voice. Eva had grown up in Middlesbrough, where she had always felt like a second-class citizen in a society suffering the pains of austerity and blaming their woes on the immigrant. People were sinking into the slime of celebrity gossip, the sexual and financial transgressions of the super rich, the mind-numbing tide of fake news. During the referendum debates in June, posters showed a million women in hijabs pressing at the steel fence marking the European border. The voters didn't vote to leave Europe. They voted to exclude the stranger, the foreigner, the Muslims.

Long before Brexit, Eva had fled to the Caliphate, where she felt empowered, energized. Every day was an adventure. With their bare hands they were laying the foundations of a brave new world. Jihad was a sacred duty. The soldiers of Islamic State weren't terrorists. That was all lies, western propaganda. They were freedom fighters creating *jannah*, the paradise on earth prophesied in the Quran. As she and Eva talked through the night on Skype, Diana felt uplifted, inspired, needed. With her training in international relations, she could bring skills to the Caliphate and show her parents that she could be a good Muslim without climbing into the marriage bed with Malik.

Diana understood the paradox at the core of the Muslim community. They wanted to be made to feel welcome in British society, while remaining – by their own volition – on the outside. She recalled playing with little girls her own age in the park. Her mother never chatted with the other women, and looked back with a vaguely distant expression if someone spoke to her. Diana came to realize that this did not arise from feelings of inferiority, but the opposite. They were special. They had been blessed by Allah, while all the other children and their mummies had not.

This intrinsic sense of difference created a metaphorical veil she had always worn, even at university. She had never had a boyfriend. She talked with boys in her study group, she would count some of them as friends, but there was never any question of going to the cinema or a club together. Young people sharing a flat, intimacy, sex. Those things, perfectly normal and accepted in modern British life, were an abomination to Islam.

Diana had a friend, a Pakistani girl, who had fallen in love with a Moroccan boy, a Muslim like her, but still it was out of the question that they could be together. They ran away and, when they were caught, the girl's two brothers murdered their sister. She had brought shame on the family and the family had demanded a blood sacrifice. It was a madness woven into the fabric of being Muslim in the western world – and worse, those crimes were rarely investigated or punished. Why should the authorities care? Each community lived by its own rules in a disconnected, parallel universe. Integration was like a ghost people spoke of but no one had ever seen.

Diana gazed out at the stars and what she saw was her life stretching out with the interminable boredom of cooking, sewing, staying home, having babies, weddings and the mosque. To wake beside Malik every day would not be a new life. It would be a slow death. All she could see in her mind's eye was his yellow teeth, his red-rimmed eyes, his dirty feet. Her parents had stolen her birthright. Eva offered an alternative, the chance to really find herself.

When she woke the following morning, the knots in her stomach had untied. Diana took her savings from the bank. She found her passport in a drawer, and crept out of the house before daybreak the following day dressed the way she always had as an English girl at college. She had a one-way ticket on the Eurostar from St Pancras to the Gare du Nord. In Paris, she caught the Deutsche Bahn for Stuttgart and Budapest, where she changed trains for Istanbul. No one asked any questions. Why would they?

She had downloaded the Find My Friends app. People had tracked her journey. Two friendly lads were waiting for her at the station in Istanbul. They drove her to the city's smuggling hub in Aksaray. There she joined several other girls in a Volkswagen panel van that took them across country to an unguarded spot in the razor-wire fence dividing Turkey from Syria. She changed from blue jeans into a long black *abaya* with a full-face niqab. She knew before she reached Mosul that it had all been a terrible mistake.

I pieced together Diana's story first from speaking with her parents and, later, after an unexpected stroke of luck, from a debriefing with Diana herself. Her parents were good people. They loved their daughter, but had made decisions about her future without taking her hopes and desires into account.

Every girl who travelled to the Caliphate and married a jihadi had their own story, but at the heart of each one was the culture clash between their daily life and experiences in Europe and the stone-wall demands of Islam. Diana told me that when her parents arranged to marry her to an older man she didn't know, she had felt humiliated, abused, diminished. The fact that she saw no other option than to run away was something I understood. The circumstances were different, every circumstance is different, but I had been abused as a child and it marks you like a scar you carry with you for the rest of your life.

It began when I was six years old.

My father had a gold-plated Hamilton wristwatch that had belonged to his father. Grandad had been a Desert Rat in the Eighth Army. He followed General Montgomery across North Africa in 1941, killing Germans along the way. Or so dad liked to tell anyone who would listen. There was a photograph of grandad in uniform on the sideboard. He was a tall man with wide shoulders and dark eyes that stared knowingly from the frame. It can't have been easy for his puny son; dad doubtless never lived up to grandad's expectations and came to resent his own son growing up a replica of his father.

Once, while dad was shaving, I picked up the famous watch and tried to turn the winder. The sound of the razor scraping at his bristles stopped. Our eyes met in the mirror and my fingers turned to jelly. I dropped the watch in the bath and my father slapped me so hard across the head, I bit through my lip. There was blood everywhere and I burst into tears. When mum came running up the stairs to see what had happened, I saw a look of terror on her face. I don't recall ever seeing my father hit my mother, but she lived in fear of his temper. For the next two years, so did I.

Once you have hit someone who is small and defenceless, you either feel sickened by what you have done or you get a taste for it. In the warehouse where dad spent his days stacking boxes, he was ordered about by the young bloke in a suit who ran the office. My father hated his job. I'm sure he hated himself. I was his punching bag. If he was in a bad mood, I would feel the weight of his hand. If I didn't move fast enough, I'd feel his boot as well.

I cried when I was six. I cried when I was seven. The tears had dried up by the time I was eight. I had grown accustomed to violence. I had plenty of fights with the boys at school, but learned to hold back. I was aware that I could hurt the other lads. What I wanted was to be hurt myself, to feel pain, because pain was at least a concrete emotion.

When you bully a child, you need someone to blame other than yourself, so you blame the victim. The intimidation feels empowering and the bully justifies his actions by saying you have an evil streak that has to be knocked out of you, that every blow is an act of kindness.

Whatever love my mother may have had for me, she kept it hidden. I found the affection I craved with the family pets, our cats and dogs, even the hens in the chicken house where I would hide when dad was on one of his rampages. Now I can look back, my biggest regret is that my education was minimal. I was always being sent to the headmaster, or sent home. I turned up to play football and cricket, but spent more time playing hooky in Warminster Town Park, where I would feed the ducks and run off my energy.

When I was 14, the local council issued a School Attendance Order against my parents. It infuriated my father, but he didn't hit me. I was bigger than him now. Two constables arrived the following day in a panda car to escort me to school. When we slowed in traffic, I jerked up the handbrake and jumped out of the back. I was quickly caught, as always.

Running away is not a strategy for escape. It is a cry for help or love, or a reaction. This time, the reaction was the last thing I had expected. I was taken before the magistrates and sent to reform school for a year.

This was a golden time for a teenage fighter. I was like a kid in a sweet shop. They were all bad boys, mostly older than me. On the second day, something was said, some slight, some jibe, maybe a joke. It didn't matter. I lashed out and took on the entire table of 16-year-olds. I didn't win that one, but they knew I had arrived. In the next 12 months, I learned that during a fight, deception is just as useful as strength, and getting in the first blow is always an advantage.

My old comprehensive took me back, not that I had been reformed. On the contrary. Locking boys up doesn't turn them into angels. It turns them into delinquents. Most boys sent to an institution have been bullied and most are unable to break the cycle, so they end up as bullies too. Now I was out, my father was frightened of me. I should have relished that, but it was sad. It was like the Arctic stood between us and every look was as cold as ice.

I was quickly bored strutting down the long corridors at school, so I hit the high road down to the park where I spent hours in the outside gym doing pull-ups and press-ups. The police came to find me. I ran away. I kept running away until I turned 16 and my school days were over. My father wanted me out of the house. I had nowhere to go and took the only option open to an unloved boy with low self-esteem, emotional and psychological problems. I joined the army – the 1st Battalion, Yorkshire Regiment – and entered the iron gates at Battlesbury Barracks.

Army life is like wearing a pair of ill-fitting boots. You put up with it. It's like reform school: demanding, demeaning, often brutal, and you rarely have any idea what's going on. From being woken sadistically at

5.30am, you are screamed at and messed about for the rest of the day. You are never entirely sure in which uniform to dress for which lesson, or where it is taking place. I learned to live with the routines and discipline without grasping why it was necessary to polish your boots before setting out on a 20-mile hike over the muddy slopes of the Brecon Beacons.

After surviving the 14-week basic training course, I had to wait more than year before I did my first of two tours in Northern Ireland. I felt totally at ease carrying an assault rifle with live ammo and was never afraid to take point when we patrolled Royal Avenue in Belfast. The Paddies took one look at me and saw that I was one of them. Not that it always worked out that way.

One night, I was with three mates in a pub and Craig, a good-looking, blue-eyed lad from south London, tried to chat up a local girl – a no-no for some reason. Someone poked someone else in the chest and spilled their beer. That's how it kicks off. We rolled out into the street full of piss and swagger, four of us against ten of them – good odds, I thought. But Craig didn't want to damage his pretty face. He ran off and the other two followed. I wasn't going to have that. I stood my ground until I was down in the gutter and got the worst kicking I've ever had.

I was stitched back together and spent the night in the infirmary. Next day, I stood weak as a used tea bag on crutches before Regimental Sergeant Major Jim Wilkes – 'Big Jim' – six feet of spit and polish with iron-grey hair and a Military Cross from the Falklands. He was the only man in the regiment I respected.

'What the fuck?' he said, and my face was so smashed up I found it hard to reply. 'How many of them this time?'

'Zen,' I replied.

'Ten?'

I nodded. He shook his head.

'You know who you remind me of? You remind me of the dumb fucker I was when I joined up.' He held up his hand, not that I had anything to say. 'It's all very well being a good fighter. What matters is to know what you're fighting for.' He took a breath. 'Do you know what you're fighting for, John?'

I shrugged. 'Self-respect,' I mumbled.

He held up his fist. 'You don't get self-respect with these,' he said, and tapped the side of his head. 'You get self-respect from what's up here.'

He stared me down and I hobbled out on my crutches.

I was astonished that I wasn't put on a charge after the punch-up with the locals, but the guys who ran off were. This small gesture, added to Big Jim's few words, had a powerful effect on me. Instead of fighting the system, I put more into it and, would you believe it, got a lot more out in return. I started boxing in the ring instead of the streets. I learned to drive. I studied martial arts, map reading and all those less quantifiable military skills: patience, tact, flexibility. I discovered I was actually quite good at soldiering and that was incredible. I had never been much good at anything.

As I began to think for myself, it struck me that in the armed forces you are a puppet, a target, a statistic. I saw blokes shot through the head and blown to bits by pipe bombs. I was on base in Crossmaglen in 1994 when the IRA brought down a Lynx helicopter with an improvised mortar, wounding three squaddies. I never really understood why we were in Northern Ireland and didn't support one side over the other. In spite of the brawls and petty rivalries, the only thing that mattered to me was my mates, boys with messed-up minds, self-doubters and self-harmers, not the officers with their hidden agendas and links up the chain to higher levels of power and control. The army is a reflection of British society, divided by class, education, even the sports we play.

After serving out my six years in the Yorks, I kicked around, failing in a succession of crap jobs in civvy street before signing on with CRG Security Solutions. I kitted myself up with some good shades and was on the first flight to Iraq. The moment I stepped out of the airport, Wayne Whitely, another old soldier like myself, handed me an AK with two magazines and told me as we set off down the BIAP that it was the most dangerous road in the world. He wasn't wrong. I had entered the Wild West, or the Wild East, my university campus for the next decade.

Baghdad in 2003 was a gold rush. President Bush had declared victory after the one-sided war against Saddam Hussein and pushed through Congress a reconstruction package worth $87 billion – including $30 billion for security. I watched from the concourse at the airport as the crisp new greenbacks were unloaded on palettes from transport planes in shrink-wrapped blocks of $250,000. The city was awash in baksheesh, new Toyotas, refrigerators, air-con units and high-speed computers with something Saddam had denied his citizens: internet porn.

Insurgents dropped bombs off bridges as we drove generals into the CPU (Coalition Provisional Authority) – the Green Zone, a pleasure park of palaces and five-star hotels with swimming pools guarded by a steel fence and a ring of M1 Abrams battle tanks. While American forces patrolled the streets in armoured Humvees, on the west bank of the Tigris builders started laying the footings for the new American Embassy in a 100-acre complex the size of Vatican City. With schools and supermarkets for the 5,000 staff, the building has 15ft Hesco-sheathed walls and is said to be the only structure in the world that would withstand an attack from a nuclear bomb.

It was a sure sign to the Iraqis that the Americans were there to stay. Since the 8th century, Baghdad has been at the crossroads of the ancient silk routes, and Iraq happens to sit on the largest oil deposits in the world outside Saudi Arabia. American air strikes had smashed the entire oil infrastructure and American taxpayer dollars paid American corporations to rebuild it – a neat way of taking money from the poor and giving it to the rich.

In Ireland, if you fired one round there was an inquiry. In Iraq that year, I drew fresh mags from the armoury every day. I learned how to use cut-down weapons and RPGs, rocket-propelled grenades. We were shot at most days and loosened up drinking spritzers with barbecued lamb at sundown on the roof of our fortress building, watching erupting bombs and internecine firefights. Bursts of gunfire sounded through the night. Tracer lit the sky like it was Guy Fawkes Day every day. The constant whine and thrum of helicopters pounded overhead and I felt like an extra in *Apocalypse Now*.

Sadr City was the most precarious quarter of the most treacherous city on earth. That's where we made night runs bringing crates of beer to fancy-dress parties on the American base. Everyone drank as if there was no tomorrow – a self-fulfilling prophecy for some – the music was deafening, nudity routine and palls of smoke from gold-speckled black hash curled through Saddam's crystal chandeliers. There were two complaints: the Picassos and Monets had already been stolen and there were never enough women to go round. Parties turned into orgies. Fist fights became firefights. Night clubs opened. Brothels opened. Iraq turned into Sodom and Gomorrah and the Sunni fundamentalists pulled on their long beards as they looked on in horror.

While we were having the time of our lives, the Shia parties, after

30 years of repression, won the general election promoted by the United States with devastating consequences. The end of Sunni rule in Iraq upset the delicate balance in the Middle East and unleashed what has to date been 15 years of carnage in wars that have spread across Libya, Egypt, Yemen, Somalia and Syria, causing more than a million civilian deaths and relentlessly, if unwittingly, damaging the interests of the United States and Europe.

The Middle East Cold War is played out between the two major powers: Sunni Saudi Arabia and Shia Iran, both oil rich and impatient to expand their spheres of influence. The Saudis are backed by the United States. Iran counts on Russia and China, the divide intensifying hostility and mistrust between East and West.

What American and Coalition forces had achieved with their invasion of Iraq was create what Saudi Arabia feared most: the completion of the Shia Crescent, a curving stretch of unbroken territory from Iran, through Shia-administered Iraq, to majority Alawite – Shia-based – Syria, and across the border to the influential Shia militia Hezbollah in Lebanon, the gateway to Israel.

No one has ever been able to explain to me why Dick Cheney, Donald Rumsfeld and the neo-cons in George Bush's White House supported a general election in Iraq when they must have known that the 60 per cent Shia majority would win that election and foster a vision of the world that was the opposite of their own.

Many educated Iraqis I spoke to subscribed to the conspiracy theory that the Americans had not been reckless by going to war. On the contrary, they had done so to trigger what's called the butterfly effect. By activating change in one state – the unseating of Saddam Hussein – chaos would be spread across the Middle East, creating instability and dysfunction: the cycle of wars, the use of chemical weapons, the deliberate targeting of hospitals, the non-stop tide of refugees that produced a sense of siege in the western psyche and the need for greater defence spending. Chaos is good business.

Iran had long been the traditional enemy. The overthrow of Saddam handed Iraq straight into the hands of Iran's ayatollahs. When Shia death squads in Iraq started to hunt down former Sunni leaders and their families – my friend Dozan Rostami among them – Sunni militias were armed by Saudi Arabia to fight back.

Many Sunni volunteers were horrified by the decadence brought by western-style democracy and found their way into ISIS, a strain of jihadi fundamentalism more extreme than al-Qaeda, where the war cycle began: the destruction of the World Trade Center on 9/11 followed by the invasion of Afghanistan.

The anarchy and lawlessness created by the West, which successive American administrations with their European allies have failed to resolve, has turned the Middle East into a wasteland of refugees, people smuggling, child prostitution, slavery, Russian renaissance, the looming threat of an omnipotent China and a bellicose Turkey itching to annihilate the Kurds.

It is a mess, a catastrophe, and it is going to get worse.

I had not reached these conclusions in 2003. What the mayhem meant to me back then was a constant source of highly paid if perilous work. Outside the Green Zone, the roads through every quarter of Baghdad were an assault course on the highway to hell. We escorted diplomats, journalists, oil men in bootlace ties and military officers doing short postings to 'stamp their ticket' and add a campaign medal to the smorgasbord of ribbons on their chests. Armed to the gunwales, we raced over the broken roads on a chicken run of IEDs shoved in drainage pipes, abandoned car tyres and piles of rubbish, while bandits popped up on rooftops and bridges spraying the air with deadly rounds that whizzed overhead like mosquitoes.

After I moved to work for Aegis, it was something of a thrill to be part of the team sent to guard the British Embassy to await the arrival of Prime Minister Tony Blair. A rocket sailed in from nowhere and landed in the car park at the exact moment Blair was due to arrive. He was late – lucky for him, and unlucky for some intelligence chief who must have lost his job.

The first time I was in an ambush was driving in from the airport with a trio of country and western singers, three girls in white cowboy hats. It was the usual pandemonium, Iraqi kamikaze drivers going the wrong way, four-vehicle packets of armoured Humvees with 3rd Infantry gunners in shades behind high-calibre machine guns. I was in the lead vehicle with Wayne driving and a decent ex-British army captain in the back seat. In the middle vehicle, the girls were escorted by two former SAS men. Bringing up the rear was another three-man team, Smudge, Dean and Jake Blackman, an ex-marine from Alabama.

We drove close and fast. On both sides of the road, plastic bottles skipped on the wind over the dusty wilderness. There were a few mud-coloured houses, mostly in ruins, some goat herders who had dropped down from another planet. Off to my left, I could see the Dora refinery with its burning flame, a useful landmark, and, in the distance, the tall marble-clad towers of the Green Zone. Nearly there, I thought, tempting the devil, and a burst of bullets about a foot above the road sliced along the side of the vehicles. It shredded the passenger-side tyres of the old Peugeot carrying the Americans.

Wayne screeched to a halt and reversed at an angle to shield the Peugeot. First rule is to protect your principals. Smudge, driving the tail vehicle, shot forward to complete the barrier. Two chancers in baggy pants and long shirts popped up on the roof of a broken building, firing as if their ancient AKs were garden hoses. Wayne was on my left. He took out the insurgent on the left as I let off two that drilled into the chest of his comrade on the right.

My stomach lurched. Everything went into slow motion. I saw the blood spurt out and hang in the air. The man I'd shot remained standing for a second, as if stunned, then deflated like a balloon as he slipped to the ground. It was like shooting at a target. But it wasn't a target. It was a man. A living man one moment. A dead man the next. My hands trembled. I felt bile rise into my throat. I controlled it until we were back at base. When I threw up my sick had an acidic taste that would always remind me of death.

Killing another human being is not something you get used to. It takes away their life and subtracts something from your own, a fine layer of your humanity. I can say that I have never shot anyone who wasn't intending to shoot at me or kill me in some terrible way. That doesn't justify anything, except we are in a war with terrorists who want to change our way of life and, ultimately, turn the entire world into an Islamic Caliphate. That's not going to happen, but we have to stop those who believe it can happen.

You never forget your first killing. It changes you. It changed me. It made me aware that my job with Aegis wasn't just a means of making a living, a good life with plenty of perks. I had responsibility to add something. If I was going to kill bad guys as part of my job, I had to be more aware of protecting the good guys, the innocent.

Those were the thoughts that accompanied me on the journey back across the desert from Mosul to Erbil.

We had failed to rescue Diana Abbasi.

Now what?

CHAPTER 8
Network

Kali adjusted the music on her iPhone. She drank some water from a plastic bottle and stretched out with her head propped on a rolled towel. She was deeply tanned in a white bathing suit, long limbed with long slender feet that moved to the music like two wriggling fish. With her dark eyes and dark hair, there was something of the primitive about her, unruly; passionate. I never knew what Kali was thinking and always imagined her thoughts were deeper than my own. Her full lips seldom smiled, as if smiles were rationed. When she did smile, it made my heart beat faster. I was happy to be home and anxious to get back to Erbil, rival feelings that went back and forth like a ping-pong ball in my head.

The Sealine rocked on the tide. A speedboat growled by, towing a girl on a single ski. She wheeled from side to side, bouncing over the waves, her long hair streaming behind her, polished by the sun. It was hot and sticky, the dog days of summer. Sirius was rising, the time of sudden thunderstorms, lethargy, mad dogs and bad luck.

Diana Abbasi was still captive in the silver dust of Islamic State. Had they discovered her attempt to flee? Had she been caned, whipped, raped?

I had no way of knowing. No way to find out. Hassan had tried to contact Apollo. His phone was dead. Destroyed probably. Cell phones are like fingerprints recording a digital stream like the curling wave left by the water skier.

More emails from families with girls who wanted to escape the Caliphate dropped daily into my inbox. If we were going to get them out, we needed better organization. A network. Finance. I believed in the old adage: if at first you don't succeed, try, try, try again. We had to try harder. Try better. And I had to fight my inclination to leap first and look after.

I snapped the cap from a Mythos. Natty and two of her friends dived in turn from the high prow. They were good little swimmers and had a system. Plunging into the sea, they drove the fish towards the back of the boat where two lines arced into the water. It seemed to be working. There were three good-sized sea bass circling in a keepnet. We needed one more for dinner.

Our guest that night was Matt Lambert. I picked him up at the Veneziano, a boutique hotel in the old city with polished stone walls and four-poster beds. We had never met but I recognized him immediately. He was standing at the top of the steps like a model promoting English style: tall, with sandy hair parted like a schoolboy on the side, a pale blue shirt the colour of his eyes, his creamy-white suit topped off with a Panama hat with a dark red and dark blue band like a Guardsman's tie. I swung the door open and he hurried down the steps.

'John…'

'Step in, that's me.'

He did so. We shook hands.

'What a pleasure. It's jolly kind to come and collect me.'

'Least I could do, mate,' I replied. 'Taxis can never find my place.'

He hooked into the seat belt. I edged into the traffic flow and turned left, heading towards the coast. We passed the Palace of Knossos. He strained his neck looking up at the crumbling ruins.

'Beautiful,' he said. 'I love this country.'

'You've been before?'

'A few times. I studied classics, before the army got me.' He paused. 'Pity about the girl.'

'Another fuck-up.'

'Don't blame yourself, John. I read your report. You did everything you could.'

He had a plummy accent and manners so honed and polished you had to wonder if he was putting it on. Then again, don't they say you are what you do? I tended to feel awkward with the Matt Lamberts of this world and was irritated with myself for having that feeling.

'Good flight?' I asked, pointlessly.

'BA. Less than four hours. I read the new le Carré. Flying's about the only time when I can catch up with my reading.'

'I always try to catch up with some sleep.'

'The old enemy,' he said. 'You sleep, you wake, and nothing's changed.'

The chirpiness slipped from his tone, which surprised me. I had assumed, without the facts, that his life ran on well-oiled wheels, well-connected, well dug in with a farm in Oxford where he raised cattle – Aberdeen Angus, he'd told me. I still wasn't sure of the purpose of his visit to Crete – unless it was an excuse to tour the ruins – and I wasn't entirely comfortable that he had sent me $5,000 when he wasn't obliged to do so.

'The 5K you sent is still sitting in a drawer in Erbil. I didn't want to take a chance flying back with a lot of cash. I'm no stranger to a body search.'

'Don't even think about it, John. It was an investment,' he said. 'In more ways than one.'

'That so?'

His tone brightened. 'I acquired some stock in a Franco-Iraqi construction company. A broker in Guernsey arranged for a law firm in Erbil to draw up the papers and added five thousand dollars as a contingency.'

'Nice work if you can get it.'

'The Iraqi economy's growing at eleven per cent. If you've got any spare cash, you can't do better. You know as well as me, there are no pensions in our line of work.'

He was right. I had never thought about that sort of thing, growing older, retiring. The big Four-O is more than just a number.

'Could be interesting,' I said.

'If you need any tips, I'd be happy to give you a lead.'

'I might just do that. Soon as I've learned how to play chess.'

I glanced out across the bay. The wind had blown up. Whitecaps broke against the rocks. The island is at the crossroads of four seas: the Myrtoan to the north, the Sea of Crete in the south, the Karpathian in the east, the Libyan to the west. We call it the Mediterranean, but each expanse of water retains its own distinct colour and marine life, its own history.

The road twisted and turned. Coronas of mist clung to the mountains. I turned on to the track leading to the villa. The plaster glowed in the last rays of the sun and I was touched as always by a feeling of pride. I wouldn't have swapped the big pink for a farm in Oxford and all the prize cows in the world.

'Hope you like fresh fish?' I said.

'I most certainly do.' He gazed up at the villa, then back at me. 'Nice place you got here.'

'My little piece of heaven.'

'I'm happy you found it, John.'

Natty opened the gates. The cats swirled about our feet as we stepped from the vehicle. Nikko, the big bruiser, stood off to one side eyeing Matt like a rival.

We had caught one more sea bass, a plump three-pounder. Kali baked the fish with garlic and olive oil on beds of rosemary picked from the garden and served it with feta salad and Kalamata olives. We sat outside beneath the stars with the cats milling around the table legs and an ice-cold bottle of retsina. I took my empties back to Yannis in Heraklion and he practised his English as he filled them from a five-foot barrel. The wine was strong and dark with the taste of the hill pines rising behind the house. Retsina goes straight to the brain. Drink a little and it gives you an edge. Drink a lot and it feels as if the retinas are being scraped off the back of your eyes.

Matt had removed his hat and kissed Kali and Ntileini's cheeks. He focused fully on whoever he was speaking to and made them feel for a moment as if they were the most important person in the world. With his blue eyes and tailored suit, he could have been a character from the John le Carré novel he was reading, the gentleman spy of Natty's imagination. They quickly found common interest in the Minoan ruins at Knossos. I was proud that my daughter had such knowledge, such curiosity, but I couldn't help being reminded of what was happening inside the Caliphate. The buildings, murals and artefacts preserved for three millennia were being dynamited to dust by the jihadis.

I had spent a few days in Palmyra in Syria, a Roman city of white limestone towers and temples built a thousand years before Christ, the touchstones of our shared history. Before the site was obliterated in August 2015, the keeper, Khaled al-Asaad, concealed some of the most important antiquities and suffered four weeks of daily torture without giving up their hiding place. The zealots cut off his head and hung his remains on one of the last standing columns in the ravaged city, a warning to those who defied Islamic State. Khaled al-Asaad was 82 years old. A hero. An inspiration. I promised myself that when I returned to Erbil, I would climb the mount to the Citadel.

Stars flooded into the sky. We picked out the constellations named for Greek gods: Andromeda, Pegasus, Ursa Major. The fish was delicious. You could taste the sea. The hills darkened. We drank Greek coffee with foam on the top and grounds coating the bottom of the cup. It cleared our heads as I led Matt up through the olive grove to the highest point, where the sea stretched out in the distance like a silk sheet shimmering below the rising moon. I had instantly disliked Matt Lambert. Now, I wasn't so sure. There was something vulnerable about him, something honest. I jumped straight in.

'It's nice having you here, Matt. It's good for Natty to have someone smart to talk to.'

'Modesty is a very suspicious quality, John. I don't think you're letting her down in that area.'

'You know what I mean,' I wavered. 'I still haven't worked out what's in it for you.'

'Rescuing young women caught up in the Caliphate?'

'Exactly.'

'What's in it for you?' he returned, standing the question on its head.

114

'I've been wondering that myself,' I replied.

There was no single answer. I had a gut feeling that it was the right thing to do. I wasn't merely in charge of my own destiny, I was shaping it. Perhaps helping to shape the destiny of Iraq and Syria. Jihad had to be stopped and I knew, as Matt Lambert knew, that every bomb dropped from 50,000 feet and every unmanned Predator guided by controllers in Nevada did not bring jihad closer to an end, but inspired more outrage and recruitment from the Muslim community.

There were two places to sit. The remains of an old stone wall and the domed hump of an ancient olive tree. We dropped down, the canopy of pale green leaves above our heads, the moon silvering the turn of the waves.

'A lot of reasons, Matt. I've got a daughter. It could be her over there.'

He looked away, out to sea, then back again. Our eyes met. He was focused.

'I know what it is to have a daughter.' He took a breath. 'I know what it is to lose one.'

A solemn tone had entered his voice; a lot of things that had been unclear were suddenly clearer.

'Lucy would have been starting university about now. She was a summer baby.' His shoulders lifted. 'We used to say she wasn't born in the maternity wing at the hospital. She was born in the saddle. Lucy could ride before she could walk. You know, she won more trophies at gymkhanas than we have shelves to put them on. Every square inch in the stable is pinned with rosettes...'

He choked up. His eyes had become glassy.

'I'm sorry,' I said.

'You don't get over it, John. Never. There is a natural order.' He made

115

a chopping motion, segmenting time. 'You expect your parents to die before you. Not your children. It throws the world out of balance.' He broke off. I could hear the trees murmuring. 'She was on Jasmine, a chestnut filly, a three-year-old. They had an instinct that was uncanny, as if the same blood ran in their veins. Watching them was like watching a bird in flight, something divine almost.'

Lambert glanced away and continued, talking into the darkness.

'We were at an event in Fontainebleau in May. Lucy had done a faultless first round and was riding back to the paddock. There was a lad of about ten on a grey colt that was too big for him. He lost control. The colt charged and Jasmine bolted. She jumped a fence, that's what she was trained to do. They landed in the path of a Land Rover towing a trailer. They were killed on the spot. Both of them. Lucy and Jasmine.' He looked into my eyes. 'We wanted to bury them together, but you can't do that sort of thing.'

Tears trickled down his cheeks. I didn't know what to say. Nothing was appropriate. I felt my own eyes welling up.

'I'm sorry, mate,' I said finally.

He brushed away his tears. His tone hardened. He was a soldier.

'It's not often in life that you get a chance to add something. Jihad isn't a war. It's an ideal. An objective. An aberration. Totally intractable. If there are young women with children, lost boys, whoever it is … if they are trapped in that hell and we can help them get out, don't we have a duty to do so?'

'Not everyone thinks the same way. Dutch intelligence wants us to leave them there and let them die. I daresay MI6 has the same policy.'

'No doubt. There is a consensus. One of the strengths of the EU is shared intel.'

'Then why the bloody hell did we want to leave it, then?'

'We are fragmenting. Political debate, social policy, these things used to be less complicated. Governments had the essentially simple task of creating growth and employment. There was a balance. The pendulum shifted from left to right, an adjustment of taxes to take a little more from the rich to give to the poor…'

'Not enough of an adjustment, in my opinion.'

'I don't disagree. But that's changed. Growth can't go on for ever. It's basic maths – the Greeks taught us that. We're polluting the earth and the oceans, the air we breathe. We compete in every city for space. We're afraid of technology, the barbarian at the gate.' He leaned forward. 'Parts of Africa are unliveable. In the Middle East, people are fleeing bombs, Islamists, the dictators we keep in power. More than a million Syrian refugees are seeking asylum in Europe. More than three million Syrians are sitting on the Turkish border. We're at the beginning of something unknowable, inconceivable. Do you know how many Muslims live in Europe?'

'Ten, twelve million?' I guessed.

'Twenty million. The majority are decent people who want to integrate and have a decent life…'

'Are you sure about that, Matt?'

He shook his head. 'No, I'm not sure. But we have to start from that premise. Every girl, every young man, who leaves Europe to join ISIS verifies our failure to assimilate and create futures for these people, our fellow citizens.' His features sharpened. 'Every person we can bring back is living proof that Islamic State is a failure. We have to change the paradigm.'

In articulating my thoughts, Matt Lambert showed the task was bigger than I had visualized, bigger than I wanted to visualize.

He rolled his arm across the landscape. 'It is appropriate that we're talking about these things here. It's where it all began,' he continued. 'Democracy is built on the essential dignity of man, on the cultivation of moral values; to live with truth, to have compassion. We cannot construct equality. We can create fairness. We've lost these values, John. We've created a kitsch society, completely vacuous, dedicated to our base instincts. Our fathers after the war created the National Health Service, the Welfare State, universal education. A safety net. What have we done? We've cut the strings, unpicked the fabric and allowed it to disintegrate.'

'Have you always thought this way, Matt?'

'No. I'm a company man. An intelligence officer. A flag waver. When Lucy died and Victoria left, I couldn't see any point in going on.' He put two fingers to his temple and pulled the trigger. He shook his head. 'I wasn't made for suicide. It wouldn't have been fair to Victoria *or* Lucy...'

'Victoria's your wife?'

'You look at each other every day and what you see is what you've lost. She went to live with her sister in Bedford, outside New York. We speak. We aren't bad friends.' He shrugged. 'Who knows?'

It was one of those moments when you light a cigarette and that first hit of nicotine puts your thoughts in order. Kali had nagged me to quit smoking, but I still missed it.

'So, we're going to bring girls out of Islamic State and build a better world?'

'I think of it as Operation Jihadi Bride,' he replied, voice firm. 'Parties like UKIP are springing up all over Europe. It's like the 1930s. We're in crisis. There's austerity. No jobs. People feel betrayed. They fear the unknown, the dark skinned, the Muslims. We're ripe for a return to fascism, in England, all over Europe. If that happens, there will be rivers of blood in the streets.'

'If what you say is right, and I don't dispute it at all, whatever we do, it's not going to make any difference.'

'Perhaps not, John. But what else are we going to do? We only get one life. We don't know how long we're going to be here living it. If we can do something, it has to be better than doing nothing.'

He had risen from the stone wall and took a step towards me. I stood. We shook hands.

'We need to build a network,' I said.

'Absolutely. First thing. And raise some money. I've been shaping some proposals, looking at relevant organizations.'

'You've been planning this for a while.'

'Everything's a question of timing. Right time. Right people.'

Matt Lambert then did something I hadn't been expecting. He gave me a man hug, holding me tight, and I heard the blast from the horn of a ship out at sea. It sounded like *hurrah, hurrah*, odd but apt.

CHAPTER 9
Managed Return

The immigration officer opened my passport without checking the photo and applied an old-fashioned wet ink stamp that smudged as he handed it back to me. I was waved through customs and couldn't help wondering as I stepped out of the airport whether it was down to good luck, or if Hassan Ghazi had been playing the puppet-master and pulled a few strings.

Elind and Usef waited in the shade, heads bobbing to zithers and ouds. The lads had put new windows in the Nissan Pathfinder, beaten out the dents and sprayed the vehicle sandy brown, the colour of the desert. They must have known we would be going back before I did. We praised Allah, tapped our chests and Elind put his foot down.

'Blimey, mate, you're not on the run from the cops, are you?' I said, and he dropped a gear as he curved on two wheels out of the parking lot.

'Thank you very much,' he replied.

Erbil hit my nostrils with the usual smells. Ripe fruit and hot spices, the dry wind from the desert, the underlying whiff of gasoline, the black gold that had made the city rich. The streets were chaotic, drivers skirting the donkey carts and camels with their rolling gait and forlorn expressions. I saw a lot of girls in military fatigues and red berets, old men with curling moustaches and tightly turned *shemaghs*. Erbil was a giant social experiment, an example of how the Middle East could be if foreign and vested interests were removed from the equation, if oil lost its charm and implications, if Sunni and Shia got over themselves.

The city unwound from the glass skyscrapers into the poor south side and I felt a strange sort of nostalgia entering the rutted lane with hanging wires and hungry dogs. Cano Ali opened the iron gates and stood back, the sun gleaming on his bald pate. He had a cherubic smile like a Chinese Buddha, hands on hips, a fag gripped in the corner of his mouth. He said something in Kurdish I didn't understand and the two lads burst out laughing.

'You're a bloody comedian, you are,' I said, and he wagged a finger.

'Practice,' he replied, his answer to everything.

Dozan put the kettle on and we sat around the big kitchen table nattering about each other's families, the flight. Hassan produced a box of pastries and I, in turn, followed the custom encouraged in the Quran by handing out small gifts Kali had wrapped in blue and white paper, the colours of the Greek flag.

For music nut Elind, I had *The Best of Fleetwood Mac*, a double CD. I had noticed Usef working on the vehicles with some primitive tools that wouldn't have looked out of place in a museum. I gave him a set of precision spanners and, the way he thanked me, I imagined he'd never been given a present by anyone in his life. I had found in the English bookshop in Heraklion a copy of David McDowall's *A Modern History of the Kurds* for Dozan. I gave Hassan an electric beard trimmer (he studied it like a rare artefact) and for Cano I had a compass in a blue velvet-lined box. I'd read a compass was a good gift for a Muslim so that he knew exactly where Mecca was when travelling, not that Cano was devout.

'To practise,' I told him.

He squeezed the air from my lungs as he took me in a bear hug, and my mind went back to that night in the olive grove with Matt Lambert. He had taken Natty to the Archaeological Museum to see the Minoan treasures the following day and we dropped him off at the airport for the night flight back to London. He had finished reading *The Night Manager*, or so he said, and gave it to Natty as a parting gift, her introduction to the world of spies, lies and impeccable English manners.

We had a plan, a strategy, or more accurately a blueprint without contracts, bullet points, forecasts or financial arrangements. Just a handshake and a goal to bring vacillating jihadis out of Islamic State. We had talked it through while the moon waned over the Gulf of Heraklion and agreed that our first step was to create a network inside the Caliphate and within the security services.

As Natty was about to learn from reading John le Carré, informers have a multitude of complex motivations for choosing betrayal: queen and country (rarely), self-preservation, blackmail, revenge, pride, to save the lives of loved ones, a desperate need to escape, for drugs or medical treatment. There's lust, of course, usually linked to a variety of deadly sins – envy, gluttony and greed, an opportunity, an offer that can't be refused, the rustle and clink of cold hard cash.

Building a network requires tradecraft, that is psychological profiling to secure informants who can provide intelligence without getting caught. You are not going to win trust and build a reputation if your assets wind up with a midnight knock on the door and their head on a spike. It isn't always practicable, but it's better if agents don't know each other. That way, they can't play Judas with the entire network, even under torture, as collaborators usually do.

We didn't have a great deal of money to spread about, but there were a lot of people inside Islamic State willing to undermine it. While Matt Lambert wrote proposals and sought finance from humanitarian organizations and NGOs, Hassan and I contacted potential assets on WhatsApp and Skype. Hassan had the most success with serving members of the Kurdish militia, the YPG. He never bothered to tell me – why would he? – but I later learned that he was a member of the party and a former YPG commander.

The YPG was highly regarded by US advisers in Syria, its reputation sealed after standing toe to toe with the US forces and defeating ISIS at the bloody siege of Kobani in 2015. This was the first time the militia had received air and ground support from the United States. It resulted in the US urging the Kurds to form a new army combining various minority groups, small Arab militias and foreign volunteers, many from the UK. The Syrian Democratic Forces, as it became known, set out with its three all-female battalions to fight ISIS on one front and President Bashar al-Assad's troops on the other.

As was well known, and Hassan made clear to me, the Kurds agreed to take American arms and do America's bidding with the long-term goal of getting US support for a Kurdish homeland, something vigorously opposed by America's NATO ally, Turkey, which defined the YPG as a terrorist organization. I did ask if the United States would ultimately betray the Kurds. Hassan answered in his usual style by pointing at the sky.

'Only Allah knows the future,' he said.

A fresh assault on ISIS was coming. War was in the air. You could sense it in the eager faces and clipped beat of the people hurrying along the sidewalk. Erbil hummed with military aircraft continuously landing and taking off. The jangle and whine of low-flying helicopters reminded me of Baghdad back in the glory days. The roads were jammed with taxis ferrying reporters to downtown hotels. The sting goes out of the sun in October. Nights can be decidedly cool. It's a good month for battle.

We were in contact with more than one hundred young women trapped in Islamic State and had every intention of bringing them out. Our network was growing and we were receiving information on strongholds, troop movements and escape routes – a major priority for ISIS leaders. With the potential of this intel, I felt ballsy enough to pay a visit to my old friend Cornelius Visser.

The Dutch did not have a consulate in Erbil, but shared space in a high rise controlled by the Turkish authorities. It was hot, mid-afternoon. I tossed out some scraps for the skinny dogs and my eyeballs began to sweat as I set out in my linen suit – no tie – on the half-mile walk downtown from the safe house. I blagged my way through the outer security gates and entered a compound guarded by machine guns. In the building's large foyer, a smartly dressed Kurd smoothed down his tache and informed me with the typical jobsworth response that no Dutch officials were available.

'It's about Laura Hansen,' I said in a loud voice.

He looked back as if I might be trouble and reluctantly made a phone call. He passed me the phone.

'I didn't know you were back,' Visser said.

'I didn't know you cared. I may have something for you.'

'That usually means you may want something from me.'

'You know something, you sound just like an Arab.'

125

'You are a very funny man.'

'I'm thinking of doing stand-up.'

'That, Mr Carney, would be a good career choice. When you die on stage, it is only your ego they kill.'

'You sound like someone with experience.'

'Mr Carney, do we ever really know anyone else?'

We arranged to meet an hour later at the Divan Hotel, same place as last time. I ordered a pint of cider. We sat facing each other across a round glass table with wilting pink roses in a vase, the light through the vertical blinds making stripes across his carved features. He stroked his lush hair and folded his hands into his lap.

'You have something for me?' he began.

'Managed return,' I replied. 'That's got to be the best way. I'm in touch with people stuck in Mosul, Tal Afar, Raqqa, Deir ez-Zor. Canadian, British, French, German, Dutch...'

'So you have formed your network?'

'It was your idea,' I said. 'These women are terrified. They've been beaten up. Raped. Gang-raped. Whatever side they may have been on, they're on our side now. It's better if we manage their return. We can arrange to have them surrender to the YPG and hand them over to the relevant embassies to face the justice system in their own country.'

'You really are an idealist...'

'Stand-ups usually are,' I told him. 'If we ignore them, they'll go off the grid. And when they make it back to Europe – if they make it back to Europe – the only people they'll be able to trust are the preachers and their old friends on the jihadi circuit. Fundamentalists. Groomers. Maniacs. We have to get them on our side. It makes no sense not to.'

As I called the waiter to order another pint, I realized the two people at the table behind me in suits and ties were Europeans, Dutch probably, and were listening in on our conversation. Not that anything I was saying was secret. On the contrary, I thought managed return was the only way and wanted it out there.

Visser sipped his sparkling water. 'What do you want from me, John?' he asked.

'Top cover,' I replied, and he dropped his cool to have a good laugh.

'Top cover,' he repeated. He mopped his brow with a handkerchief. 'In exchange for what, exactly?'

'Intel. You can make a name for yourself. You arrange to give my team some security, and you can get first go at the debriefs.'

I sipped my drink. Visser shook his head as he looked back at me across the pink roses. I didn't think for one moment that I was going to get cover through the Dutch secret service, but I read in Visser's expression a respect he had not shown until that moment.

'It's a chance for you to do the decent thing, Cor,' I continued, and his response was about the most honest thing I ever heard come out of his mouth.

'I do not have a view. I do not make decisions. I do the bidding of my government. Our nationals who volunteered to make war against our interests are enemies of the state. They have to face justice.'

'So, we're on the same page,' I said. 'That's what we want for Laura Hansen. Get her home. Let your judges decide on her future…'

'Do you think we are barbarians, John?' he asked, and leaned forward. 'Laura is back in The Hague, as are her children. I am surprised you didn't already know that.'

'So am I.'

'A gap in your network?'

'It's a work in progress. We'll fill it.' I glanced over my shoulder at the two blokes listening in behind me and raised my voice. 'We're going to do exactly what I've told you. Just do the decent thing and give us some cover. Give the people we bring out a chance to start again. That's what you do in a civilized world.'

He nodded for several seconds. 'I will pass your request up to the powers that be,' he said, pointing at the ceiling.

I finished my pint. We stood and he shook my hand. I turned to leave and then turned back to the two men at the table behind us.

'Hope you got all that,' I said.

I strode back through reception. A TV crew was checking in with stacks of silver cases. I heard a woman with yellow hair and a gash of red lipstick demand 'a quiet room at the front of the hotel'. Her accent told me the invasion to unseat ISIS would start any day. American reporters have sources inside the Pentagon.

It was excellent news that Laura and her kids were out. It had clearly pleased Cor Visser that I didn't already have this intel. I learned from Hassan when I mentioned it to him later that his man in Asayish had been transferred and he was making new contacts. This was standard. Those who lie for a living are shapeshifters in a world constantly in flux; good guys become bad guys, bad guys disappear, usually into the earth, sometimes to their secret apartments in Switzerland or Cannes or Kensington.

The hours had vanished. The day was cooling off. I had half a mind to visit the Citadel, but that would have to wait. I scrolled through my contacts and hit jackrabbit.

'Fancy a drink?'

'You don't have to ask twice,' he replied.

I took a cab and found Jack Fieldhouse with a pint of Roj and a bowl of pistachios, listening to the parrots chattering in the pomegranate trees at his favourite bar.

'You're a sight for sore eyes,' he said. 'Still saving the world?'

'Someone's got to.'

I told him we were building a network and intended bringing out as many people as we could from the Caliphate. He sat back stroking his square jaw.

'You know Roy Underhill?'

'Know the name.'

'Navy SEAL, Texan. Big bastard. He stayed on in Mosul with his lady and a couple of kids. Been living underground the last twelve months.' He swigged down his pint and clicked his fingers for a refill. 'He's got info on tunnels, arms caches, stolen treasure, artefacts.'

'Fuck me.'

'We'd need a team and some trucks to bring it out.'

'You serious?'

'Absolutely. Buy a nice little place in Crete and live the life of Carney.'

We clinked glasses and went for the second pint.

'In the meantime…' I said, and paused, 'tunnels, arms caches, escape routes?'

'I'll text Roy with your number.'

I placed my beer down on the table. 'Iraqi intelligence must have this info, tunnels and stuff?' I said.

'Not sure, John. Roy plays the game his own way. He's a one-off.'

CHAPTER 10

We Are Coming, Nineveh

You forget about the dust. It hangs over the landscape like a ragged curtain. It scratches your throat. The air tastes of sulphur, saltpetre, cordite, burning rubber and burning oil from the pipelines sabotaged by ISIS to disrupt aerial surveillance.

The noise is constant: the clatter of machine guns, the whoop and thump of mortars, the ricochet of stray rounds bouncing off vehicles like jangling keys. You hear wailing dogs, weeping children, screaming mothers. Battle is no place for mothers and their babies. They see things no one should ever see. Children who survive will have lost something that will never be found. They will have empty eyes, a blank stare, a void in their very being.

The advance was impeded by snipers – young men in trainers, fast on their feet, faces glazed in gun oil. I watched a lad in his teens in the upstairs room of a house shooting wildly. Then he stopped, as if frozen, and slumped across the empty window frame, dead from a head shot. He hung motionless, hands outstretched, blood dripping from his fingers, the tail of his turban flapping in the breeze. There was nothing heroic about his death. He was just another nameless jihadi the Kurd support units would bury in an unmarked grave.

I had always felt invincible. I didn't feel that way any more. I had a wife and daughter. Ntileini was back at school. I wasn't there to take her or pick her up. I wasn't there to hear her stories, to share her doubts and dreams. I missed the market run with Kali, that first sip of beer at sunset, the sound of the wind whispering in the olive trees. I missed the cats with their shiny eyes and curious expressions.

I glanced along the line at Hassan, Dozan, Cano Ali, an unlit cigarette in his mouth, his large head squeezed into a helmet. We were hunkered down inside a shattered farmhouse and, for all the dust and danger, I couldn't help thinking we were in the right place at the right time. How you live your life is a question of choices. You do your best to make the right ones and make sure you fix it when you don't.

The operation to retake Mosul was dubbed 'We Are Coming, Nineveh' by the Iraqi prime minister, Haider al-Abadi. It launched on 16 October 2016, two years and four months after the Islamists had seized the city and chased the Iraqi army in shame back to Baghdad to lick their wounds.

For two years and four months, ISIS had ruled with the whip and cane, the machete and AK-47, with blood on their hands and balaclavas covering their faces. Thousands of recruits – three, ten, twenty, the numbers varied, no one knew exactly – had reached the self-proclaimed Caliphate from all over Europe, the States, Canada, Australia. They were, for the most part, young people who had set out to give meaning to their lives by joining what they believed was a holy war and had turned into an assault on our very humanity.

They had made wrong choices, and out there in the lead storm were young people who had changed their minds. I had their names and profiles on my laptop. I just had to find them and bring them out.

Coalition air targeted ISIS strongholds out of sight above the battlefield as the Iraqi battalions backed by the Peshmerga and YPG made slow progress through the minefields and smoke. The Iraqi bomb disposal teams were equipped with Casspir armour-bodied de-mining vehicles and supported by volunteers, mainly British and American ex-soldiers. They had helped smash the country in Bush-and-Blair's ill-conceived Operation Iraqi Freedom and had returned to try and put it back together again. They were usually damaged men with old wounds who trusted in the axiom that the only thing needed for the triumph of evil is that good men do nothing.

Single rounds from another sniper – he must have had some training – drilled into the wall of the farmhouse. As he changed position, the gunfire stopped for a few minutes, then started again, pinning us down 140 metres behind a unit of YPG militiamen. The village was surrounded. The jihadis left behind had either been ordered by their commanders to hold on at all costs, or were prepared for martyrdom. Whatever the motive, this was the last day they would spend on this earth and they were intent on taking as many apostates with them as they could.

There was a moment of quiet. I heard the cluck of chickens. Battles draw breath. You wipe the dirt from your eyes. You change mags. You swig down some water. The smokers light fags. That's what Cano did, and I watched the blue smoke drift around the walls. The house was little more than a barn. It smelled of animals. There was neither table nor chairs, no books, just rolled mats that served as beds, a metal bucket half full of dusty water, a jar of olive oil, some red peppers on a shelf, blackened pots and kettles on the open stove. They burned kerosene for light and fuel. There were no trees as far as you could see in any direction.

Three shots drilled through the eye of the empty window and bounced around the walls. By squatting behind a pile of masonry on one side of the frame, I had a good sightline to the YPG. They responded with a volley of machine-gun fire that kept the shooter's head down. The unit had taken over a three-storey house with an ornate entrance, the local clan chief's most probably. Off to our right were two wooden sheds and a row of chicken coops. A dead camel lay outside, its guts spilled in the dirt.

As I studied the row of buildings, the door to the farthest shed opened, then closed again. In that second I saw a woman, head to toe in black, face covered, a shadow that appeared and disappeared in a way that made you wonder if your mind was playing tricks. I stretched up to take a closer look, and a hand on my forearm dragged me down again. Hassan waved a finger at me.

'There's someone in the shed, over there,' I said. 'A woman.'

'It could be a man in a niqab. It would not be the first time.'

I grabbed the binoculars from Dozan to take a second look and watched as the same figure appeared in the doorway with a boy of about six or seven. I knew it was a woman by the way she held her two hands on his shoulders. It was a feminine gesture, protective yet deferential. The shed was some 70 metres away, a ten-second dash for a decent runner. I could make it in 20.

The woman must have reasoned that if snipers were pinning us down, we were her best chance. Before I had decided what to do next, she hurried the child out of the shed. They stepped over the camel and ran towards us. The boy gained quickly on his mother. You can't stretch out your legs in a ground-sweeping *abaya*, and she threw it off as she ran. She freed her head from her niqab and the way her loosened hair trailed out behind her reminded me of the girl on the water ski that day when we fished for sea bass.

These instantaneous actions are like a speeded-up film. You don't think. You act. It's all instinct. I leapt through the vacant space left by the missing door and raced towards them. The woman had caught up with her son. I scooped him into my arms and we sprinted to the farmhouse with bullets snapping into the dirt around our feet.

YPG mortars rained down on the position held by the sniper. Then there was silence. They had found their range.

The woman had squirrelled into the corner with her boy.

All she could say was *'Merci, merci, merci.'* She held her son tight in her arms. Her body rocked and trembled as if years of tension had built up inside her and it was erupting in heaving sobs.

She was the first renegade bride we had actively freed from Islamic State. We had almost certainly saved her life, and that made everything worthwhile.

Dozan gave them water. They drained the canteen. The woman kept looking at me and shaking her head.

'Je suis française,' she finally said.

'English,' I replied, and her change of expression, a sudden look of hope, seemed to say she had glimpsed the road home.

She managed to tell us her name was Marie-Claire and she came from Lyon. She was pale and drawn, about 25 years old. Her son, Haaroon, was a skinny little boy with alert, pensive eyes that regarded us with more interest than fear. Dozan understood more French than me, but not enough to get anything useful. It is a curse not speaking other languages; in a broken world it's more important than ever.

We sat around for 40 minutes while the gunfight continued. The woman flinched when the explosions were close. They drank all the water we carried. Cano Ali produced a bag of dates from one of his pouches and the way they stuffed them down they clearly hadn't eaten for some time.

Without her black garments, Marie-Claire looked like she had come from the gym, in blue sweat pants with a double white stripe down the legs and a blue top zipped to the throat. She had no shoes. Haaroon wore grubby sneakers, torn shorts and a T-shirt that might have been red once but had faded into the colours of the sunset.

When Hassan heard from his contact that it was safe to leave the area, we headed back on the de-mined corridor marked through the desert to a holding station on the Kurdish border. Dozan drove the second vehicle. I sat in the back. Marie-Claire clung to my hand like a drowning person to flotsam. She rattled on non-stop, a great tide of words she'd been holding in for a long time. I didn't understand a thing.

We arrived at a camp set up with new tents stamped with the blue letters *UN*. The smell of burning oil still hung in the air 30 miles from the village. You could hear the dim resonance of explosions and the grey smoke drifting along the horizon had the look of old galleons at sea. The red, white and green tricolour of the Peshmerga flickered limply on a pole above a temporary barrier set up among some portable metal cabins.

Hassan ducked out of the lead vehicle. The official at the entrance came briefly to attention. They shook hands and touched cheeks. At the outset of the operation, we had gained permission to follow in the wake of the advance to gather up stray refugees. Not only had the YPG – an integral part of the Peshmerga – been sympathetic, they let us refuel and take on water.

I debussed with the woman and her child. I walked her to the official.

Hassan introduced me, speaking English, and we shook hands.

'Mr Carney, I am pleased to meet you,' the man said, and saluted.

I turned to Marie-Claire. '*Au revoir*,' I managed in French.

A faint smile touched her lips, and I was amazed as always how a few words in a stranger's language reminds us of our shared humanity. She put her arms around me and pressed her head against my chest.

'*Merci beaucoup*, Mr Carney,' she said. 'Thank you very much.'

A woman in uniform waited outside one of the cabins. The official at the gate pointed. Marie-Claire took Haaroon's hand and made her way towards her. She didn't know what lay ahead, the cross-examinations, the accusations, the long hours of debriefing. She didn't know if she would ever make it home. But she looked relieved to have escaped Islamic State.

I put my Ray-Bans on and gazed out across the rows of empty tents. It was like a ghost town, or a photograph, clean, smart, structured. I would stand on the same spot two years later when more than a million refugees filled those tents and overspilled into a vast makeshift shanty town. There would be more tin cabins, and the flags of humanitarian organizations would be flapping against the blue sky.

'Shall we?' I said to Hassan, and he nodded gravely, as if deep in thought.

'She will be safe here,' he replied.

'Shame we didn't find her a pair of shoes.'

He nodded. 'They take their shoes,' he said. 'You can't leave the house without shoes. You cannot run away without shoes.'

He looked up at the pale splash of washed-out sun as one might their wristwatch, then shook hands again with the official. They were comfortable with each other, comfortable in their own skin. I thought for some reason of that night in the olive grove with Matt Lambert.

Two Englishmen meeting for the first time instantly seek the differences between them, the incompatible, the message in the other's accent. Only our common cause and the story of Matt's daughter had led to that awkward hug.

I climbed into the Toyota Previa beside Dozan and we followed Cano Ali back into the battlefield. We wore desert tan Kevlar body vests with multiple pockets, and helmets painted with the letters *YPG*. I kept my *shemagh* around my neck, ready to hide my English face, and travelled in the second vehicle in case we were stopped at road blocks or spotted by bad guys. ISIS recruits had no love for the Kurds, but a *kaffir* was a better prize.

We'd got rid of the 4x4 pickup in exchange for the eight-seater Previa. We'd bolted steel plating around the sides, the same with the Nissan Pathfinder, a good workhorse, but the undercarriages on both vehicles were soft skin and about as useful as orange peel if struck by an IED.

Visibility was negligible with plumes of dust rising into the air. We kept a few hundred metres between us to minimize the target. Our main concern wasn't ISIS patrols, they had scarpered back to Mosul, but Coalition aircraft. Elind and Usef had painted the car roofs in the red, white and green of the Kurdish flag, but stray vehicles outside the main body of the advance remained tempting for pilots on the way back to base with a couple of bunker-busters still in their bomb bays.

The dust had settled by the time we got back to the village. It must have had a name. I never learned it. The smaller the village, the longer its name. There were hundreds of tiny hamlets, often inhabited by one extended family, each with between ten and fifty dwellings, some fields and orchards irrigated by water systems unchanged for centuries. They kept chickens for eggs, goats for milk, cheese and meat. They stretched skins to make leather pouches and traded the negligible excess for fabric, shoes, metal tools, tobacco.

I doubt that any of these desert people had welcomed the coming of the fundamentalists with their rigorous interpretation of the Quran. Men were forced to grow beards to a certain length. Women were made to remain at home fully veiled in regions where women traditionally wore vibrant costumes and worked together in the fields, faces uncovered. Some clans were adorned with tattoos, marking them as belonging to the tribe.

ISIS rule brought men with assault rifles, female 'moral' police with long canes, rationing. Local boys were press-ganged into the cause and girls as young as 12 were taken by ISIS commanders in *nikah mut'ah* – a short-term 'pleasure marriage' permitted under Sharia law, historically so that a man on his travels could take a wife for the night, legitimizing prostitution and rape. These girls gave up their virginity for jihad and would live in shame, unmarried, outcasts for the rest of their lives.

Now that the village had been liberated and the Iraqi army had moved on, the people appeared like zombies from out of the rubble. They wandered around with sloped shoulders and numb expressions. They gazed with empty eyes at the smashed roofs of their houses, the abandoned vehicles, scrap that would never be removed, at the shiny sea of brass shell cases scattered in the dust.

I watched a sun-worn, skeletal man in rags standing over the dead camel. Tears ran down the furrows on his cheeks. A boy in an oversized army helmet climbed into the driving seat of a wrecked armoured vehicle and jerked the steering wheel back and forth. Another was collecting shell cases. I saw a girl of about seven wearing yellow bows in her hair and it made my eyes well up.

The men – they were mostly old men, or young men prematurely grown old – stood in huddled groups smoking. Food was scarce but there was always rolling tobacco. The women returned to their houses to see what they could salvage. No one took any notice of us. We were witnesses to their grief, and grief is a private thing. I thought about taking photographs of the scorched earth and ruins, but didn't.

The origin of wars is traditionally land and treasure. There was nothing here worth fighting for. The Islamists didn't want the land. They were fighting, as President George W Bush said in a speech to the UN in 2005 to justify the invasion of Iraq, for hearts and minds. Islamic State wanted to turn the hands of the clock back to the time of Muhammad and live by Sharia law in one Great Caliphate. Their struggle was between the Quranic past and the digital future.

The war they were fighting could never be won. But it seemed clear to me that neither could it ever be brought to an end. It doesn't matter how many bombs we drop on the Middle East, how many children are mutilated and killed, the jihadis like the phoenix will continue to rise from the ashes and the refugees and asylum seekers will keep coming. Once they have seen on their mobile phones the way we live, they will look out across their deserts and wastelands and make the journey west.

The battle to retake Mosul was the biggest military operation in Iraq since US and Coalition forces toppled Saddam in 2003. More than 50,000 Iraqi troops and police were in the field with US advisers and the Peshmerga, the combined Coalition forces advancing on three fronts from the south, north and east.

On the first day of the operation, Kurdish forces claimed to have captured nine strategic villages and 80 square miles of territory. A US State Department official asserted that the offensive was 'ahead of schedule'. We also received reports from our network inside Mosul that Islamic State was 'absorbing the momentum' like a heavyweight boxer and preparing to 'crush the crusaders like scarabs'.

There was some truth in this.

During the next three days, we followed the YPG as they cleared the land mines and fought their way through the outlying ISIS strongholds on the road to Nineveh. The people we scooped up and delivered to the border camp had managed to hide in barns and cellars. The majority were Iraqi, mostly women and children, a few ancient men with white whiskers. They had been rounded up and were force-marched alongside of ISIS fighters withdrawing with their rocket launchers to the city. Older boys and men of fighting age – field workers, goat herders, small traders – vanished, never to be seen again.

The road we travelled on stank of death. We saw heaped-up corpses wreathed with flies, the victims executed by shots to the back of the head. I would learn later that 8,000 families had been abducted by Islamic State. Hundreds had been killed, a goad to urge the others not to falter.

We stopped on a low sweeping rise at the edge of a wrecked olive grove. I stepped out to get some air and climbed on to the car roof with binoculars. It was an astonishing sight. The jihadi butchers in black masks were cowering behind the human shield of mothers with babies while the Peshmerga looked on hopelessly with itchy fingers. It was a stark reminder, not that we needed it, that all who are touched by terrorism are victimized by it. Like the Kurds, I was frustrated that we could do nothing, and the anger had balled up like a fist in my chest. It doesn't matter how many times you see the horror show, it always feels like the first time. You feel shame as a human being witnessing this depraved aspect of humanity.

'Come down now, John. You are a target.'

I tossed the bins to Hassan and slipped down from the roof. I stuck the buds in my ears and listened to Blondie on my iPhone while we waited. My companions sat in the shade of the olives where there was a faint breeze. They showed no emotion. Perhaps they saw the bigger picture. That all the death and devastation had some divine purpose: for Kurds, a homeland.

The jihadi caravan slipped from view and we rolled on behind the YPG. The sun was falling. The shadows stretched. Tall buildings filled the horizon. We were close to the heart of Islamic State.

Before entering the outskirts of Mosul, we passed through the ruins of Nineveh, the ancient Assyrian capital and likely resting place of the Three Wise Men on their way to Bethlehem. We know the name Nineveh from the Old Testament. Jonah, before being swallowed by a whale, was first sent by God in 1,000 BC to warn that the city would be destroyed if its decadence and depravity persisted – a prediction that would come to pass through the hands of time and the bombs of ISIS.

Christians had lived in the area around Nineveh since the time of Christ. More than 30,000 of their number had been systematically beheaded and crucified since the declaration of the Caliphate. The church built at what was believed to be the tomb of Jonah – also a Muslim prophet – was later turned into a mosque. One of the jihadis' first acts was to destroy it, along with all the libraries and places of worship.

The Nineveh Christians spoke Syriac, a dialect of Aramaic, the language of Jesus. Before and after the Muslim conquest, scholars had translated the works of the Greek poets and playwrights, largely preserving them for many centuries before their rediscovery by Europeans. The plots of some of Shakespeare's plays borrow from these translations. Our democracy, our very culture, can be dated back to those Syriac-speaking Christians, their descendants now most of them dead, the survivors scattered, 3,000 years of history obliterated.

We spent the night in the ruins. We had internet access, thanks to the YPG, and connected with our network inside Mosul.

Two things of importance came up.

First, the Peshmerga were bogged down on the outskirts of the city. Every time they tried to proceed, ISIS gunmen popped up behind them and trapped them in a deadly crossfire. It had cost a lot of lives.

Second, a Frenchman recruited by ISIS was anxious to escape with what he promised was 'valuable information'. He was less than two miles away in an area close to the Tigris.

I managed to get a call through to Roy Underhill. The moment he picked up, the phone went dead and I had this awful guilt feeling that the call had stirred some ISIS assassin who had instantly shot him. I was thankful that he called back ten minutes later.

'I was in my crypt, buddy,' he said, southern US accent. 'Are you coming to bring us out?'

'Absolutely, mate, if that's what you want.'

He laughed. Underhill had been in Mosul when it was overrun by ISIS and had remained – true to his name – underground with his local wife and children for the last two years.

'I knew it was only a matter of time. I'm hanging on for the tickertape parade.'

I told him the Peshmerga were being held back by gunmen appearing behind the advance.

'They've built tunnels everywhere, John. They need to find the exits and block 'em before they advance.'

'Do you know where the exits are?'

He was silent for a moment. 'I can probably find out. Give me two hours.'

The sun had gone down. The sky was streaked in pink and green stripes. The surviving temple walls turned golden and I could feel all that history seeping out of the ground below my feet. Nineveh is the cradle of civilization. The Assyrians were the masters of the Iron Age, architects and craftsmen; they created the first written language. Everything began here, and would end here if we weren't careful. I put my vest on a block of stone as old as time and gazed up at the stars. There seem to be more stars in the Middle East. They shine brighter.

True to his word, Roy Underhill reconnected. He sent a text on WhatsApp with details and descriptions of tunnels in the east of the city. I sent the text straight on to Hassan and woke him from his sleep.

I hadn't seen him smile much that day but he smiled now, his white teeth shiny in the moonlight. He sat cross-legged in his baggy pants. He stared up at the sky, then back at me.

'You have done well, Mr Carney,' he said.

He sent the text on and received a call two minutes later. I listened as he spoke in Kurdish. He slipped the phone back in his vest.

'There are a lot of angry Kurds out there,' he said.

'I thought they'd be pleased.'

'They will be pleased, as you say. But first they are angry. They are being woken from sleep so that they can go and look for tunnels.'

'There's something else…'

'There is always something else.'

'There's a French bloke not far from us,' I pointed. 'If we can bring him out, he's got some valuable information.'

I stretched out for some kip. I felt pretty pleased with myself, I must admit. It was through networking that Jack Fieldhouse had led me to Roy Underhill, and Roy had provided intel that, as I far as I knew, the YPG and the Iraqi army did not have. The fact that this was going to save lives justified my being there under the Nineveh stars. I closed my eyes and slept five solid hours.

CHAPTER 11

Exodus

A US Army Growler swerved into our temporary camp shortly before noon. As the dust settled, an Iraqi captain with a clipped moustache stepped from the passenger seat. He adjusted the line of his beret and lifted his right arm in a shuddering salute. Swinging from the fingers of his left hand was a white box tied with green ribbon.

'I am seeking a Mr Carney,' he said in English.

I shuffled to my feet. 'Now what have I done?' I answered.

He wasn't sure what I meant and smiled as he gave me the box. 'It is a small gift from the colonel.'

'You kidding me? How'd he know it was my birthday?'

'No, no. He wanted to say thank you very much.'

I rattled the box. 'It's not a bomb, is it?'

'No, no. I assure you. It is a gift…'

Dozan Rostami stepped between us. 'Excuse me,' he said. He moved the captain aside. They spoke for several minutes, a stream of Arabic I couldn't follow, then shook hands. The captain made sure his beret was straight and his driver screamed out of Nineveh back towards the highway.

The box contained a dozen freshly baked pastries, a miracle in the midst of the biggest operation by Iraqi forces since Saddam's doomed march on Kuwait. Cano Ali dipped straight in, grabbing two, one in each hand. I offered the box to Hassan, then Dozan. He didn't meet my eyes, and wore the solemn look usually reserved for conversations with his wife.

'*Shukran*,' he said stiffly, and turned away.

Cano Ali made coffee on the primus and we kept to the shade of a canvas sheet hooked between the two vehicles. Dozan summarized the report from the frontline, switching smoothly between English and Arabic. Using Roy Underhill's rough coordinates, de-mining teams were locating and closing down tunnels, delaying the advance. It explained why we had been stuck in Nineveh all morning and would remain there for the rest of the day. The Iraqi High Command had underestimated the will and firepower of ISIS when they were driven out of Mosul and were taking no chances in the battle to retake the city.

Via the YPG satellite connection, we had spent the morning linking jihadi brides with our informants inside Mosul. Dozan contacted his web of former colleagues in Saddam's old officer corps and Hassan had a network of assets in the Kurdish community. We cross-referenced fresh intel before sharing it with the Iraqi National Intelligence Service (INIS), the agency formed under the guidance of the Coalition Provisional Authority in 2004. It was a courtesy to pass information directly to the Iraqis – thus the box of pastries – but we knew full well that it would be shared immediately with the CIA.

Having my profile in a CIA dossier was potentially beneficial while I was an asset; precarious when the situation changed. As it would. As it always does. Someone clearly had a sense of humour when they chose the motto 'Always Out Front' for the US Military Intelligence Corps

(MI). The secret service community is by nature secretive, vindictive, two-faced and *never* out front.

We finished the pastries. Cano Ali rolled the green ribbon into a wheel and slipped it into his vest. He would use it to decorate a box of baklava or give it to one of his daughters to tie back her hair. Everything was recycled. Every bent nail was straightened. The jihadis had destroyed the irreplaceable Assyrian antiquities at Nineveh, the fifth-century Syriac monastery of St Elian, the Roman temples of Palmyra – but before setting the explosives at each site, they had dislodged the statues and packed the removable artefacts in sacks to sell on the international market.

What I couldn't understand was why, when each new rising power, whatever faith they professed, had preserved the traces of our shared history for thousands of years, Islamic State then emerges with the warped dream of changing the past by destroying the world's greatest archaeological and cultural treasures. If the militants had a genuine vision of reviving the pure Islam of the Prophet, as they wanted recruits to believe, that would at least answer my question. But carvings with human faces are forbidden as idolatry. Reaping and selling the Nineveh relics was deceitful, a compromise, a fault line at the very foundations of their ideals.

It was fortunate that the Nineveh ruins were extensive and spread out over a large area. You could pick out the cavities and fresh heaps of marble dust, the tracks of bulldozers, but most of the ornate façades that remained stood firm.

The internet was down. I was bloated with pastry. My limbs ached from lack of exercise. I wrapped my head in my *shemagh* and wandered through the site towards the road. I stopped to photograph a relief I'd noticed earlier. It showed a line of men with square-cut beards in short skirts aiming spears at an oversized lion. The figures were remarkably well preserved, the faces of each one similar but different, more similar than different from how we look today.

Guns rattled in the distance, a constant pitter-patter like heavy rain on windows. Corkscrews of smoke spiralled into the air. I climbed a low mound above the main road leading west out of Mosul and felt a sigh rise through my chest.

The previous day, I had watched hopelessly through binoculars as women and children were herded into Mosul as human shields. Now, I looked down as another stream of women and children fled the city like giant snails with their world on their backs. People from the eastern suburbs liberated by Iraqi and Kurdish forces had gathered their meagre possessions and abandoned their homes before they were turned to rubble. Most of the women were in black, but they had torn off their niqabs and turned their faces to the sun. Under the Caliphate, they had lived in shuttered rooms and cellars with their heads hooded to please Allah – or, rather, the fundamentalists.

The children were skin and bones, dressed in rags, with long switches they used to guide withered goats with angry faces. Donkeys rattled by bearing pots and pans, rolls of bedding, the passing absurdity of a padded chair with gilt legs that would find its way to the entrance of a UN tent. I pictured an old man staring impassively like King Canute out at a rolling sea of red sand.

Walking alone was a man in a black suit carrying nothing but a violin case covered in stickers. He had fresh cuts on his cheeks and must have shaved off his beard that morning with an old razor. His head nodded up and down as if he were hearing a piece of music banned as *haram* and suddenly playing again in his memory. There were few young men.

150

They had been left behind, soldiers, jihadis, dead in shallow graves. The old men with sunken cheeks wore the glassy expressions that attract war photographers, as if the lines and defiles of their faces described the contours of lost kingdoms and the emptiness at the heart of their broken world.

I saw a girl of about six in a red dress carrying a chicken. She was whispering words of comfort to the creature as she skipped barefoot in the silvery dust. I waved. I didn't expect her to wave back, and when she did, she dropped the chicken. It flapped away. She scurried after it and, as she gathered it back in her arms, I felt a shot of hope, of optimism, of faith. I needed to be reminded – constantly – that something good might come out of so much that was arbitrary and inhuman.

The Middle East was like a giant jigsaw puzzle that had been thrown into the air. Where the pieces landed, and how we reassembled the picture, would determine not only the lives of the families escaping from Mosul, but the lives of every one of us. The scene that morning on the Nineveh highway was just one wave in a sea of waves as millions of refugees set out to start again somewhere safe without terrorists, drone attacks, bombed hospitals, hungry babies, collateral damage.

The people snaked along the verges at the side of the road as a steel chain of troop convoys raced in the opposite direction towards the banks of the Tigris. I saw a platoon of armoured black Humvees carrying the Golden Division, Iraqi commandos famed for their black uniforms and faces hidden by skull masks, emulating the enemy and just as terrifying.

They were followed by a column of Toyotas, the flatbeds jammed with fighters from Hash'd al Shaabi, the Popular Mobilization Forces (PMF). These were Iranian Shiite militias created in 2014 in response to the fall of Mosul by Iran's spiritual leader, the cleric Ayatollah Ali al-Sistani. The PMF had been accused of ethnic cleansing in the Sunni areas they had liberated, but the allegation had been countered as a fabrication conceived in Tel Aviv by Mossad, the Israeli secret service. Hash'd al Shaabi flew under yellow, green and black insignia similar to that of Hezbollah, the powerful Lebanese militia, nemesis of Israel and hostile towards the United States.

The puzzle was complex. There were many different military forces in the theatre of battle and sometimes they changed sides. The call to arms against ISIS had united Shia and Sunni recruits on the same side against Shia and Sunni militias with different agendas. In the ranks of the PMF was a battalion of Iranian Christians. Volunteers had joined the battle from Saudi Arabia, Jordan, Egypt, Syria, Turkey, Russia, Indonesia. The Kurds were on the front line. US air controlled the skies. The ants' nest had been poked with a stick in 2001 when the United States bombed Afghanistan in reprisal for 9/11, and all the evils festering for centuries from the Hindu Kush to the Mediterranean had erupted like pus from an infected boil.

And who was suffering most? Muslim women with their Muslim children, driven like cattle and treated as pawns in a chess game I didn't understand and couldn't play.

It cheered me up when Dozan climbed the mound beside me. The feeling didn't last.

'Bloody chaos,' I said.

'It is, John. It is.' He pointed down at the fleeing masses. 'We can say that among those people are some who have got away because the bomb disposal units have closed the tunnels.'

'That's what we're here for.'

'It is something to be proud of.'

I caught the gravity in his tone. He had avoided looking at me as he shared the report from the intelligence captain.

'So, what are you saying?' I asked him.

'You are my brother, John.'

'Damn right…'

'Brothers can tell each other when something is not…' he paused, 'when it is not exactly right?'

I looked back at Dozan. 'Yes they can,' I assured him.

'It is the English way, I know, I remember from my flying days. You make everything a joke. It is too much. Some things are not funny.'

'Always best to keep a sense of humour.'

'Not when it is inappropriate.' He took a breath. 'I would die for you, John. You know that.'

'I'd do the same, mate…'

'You are doing something important. You are the only European here. The last English man. You are our general. Where you go, we will follow. It is not funny. It is not a joke.'

He took a grip on my shoulders and stared into my eyes. I felt chastened and I felt humbled. The captain with his pastry box tied in ribbons had stirred my old hostility towards officers with clean boots and trimmed moustaches. I was still fighting old demons.

'Some news,' Dozan continued, and his expression changed. 'Hassan has intel on the placing of an arms cache. Perhaps your contact can confirm.'

'We've got the internet up again?'

'What do you say? Up and running.'

We touched cheeks and made our way back to camp.

'Thank you,' I said, and he stopped.

'No, John, it is I who must thank you.'

Mosul, the fortress capital of the Islamic Caliphate, is a dry dusty oven of a city with a population of almost two million, the same size as Birmingham, Liverpool and Manchester combined. It rises over the Nineveh Plains 250 miles from Baghdad and 120 miles from Erbil. It is one of the oldest cities on the planet.

Until 2003, Mosul was ethnically diverse, with communities of Turkmens, Yazidis, Assyrians, Armenians, Christians, Sunni and Shia Arabs. The city had a famous medical college, one of the largest educational and research centres in the Middle East, a celebrated school of painting – specializing in miniatures – and a society of intellectuals, writers and philosophers. In the 1930s, before Iraq gained independence, the great crime writer Agatha Christie lived with her archaeologist husband close to the ruins.

The first stones of the Assyrian Empire were laid in Mosul 2,500 years before Christ. The old quarter is a warren of ancient monuments and winding narrow passageways surrounded by an ocean-sized sprawl of grey apartment blocks. In these streets, in July 2003, Saddam Hussein's thuggish sons Uday and Qusay were killed in gun battles with Coalition forces. The US 101st Airborne Division had taken charge of Mosul and given out contracts to local builders to reconstruct the city after Operation Iraqi Freedom destroyed it.

The last convoy of American troops left Mosul in December 2011 and the Iraqi government took control. By then, the seeds of Islamic State had taken root and were flourishing. Jihadi fighters, drunk on the

Islamic myth of Armageddon and the prospect of Paradise, drove out the army with its ill-prepared officer corps and seized power in June 2014. The people of Mosul – painters and teachers, politicians, the violinist, scientists and nurses – were effectively prisoners forbidden to leave the city unless they provided bonds in cash, property or family members. Sharia law was ruthlessly applied. Women could only be seen in public covered from head to toe, wearing gloves and escorted by a male relative. Men grew beards and bent their backs in prayer five times a day. Homosexuality, promiscuity, adultery, booze, dancing and music were punishable by cane, whip, severed hands, decapitation and crucifixion.

Minority groups were tortured and killed. Babies were stolen and women were forced into jihadi marriages and prostitution, which often amounted to the same thing. Before the Iraq War, some 70,000 Assyrian Christians had lived in Mosul. No more than a handful remain in the city today.

The 600,000 members of the Yazidi community had it worse. Their religion can be traced back to ancient Mesopotamia and preserves practices Islamic State considered pagan. Imams described the Yazidis as 'devil worshippers' and targeted them for 'purification', meaning extermination. Men were beheaded. Women too old to be auctioned as slaves or concubines were butchered and thrown into mass graves. Girls as young as eight were gang-raped. Boys were brainwashed and transformed into suicide bombers.

Today the Yazidi faith is extinct except within small communities in the Kurdistan refugee camps, the 1,100 women and children given sanctuary in Germany, and a few hundred survivors taken in by Canada and Australia.

The killings occurred between 2014 and 2016. They were reported by fearless journalists and TV crews. Unlike the slaughter of innocents in the Dark Ages, the Inquisition, the Holocaust, the Yazidi genocide was screened in our living rooms. It was bloody and surreal. We watched as if it were a Hollywood film and did practically nothing to end it or to aid the survivors. In our modern times we have grown a new form of cataracts. What we see with our own eyes has become 'virtual', cloudy, fake news.

We were not fighting a war in any normal sense. We were fighting a virus, a plague. A strange psychopathic evil had infected Islamic State commanders, spiritual leaders and recruits. The rape and slaughter of children was justified by perverting selective passages from the Quran. The death cult had created an extreme and radical violence, a blood lust, the Caliphate myth recast as a modern-day parable of nihilism and heroism.

The European jihadi brides I had spoken to over Skype had seen the butchery and barbarism on a daily basis for months, some for years. They wanted their lives back. They weren't terrorists. They were romantics, naïve, immature. They wanted to come home – at any price. It was my belief that if de-radicalization programmes were in place and they were treated with respect, they would be an asset, not a threat.

We followed a unit of YPG volunteers as they fought their way through the eastern suburbs towards the river. The five bridges that spanned the Tigris and linked the two halves of Mosul had either been destroyed or were booby-trapped and too dangerous to cross. Engineers constructed pontoons while jihadi mortars rained in from secure bunkers on the far bank. The river was fast flowing, but refugees braved the bullets to negotiate the currents on anything that would float. The eastern embankment was in ruins, bombed by Coalition air, dynamited by ISIS, shelled to powder by Iraqi gunners before the infantry inched forward a street at a time.

An army of 50,000 sounds significant, but the same number of people fill stadiums to watch football across England every Saturday and disperse in an hour after the match. Could an army of 50,000 take a city the size of Birmingham, Liverpool and Manchester joined together, every block filled with women, children, the old and the sick?

When we talk about the 'front line', we imagine the lines of trenches in the First World War. In street fighting, the front line is the space in front of your nose. Our intel had been vital in closing down tunnels, but once Iraqi and Peshmerga troops had taken a street, there was nothing to stop enemy fighters from creeping over roofs and through shattered buildings to come up behind them.

The noise is always a surprise and always the same: like a train crash that goes on for ever, the beating hack of machine guns like a million out-of-time drummers, the discord broken by the metallic rush of a sniper's bullet ripping the air close to your ears. No amount of water can clear the dryness from your throat. Cheaply made buildings are 90 per cent dust and sand. It hangs in the air like soup.

I saw a T-shirt that said 'Just Do It' drying on a surviving washing line. Beyond, stretching to infinity, bombed buildings seemed to reach the curve of the earth before disappearing in the drifting miasma of sulphur-coloured smoke.

After an exhaustive barrage in a dense city, when the enemy retreats and the liberators advance, survivors coated in ash-coloured dust emerge like the living dead and pick their way over the ruins. People have dried blood around their ears. They are deaf. They are voiceless, bewildered, blinded. They don't see you. It is as if you are not there. You are a shadow, a mirage, a stranger from the strange land outside the city walls. Rats and roaches scamper over the rubble. There are dead and wounded animals: dogs, goats, donkeys, horses. I saw a dead monkey like a human baby and it felt as if a knife tip had nicked my eyeballs.

I watched a man holding the hands of two little girls dressed as mini-women in *abayas* dart from one ruin to another. Two girls in black carried a wheelchair with an old woman clutching a transfusion bag dripping blood into her arm. I saw a woman on crutches lurch by on one leg and had the same feeling that had touched me observing the women with pink headscarves at the refugee camp in Aski Kalak – that it was the women who would shake off the past and rebuild new lives for the children.

Maybe that was just optimism? I held, at the same time, the thought that children who had lived through the carnage, the injustices of Sharia law, the days without light, would never be free of the memories. Dozan Rostami was right. There was nothing funny, no bright side, no yellow flower blooming among the ruins.

We rested on the ground floor of an apartment block two streets behind the YPG in a room containing begrimed pots, plastic furniture, filthy mattress rolls, rags of abandoned clothing, an empty bamboo cage. I wanted to believe the bird had been released. There must have been dead people in the basement. I knew the smell. Rotten meat overlaid with bad eggs and human shit, a faint pinch of something sweet, like cheap perfume, a solid wall of stink that clings to your nostrils and your clothes.

How we ever conducted war without mobile phones I cannot imagine. I had remained in contact with Jean-Paul Renaud, the Frenchman with intel. A bomb exploded close by and in the relative tranquillity that followed, I sent him a text. My phone pinged immediately with his location, which I checked on the GPS. He was two streets away, on the third floor of a building surrounded by the YPG.

Renaud was a former teacher in La Goutte d'Or, a predominantly Muslim quarter of northern Paris. He suffered mild autism, not that his lack of social or communication skills had prevented his conversion to Islam. He had been 'groomed' by a fundamentalist imam in Paris and travelled to Mosul via Turkey with a group of seven new recruits. He claimed never to have been a fighter, but a translator and language teacher. While he understood that he would face terrorism charges in France, he had got it into his head that once he revealed the 'valuable information' he had on the 'secret plans' of Islamic State, the authorities would go easy on him. That remained to be seen. First, we had to get him out.

We crawled from our odious-smelling hole. Cano Ali, spine pressed against the pockmarked walls, kept his eyes peeled as he led the way along the sides of the wasted buildings to the crossroads at the end of the block. According to the information Hassan had received from the YPG, the area had been cleared, but snipers lurked in the ruins waiting for easy targets. Shots rang out all around us. I could hear the dull snap of detonations without the retort or thud of rounds landing. That meant nothing was close. We had not been seen. You learn to sense danger, and soldiers get killed when their senses are disorientated.

We were one block from Renaud.

Cano Ali looked both ways, then zigzagged across the open space. In this manoeuvre, it is the men following who run the greatest risk. A hidden gunman may have seen the figure from the corner of his eye, then turned his sights on the crossing.

Not today, thank you. We made it safely to cover and continued, tight to the half-demolished walls, to the next intersection. I called Renaud.

He babbled on for two minutes in a stream of good but broken English before he shut up and listened to my instructions.

'I can see your block. Do you understand?'

'Yes, I understand. When…'

'Jean-Paul, be quiet and listen. Do you have something white, a sheet, anything you can use as a flag?'

'I have a white towel…'

'That is good. Can you wave it out of the window right now so I can see exactly where you are?'

'Yes…'

'Do it now. Quickly.'

I waited for a couple of seconds and the towel appeared about 100 metres ahead of us.

'Good, I can see it,' I said. 'Now, listen. Leave the building holding the towel in your two hands stretched above your head. That will show you are not armed.'

'I have never been armed. It is the truth.'

'I know that. The militia and the jihadi snipers, they don't know that. Do you understand?'

'Yes, I understand.'

'Come out of the building, the towel above your head. Turn to the left and walk without hurrying along the street. We are waiting for you. Do it now.'

I wrote this conversation down in my notes later that same evening. I did my best to record the exact words that had been spoken.

Of course, I could have played it differently. I could have made my way to the building and brought Jean-Paul Renaud out myself.

I didn't. I made a call. It turned out to be the wrong call.

What I didn't know until later was that a sniper on the top floor of the building had been holding up the YPG advance. They had taken two injuries, one death. When they saw Renaud creep hesitantly from the building, they thought he was the sniper, out of options and looking to surrender.

Halfway down the block, 50 metres, five seconds from where we were waiting, six guys from the YPG militia jumped out of their hiding place. They battered Jean-Paul down with their rifle butts. They slipped a live grenade down his shirt and bolted for cover.

CHAPTER 12

Mouth of the Serpent

My adrenaline spiked. Anger sweat gushed from my armpits. I really wanted to hit somebody.

We stood in a sea of devastation, ears ringing from the explosion. Scraps of blood and flesh clung to the walls. There was nothing to pick up, no wallet or dog tags, nothing to say Jean-Paul Renaud had been in Mosul or had ever existed. I would, through the grapevine, let his family know he had died, and they would resent me for not saving him.

The air tasted of burnt meat. My hearing came back slowly as if sensing something in the distance moving closer. Drones hummed faintly overhead. Guns crackled. Mortars looped into the sky and landed with dull thuds. The sound was muted, several blocks away. You can't say the danger had passed. You never knew when an injured jihadi might rise from the dust and have one last pop before martyrdom.

Hassan had entered the protection of a crippled building turned to debris. The Assyrians built walls to last five thousand years. Modern Mosul had been raised on breeze blocks, plasterboard, watery cement stirred with red dust from the desert, everything flimsy, tenuous. Like the Caliphate.

'John, come. Come,' Hassan repeated, raising his voice.

'What the fuck?' I said as I joined the others.

'We are fighting a war…'

I glared back at him. 'Losing a fucking war, you mean.'

Cano Ali stepped forward and tapped my vest with the back of his hand. He said something I didn't understand.

'Call Roy Underhill,' Hassan translated. 'He may have information on the arms cache we're looking for.'

Cano stared at me as he lit up. I took the fag from him, dragged the smoke deep down into my chest cavity and let it out slowly. I could see my reflection in his eyes when he took the cigarette back.

I got Roy on WhatsApp. He was two miles away, behind enemy lines. The Peshmerga were pushing closer, but his zone was well defended with rings of IEDs, armoured vehicles, field guns. I asked him if he knew of an arms cache in his area.

'Buddy, they've got arms stashed everywhere. What do you think these mothers spend their dollars on, new schools?'

'Anything specific? The Kurds tell me there's a warehouse full of tanks.'

'Ah, that arms cache!' he exclaimed. 'There's a church three blocks from me, it's Coptic or Greek. They've got more assault rifles than you can count on all the fingers from all the hands they've cut off. There must be at least a dozen T-62s, the old Soviet battle tank. They've got a few Abrams as well.'

'Captured from the Iraqi army?'

'You got it. We left a black hole when we pulled out and ISIS was ready to fill it.'

'You're not criticizing American foreign policy are you, Roy?'

164

'Whoa, you kidding me? Best American war in my lifetime,' he said. 'I'll send you the church coordinates.'

'Appreciate it…'

'One more thing. There's a girl here, Sophian. Like Sophia with an extra n. Australian. She's got a baby and wants out, like yesterday…'

'Can we get to her?'

'I told her to wait till we were liberated by you guys. But the baby needs treatment for something or other. She figures better now than later.'

'Hey, what the fuck man, we're up for it.'

I had spoken without thinking. Not for the first time. My phone was on speaker. The guys gathered closer. They nodded their heads as we made a plan. A hospital was situated two blocks from Roy's basement. It was in the same square as the church holding the arms cache – chosen by ISIS to hide their heavy armour, as US 'precision' strikes avoided places of worship. That explained why the hospital was still functioning. While the battle played out on the outskirts of Mosul, life carried on as normal in the city centre – slave auctions, beheadings, training eight-year-old boys to strap on suicide vests.

'I can drop the woman and baby off at the hospital if you can come and get her,' Roy said.

'Won't you be seen?'

He laughed. 'Not me, brother. I'm black.' I didn't respond for a second and he laughed again. 'They think of *kaffirs* as white guys. You a whitey?'

'Irish. More pink than white.'

'Then you take care.'

'I'll do that, Roy.' I glanced at Hassan, Dozan, Cano Ali. 'Two miles. We'll be there in one hour.'

I clicked off. Cano Ali snapped a fresh mag into his AK, turned the dial on the selector and dropped one in the chamber.

'What the fuck,' he said, aping my voice, and the tension drained away.

We followed him out of the derelict building and back a half dozen blocks to where the vehicles were hidden in the ruins. You could hear the tramp of our boots, our footfall raising eddies of silver ash. The dead we passed along the way were already losing their individuality. Expressions fade, faces glaze, the dust claims them, like it says in the funeral oratory. They weren't jihadis or prisoners or enemies. They were just corpses, men, women, children, animals. If hell has a smell, that smell hung in the air.

We stripped out of our Kevlar vests and wrapped our heads in *shemaghs*. I glanced at my companions. If you were casting jihadis for a film, you'd show these guys the door. Cano Ali could have passed for a sumo wrestler, big, bald, clean shaven. Dozan, with his handlebar moustache and carved cheekbones, was exactly how he appeared, a Sunni pilot trained by the RAF. Hassan Ghazi looked like a pasha.

We heard the whistle of a stray rocket and ducked our heads by instinct as it bored into an empty building. The way it collapsed in on itself made me think for some reason of the Twin Towers free-falling over the streets of New York, setting off a chain reaction that was annihilating the cities of Iraq brick by brick. It was a weird decision, the reasoning still not exactly clear to me, that after the al-Qaeda attack on 9/11, the Bush White House decided to oust Saddam Hussein. Most of the hijackers came from Saudi Arabia and, at that time, Iraq was unique in the Arab world for not having cells of Islamic terrorists. Islamic State was born out of the insurrection that followed the Coalition invasion.

We slipped into our Ray-Bans. Cano Ali, in the lead vehicle, set off over the rubble. Hassan called his YPG contact to inform him of our dubious task and to ask for cover where possible. He gave me the report as our two-car packet crept over the gutted streets between crumbling buildings, around corpses, through the acrid smoke of burning oil dumps.

I was in the Previa's passenger seat beside Dozan. He was as good as his word. They all were. They were risking their lives to rescue one Australian girl and her baby. It made no sense when there were thousands of people emerging from cellars and fleeing towards the river. The thing is, combat rarely makes sense. It rarely goes to plan. You do what you do because it seems right at the time and, even when you are doing it, there's a small part of you that says this is madness.

Roy Underhill's position was two miles into enemy territory to the west of us. We turned right and left through the lattice of skeletal buildings; I thought, this is what the world will look like after a nuclear war. Some roads were blocked and we had to back up and try a different route. A have-a-go jihadi left behind leaned over a rooftop and let off a couple of shots. Hassan replied with a long burst from the weapon he kept lodged against the door frame in the Toyota. The gunman dropped from view, dead or staring up at the sky wondering if heaven was up there beyond the drifting clouds of choking smoke.

We caught up with the YPG unit – those who had killed the Frenchman – and stopped. I felt like getting out and giving them a piece of my mind, but there was no time for that. Their officer exchanged a few words with Hassan. They slapped hands and we continued into the mouth of the serpent. The Kurdish flags painted on the car roofs had been vital behind the lines. Now they were a red rag to the bull.

I stayed in contact with Roy until he left his hideout to transfer Sophian to the hospital.

'Hey, man,' he said, like it was an afterthought. 'Hope you've got room for another one?'

'Another what?'

'Another girl. She's already tried to get out once. She's dead keen to have another go.'

'More the merrier, mate,' I told him.

He gave me a description of himself. I described our vehicles.

'Okay, brother,' he said. 'I won't say good luck, it's bad luck.'

We would maintain cell-phone silence for the next 15 minutes until we reached the hospital. Roy had not described the girls, but I knew what they'd look like: in black from scalp to gloves to ankles and accompanied by a male 'relative', a dark-skinned man with a black beard, white turban and *thobe*, the costume of Saudis and holy men.

The YPG raised a smokescreen with a mortar barrage west of the hospital. At some point, we crossed the invisible line and snaked three blocks through enemy territory. I spotted machine-gun nests and lookouts – dickers we called them in the old days. Either they didn't recognize the Kurdish colours, or they'd assumed no one from outside the Caliphate would be crazy enough to be driving in.

We turned a corner and, to our complete surprise, entered a busy street full of pedestrians, surrounded by rubble piled up in barricades. There were people coming and going, cars honking, a couple of market stalls with limp vegetables. The crowd parted as a pair of fighters strutted by with rocket launchers over their shoulders. They were young lads with fierce expressions and scraggly beards. I would have leaned out of the vehicle and shouted at them to fuck off back home to their mums, but Dozan wouldn't have approved.

He tapped my leg and pointed.

The hospital was up ahead, grey, unadorned, with a flat roof. Holes gaped, with flapping shreds of curtains where the windows had blown out. The buildings beyond the hospital clung together like a fallen house of cards. The interiors had turned to dust and what remained was shaky stacks of concrete girders with twisted iron stays, a dystopian cityscape of utter devastation. You could not imagine how people lived here, survived here, raised children here, how human beings had come to this.

I shook the thoughts out of my head. My finger rested on the trigger of a folding-stock AK. My throat burned from the filthy air.

A path had been cleared through the debris around the hospital. People carriers arrived and departed in Middle East fashion, drivers blaspheming and blasting their horns, the nose of every vehicle trying to push its way through the confusion. Cano Ali joined in, waving his fist out the window.

I spotted Roy Underhill, hands behind his back, a benign countenance, a head taller than anyone else, his gaze moving along the line of cars. My face was covered except for my eyes, but his faint nod said he had recognized me.

He strode through the throng. Two women in black, one with a baby, bobbed along submissively in his wake. He opened the sliding rear door and waved his hand dismissively as they climbed in. He snapped the door shut, peered in my window, then across the road in the direction of the church.

'It's called St Thomas's. Take care, buddy.'

He turned and was gone.

Cano Ali had deliberately blocked the exit. He sat on the horn until Dozan was able to wriggle through the turmoil and lead our packet back the way we had come. Dozan had taken the lead because he was skilled at manoeuvring through tricky situations, but more importantly, he had a baby on board. By the time the lookouts spotted us, it was the second vehicle that would catch the crossfire.

Some men risk their lives to save unknown babies. Some men throw live babies into burning pits with their dead mothers. British intelligence would tell me that anyone who had joined Islamic State was considered an enemy of the state and should be executed. Members of humanitarian organizations wanted to bring these people home to de-radicalization programmes and fair trials.

I thought of the two teenage boys with rocket launchers. They would be dead within the week, and what would it have all been for?

Hassan had alerted the YPG that we were coming out and a fresh fusillade of shells thumped into the walls along the route. Visibility through the dust storm was down to a few inches, shielding us from the jihadi machine guns. They were keeping their heads down and the few bursts they let off pinged from the vehicles without doing any serious damage.

In 15 minutes we were back to the relative safety of the Kurdish lines. We kept going, zigzagging our way through the contemporary ruins of Mosul to the prehistoric ruins of Nineveh. My head was hot and sweaty. I removed my *shemagh*. The girls had not spoken a word. I glanced over my shoulder. They were motionless like two black statues holding hands. The baby was silent. Traumatized babies don't cry.

'You can take your headgear off now if you want to,' I said.

It was a couple of seconds before they did so. It was obvious which of the two girls was Sophian, she was holding the baby. It was even more obvious who the other girl was. Her photograph was in her profile on my laptop. I must have looked at it a hundred times.

'Diana Abbasi,' I said.

'Mr Carney.'

The sun was setting by the time we got back to Erbil. As we pulled up at the metal gates, it felt like we were arriving home. We'd been on the road five days, sleeping rough. I'm getting too old for all this, I said to myself.

Hassan had agreed after some arm-twisting that we would keep the girls in the safe house overnight, conduct a casual debrief, then take them to the authorities in the morning.

Dozan, before going home to spend the evening with his wife, helped me move an extra bed into his room. It was the largest, with shuttered doors leading to a balcony above the palms at the front of the building. The room had a large sofa, a low table with rose petals floating in a bowl of water and miniature raffia baskets on a shelf. Water stains ran in contours over the walls, but the space in the glow of the kerosene lamp was pleasant enough and the girls gazed about them as if they had arrived at the Ritz. I shut the door and left them to catch their breath.

Cano Ali had left on an errand and Hassan joined me in the kitchen with two bottles of warm beer. We had a dilemma: whether or not to confirm that St Thomas's Church was a repository for heavy armour. The hospital was still in service. The last thing I wanted to hear was that stray bombs had blown it off the map.

We had to weigh that possibility against the fact that intel is a commodity to be bartered and exchanged. The Peshmerga had allowed us to follow the offensive; they even watered and fed us. The YPG had set up a barrage to assist our way in and out of enemy territory. We had contributed updates on tunnel locations. I thought that was sufficient for now and we should hold the info on St Thomas's for at least a few days. Hassan argued that the advance on the area would take place in the next 48 hours. Every scrap of intelligence would aid the operation.

The slow beat of his amber beads ended. 'Your American friend would not have shared the coordinates if he did not want it to be passed on.'

'It could cost lives, Hassan.'

'As in everything we do, John.'

I sipped my drink. 'Where'd you get these beers from?' I asked, and he tapped the side of his nose.

'Contacts,' he replied.

'Next time we're in the bazaar, we should look for an ice box.'

He touched his nose again. 'I might just have a contact.'

'I bet you bloody do.'

His phone was on the table. I swallowed the warm beer, plonked the bottle down and pushed the device towards him. He made his calls: Iraqi intelligence, his new contact in Asayish, and finally the Kurdish authorities dealing with jihadi brides.

I changed out of my dusty clothes and Skyped Kali. She was following the battle for Mosul and knew more about the offensive than I did. I assured her we remained behind the lines and she was pleased to hear that I had brought out two women and a baby. She wanted to know what was going to happen to them. That was the big question, the question everyone was asking, and no one seemed to have an answer.

'A detention centre for a while,' I said. 'Then, who knows…'

I looked back into Kali's dark eyes. We were silent for a moment, then she leaned forward until her lips touched the screen.

Diana and Sophian had washed in the clanking apparatus we called a shower by the time Cano Ali returned with his backpack stuffed with milk formula, fresh fruit, grub for dinner and an electric blender to puree baby food. In a separate bag, he had some baby clothes and, wrapped in recycled paper, a selection of four dresses, underwear and sandals.

Hassan inspected the collection and nodded shrewdly.

'Ah, so now you are robbing your own daughters,' he said.

Cano gave me the bag of clothes and marched off to the kitchen without a response. I climbed the stairs to the girls' room and knocked.

'Some clean clothes,' I called. 'They're outside the door. Dinner's on the go.'

When they finally appeared, Sophian and Diana had transformed from unidentifiable black sacks into normal young women in the embroidered dresses of the Kurds. I had seen women fully covered all over the Middle East, in London and Manchester, but it only occurred to me at that moment that the *abaya* and niqab are inhuman, unnatural and vaguely sinister.

Sophian and Diana were painfully thin, with pronounced cheekbones, stick wrists and haunted expressions. With their freshly washed hair and bright clothes, I was going to say to them 'you look great,' but that's no longer PC and I kept quiet until Cano brought a steaming pot of bean soup to the table. They ate without speaking or looking up, one plate after another. Cano had pureed vegetables for the baby, a boy of six months named Yusuf. He took him from his mother's arms and, as he fed him with a spoon, the boy stared back at Cano with big empty eyes.

'I've never seen him go to anyone,' Sophian said, and Hassan translated.

'Practice,' Cano told her. He held up four fingers. 'Four *habibi*. Four girls.'

Everyone smiled. The ice had broken.

I glanced up as Hassan left the room and a picture of Roy Underhill came into my mind, the way he had glided through the crowd like a sheikh, hiding in plain sight, risking his life because the world only stays in balance when good people do what's right.

Cano cleaned up. He then left the house, waving his hand back over his shoulder.

'*Ma al-salamah*,' he called.

Hassan must have been waiting for him outside beneath the palm trees, his favourite spot. They exchanged a few words, the car doors slammed and I heard the vehicle disappear into the night.

I made mint tea and we sat at the table nursing the glasses. Yusuf slept. Sophian laid him on a soft chair. There were tears in her eyes when she sat again.

'Thank you,' she said. 'Thank you.' She glanced at her baby. 'I had to get out for him. You can't imagine...'

She broke off. Tears flowed down her gaunt cheeks. She sobbed. It was contagious. Diana sobbed too. This was my debrief, two young women overcome with relief, the tension pouring from them like an electric current.

'What can't I imagine?' I asked softly.

Sophian brushed at her tears with the back of her hand. She shook her head. 'It's like a story on another planet. You know, like *Star Wars*,' she said. 'Women are just baby factories. We're pieces of meat. They have no respect, no kindness, no...humanity.'

'They raped me,' Diana added, lowering her eyes, saying the words that must have been festering inside her, a great poisonous ball of shame and rage. 'They raped me every day. Not one man. Two or three or four. I was a virgin...' She looked up with a forlorn expression. 'No one will want me now.'

They cried again. They were going to need a lot of tears to wash away all the anger, the suffering. Sophian and Diana were victims. They didn't need to be de-radicalized. They reviled Islamic State. They wanted Islamic State with its clerics and commanders and boy soldiers wiped from the face of the earth. If counter-terrorist officers understood that, they could learn from these girls. They could teach them how to turn others. They weren't terrorists. They were potential assets.

'We were promised heaven,' Diana said. 'It turned into hell.'

'Worse than hell,' Sophian added.

She took a sip of tea and put her glass down. Her cheeks bloomed with colour as she told me her story. Sophian had travelled from Australia to England, from Turkey to Iraq. She had grown up in Hurstville, the Sydney suburb where her father owned an electrical franchise. They had a large house in its own plot of land, new cars, gold jewellery. Her life had been privileged but superficial, she said, the endless pursuit of qualifications and money, marrying into the right family, constantly seeking admiration and regard in the eyes of the community.

'There is nothing Islamic in that,' she stated. 'The Caliphate promised true Islam, a world where men and women would live in the way set down by the Prophet. It wasn't true. It was a lie. It was all a lie from beginning to end. But that's what we believed. We didn't come here to be with good-looking boys we'd met on the internet. That's the male view, the propaganda.'

Diana was nodding furiously. 'We thought we could create a new identity, a new reality.' She paused for a second. 'We face race hatred every day. In London, every time I wear a headscarf on the bus or the tube, someone will screw up their face at me. Women as much as men.'

'But you didn't want to marry someone chosen by your parents?' I reminded her.

Diana lowered her eyes. 'That's the problem for people like me, like us,' she replied. 'I don't belong anywhere, not here, not in Pakistan, not at home.'

'Still you want to go back?'

'Of course. I'm English. I was born in London.' She gathered her thoughts. 'When I was at university, I was shocked that students from private schools didn't mix with students from ordinary schools. They're all English, or British, but they speak a different language. They listen to different music. They are two separate groups in their own little boxes. I'm in another box. We all stay in our own boxes. There is no such thing as integration. It's a word we use for a society that is disintegrating.'

'You know about Brexit?'

'Yes, even here.' She shook her shoulders. 'Or there, I should say. People only feel comfortable with their own kind. It shouldn't be like that, but it is like that.'

I had heard these things before. I would hear them again. The Islamist groomers knew how to fish in the wells of disappointment and disillusion. There was no simple reason why so many women – thousands, how many thousands is unclear – from across Europe, from as far away as the United States and Australia, had left their homes to be a part of the Caliphate. Many came as jihadi brides. Others came in search of paradise or adventure. They came to escape parents, arranged marriages, their tedious lives in suburban towns, a perceived lack of opportunity, a sense, rightly or wrongly, of racial hatred and rejection. They came because they wanted to feel that sense of belonging they had not felt in their own countries and communities. I could understand that.

In Mosul, Sophian and Diana had lived in a communal house administered by the female brigade known as al-Khansaa, zealots with canes who watched other women to make sure that they were not wearing makeup, showing bare skin, or hiding a mobile phone, and flogged the soles of their feet if they caught them in any number of forbidden acts.

'It's like I said, science fiction. The communal houses are just brothels,' Sophian said. 'We were unpaid prostitutes, concubines for men who wanted a pleasure marriage. You can't wear lipstick, but you can sleep with a different man every night.'

'Guns and sex. It's revolting. It's a bad joke,' Diana added. 'If that's what it promotes in the Quran, then I am not a Muslim.'

They looked at each other and nodded.

Most of the women had journeyed to Mosul of their own free will. Some had been dragged off against their will. Among the al-Khansaa brigade were women who had taken the lead and persuaded their husbands to join ISIS. They believed it was their duty to have children and bring them up prepared to fight holy war. They celebrated when their husbands became martyrs and their sons were old enough to turn themselves into walking bombs. The al-Khansaa women were aware that the firepower of the United States behind the Iraqi military would ultimately defeat Islamic State. Their mission was to keep the myth of the Caliphate alive until it rose again.

'Will it rise again?'

They nodded in unison.

'In North Africa,' Diana said. 'They have escape routes planned…'

'Do you know where they are?'

She shook her head. 'No. Once you are in the Caliphate you can't get out unless you are one of the special people. We're just scraps, the crumbs, jihadi whores…'

Tears welled into her eyes again.

177

'You're out now, Diana. There's going to be a lot of bullshit. You know, with the authorities. But we will try and get you home.'

'Thank you…'

'Do you know anything more about North Africa, the Caliphate rising again?'

'Just rumours. There's a big poor population in Africa. That's where the radicals will spin their lies and sow their poison seeds.' She looked into my eyes. 'There will be more wars, more killing, more refugees. It's never going to end.'

The baby woke and Sophian lifted him into her arms. I made more tea. I fancied a beer but had no idea where Hassan kept them, if there were any. I asked Diana how they had managed to leave their hideouts that day for the hospital.

'It's chaos now. Food shortages, bombardments. It's falling down around their ears,' she replied. 'The boss women are too busy thinking about how to save their own skins to watch us all the time.'

'How did you make contact with Roy Underhill?'

Diana released a faint smile. She had precise features, with green eyes and fair hair, a typical English girl who didn't feel as if she belonged, a fault in her or a fault in society, I wasn't sure.

'He repairs things in the house. Like a handyman. He's always nodding to himself and chanting verses from the Quran,' she continued. 'But it's an act. He knows intuitively who he can trust and who he can't. And when he trusts you, he tries to help you. He gave me a mobile phone so I could call home…'

I remembered the distressed email from Diana Abbasi's mother, our failed attempt to bring her out with the help of the fixer, Apollo, who needed $5,000 to smuggle his son to England. It was when we drove back empty handed across the desert that I knew we had to build an effective network to undermine Islamic State.

'There's something else,' Diana volunteered. 'Women were never encouraged to be suicide bombers or fighters until the last couple of weeks. Then it changed.'

She glanced across the table and Sophian continued. 'The imam suddenly started talking about Nusaybah bint Ka'ab, the woman who picked up a sword on the battlefield to defend Muhammad when he was surrounded by enemies. They want us to be *mujahid*, like the female warriors of history.'

'When the Caliphate falls, they want the women to go back to Europe and kill themselves in attacks.' Diana shrugged her thin shoulders and repeated the phrase she'd said before. 'It's never going to end.'

It was late. The girls were tired. I was tired. Sophian came to her feet. Yusuf opened his eyes for a second and closed them again. I remembered Ntileini doing that in her cot and had always wondered if babies dreamed and, if they did, what they dreamed about.

'He's going to be a surfer, not a suicide bomber,' she said.

'Good to hear it,' I replied, and pushed my chair back. 'You can bang on my door if you need anything.'

We said good night. The girls climbed the stairs with bottles of water. I checked all the doors and turned off the lights. I dropped down on my narrow bed with my feet over the end, staring at the shadows crossing the ceiling. I heard a dog bark and it reminded me the strays needed feeding.

CHAPTER 13

We Are at War

The Citadel in Erbil is a fortress city on a steep *tell*, a man-made hill created by many generations of people living and rebuilding on the same spot. Nomads came to the region 5,000 years before Christ, and colonizers from countless tribes have fought their way to the mountain top ever since.

According to the tourist guide, the Citadel was first mentioned on clay tablets in 2,300 BC and is the longest continuously inhabited settlement on the planet. The Assyrians occupied the stronghold for 1,000 years before being toppled by Alexander the Great on his long march to India. The Greeks were followed by Romans, Christians and Mongols, each culture leaving their own artefacts, architecture and wall paintings.

It was a clear dazzling day, the sky a sheet of blue, the sun beating down like it was still summer – 30 degrees and the only shade close to the walls. I stood with Cano Ali on the lip of a hole where a group of archaeologists were dusting off clay shards from a fire temple built to honour Zarathustra – the tutor of Pythagoras, I read, and founder of what is thought to be the first monotheistic religion. I took some photos for Natty. After her day out with Matt Lambert, she was more interested in the ancient world than ever.

We cooled off visiting the Grand Mosque, then strolled through ruins in various states of decay and restoration. Cano told me in Arabic what each different civilization had built, when and what it all meant. He spoke slowly, pronouncing every syllable, and made me repeat words so that I would remember them. I didn't know Cano was so well up on Erbil's history, but then, Cano never ceased to surprise me.

Only when I was lying in bed listening to the dogs whining in the street outside did it occur to me that my comrades had left me alone the previous evening so that Sophian and Diana would feel more comfortable without their presence. Of course, the guys were happy to go home and spend some time with their families. But their first consideration was to give me the space to undertake the debriefing.

They arrived back before breakfast. Hassan had brought pastries, fig jam, a bag of oranges. We sat down together at the big table with a pot of coffee. Cano fed Yusuf with pureed fruit. It was little more than 12 hours since the infant had left Islamic State and already there was laughter in his eyes as he looked up at Cano pulling faces, like father and son with their full lips and shiny bald heads. Cano put the remains of the puree in a glass jar sealed with a square of greaseproof paper which he tied with green ribbon.

The two women in their Kurdish dresses seemed ready to face what they knew was going to be an uncertain future. Their liberation from Islamic State would have given them a surge of optimism and purpose. But the reprieve is temporary. Within a few days, they would feel the onset of PTSD – post-traumatic stress disorder, a condition for which there is no cure except patience and understanding. In extreme cases, and I can't think of anything more extreme than rape and brutality in a war setting, the stress remains present for the remainder of one's life. The one thing to avoid when people have PTSD is pressure to talk about the event that caused it. That was the very pressure they were about to face.

Cano kissed the baby's head and placed him back into his mother's arms. While we set off to visit the Citadel, Hassan and Dozan had escorted Sophian and Diana to what was called the Community Centre in Kasnazan, ten miles from Erbil. The facility was financed by the Danish Refugee Council in cooperation with the British government's Department for International Development. It was supposed to be the one place where refugees from war zones received psychological support and legal assistance. Not that I had much confidence that the service still operated as it had been planned.

The Danish government had been sympathetic to Syrian and Iraqi asylum seekers when the project started in 2014, but the stance had hardened the following year when the anti-immigration Danish People's Party became the main opposition in the national parliament. People were compassionate when there was a trickle of evacuees, but once the numbers multiplied, populist parties gained traction, warning of the dangers of alien hordes bursting through the borders.

I was glad my visit to the Citadel was done and dusted. Cano Ali was clearly proud of Erbil's World Heritage site, but it wasn't a patch on Nineveh and, in the end, one pile of ruins to me tends to look much like another.

We drove back into the city. I had a meeting at the Divan Hotel, and had no idea why Cano made a detour and parked at the Qaysari Bazaar.

I pulled out all the stops to ask in well-modulated Arabic what the hell we were doing there. He brushed impatiently at my lapels, replied in a fiery tirade I didn't understand, and I could do nothing except follow in his wake as he marched through the labyrinth of ripe tomatoes and old men smoking hubbly-bubblies.

The penny dropped when we arrived at the door to Hassan's tailor.

After the kissing and enquiries about everyone's family, tea was served in tiny glasses. The two Kurds chatted amiably and I stood behind the changing-room curtain in my boxers waiting while Mazar Ghazi ironed my linen suit. My boots were polished by the shoeshine boy, conveniently squatting outside the shop when we arrived. I dressed. Mazar produced a pale blue shirt and Cano unfurled a dark blue tie from his pocket like a conjuror bringing a rabbit from a hat. His eyes gleamed as he turned me to the mirror.

'You've been playing me like a cheap violin,' I said, and of course he had no idea what I was talking about.

'Very good Englishman,' he replied.

Cano flipped a coin which the shoeshine boy plucked from the air with two blackened fingers, and we strode back through the bazaar. Cano bought bags of pomegranates and grapes for his *habibis* and tore through the traffic as if we were bank robbers.

My meeting was with Oliver Posh-Something, our man from MI6. He had called while we were eating breakfast and insisted we meet 'without delay'. I had been tempted to put it off, just to be difficult, but we were going back to Mosul in a couple of days and, like a visit to the dentist, it was best to get it over and done with.

Cano swerved to a halt at the hotel entrance.

'Good Englishman,' he said again.

I climbed the steps and almost fell over a pile of silver cases as I stepped into the giddy cool of the air-conditioning. It was a madhouse, with pressmen greedy for scoops, TV cameras the size of small boats, translators and fixers, lady anchors in bulletproof vests.

An English freelancer I knew shouldered his way through the crowd and stuck out his damp palm. Rob Dyson was a young guy trying to make a name for himself without contacts, family in high places, all the stuff you need just to get a break. He was sweaty, with thick-lensed glasses, one of the arms held with sticky tape.

'Hello, John, you look smart,' he said.

'Gotta turn it on for the ladies, right?'

'I thought you were married?'

'Who told you that?'

'You know I can't reveal my sources,' he answered, and we laughed. 'You wouldn't have anything for me, would you?'

'Not right now. But I'll keep you in mind.'

'Anything…'

'Rob, when I've got something, you'll be the first to know.'

He grinned. 'That's great, thanks,' he said, and his tone changed. 'Problem is, no one really knows what's going on out there…'

'You name it, it's going on.'

We shook hands again and he turned back into the din of the gossip mill. I felt three parts smug and seven parts depressed that I knew exactly what was going on in the firebombed streets of Mosul. The death of a bad dream. The death of innocents on a daily, hourly, minute-by-minute basis: women and babies, Peshmerga volunteers and child jihadis, doctors, aid workers, advisers, bomb makers blowing themselves into the heaven constructed by false prophets and delusion. Rats and mangy dogs scavenge on corpses. A mother runs with her seven-year-old daughter from a collapsing building into the sudden explosion of a stray mortar falling at that time and that place by the act of an uncaring god. Your nasal passages burn from cordite. Your throat is dry like ash. Your eyes sting. You've got a cut-down AK-47 lodged in your right shoulder and you're burning to shoot somebody who needs to be shot.

Everything the reporters got their hands on was Photoshopped, rumour, hearsay. TV news was mere snapshots, glimpses like the view from a train. You could watch every item from beginning to end, but it was too random, too abstract to stick in your head. Newspapers and online websites sought out the sensational, firefights, bodies tossed in mass graves, children with eyes burnt out from chemical weapons. All these things were happening, but they were isolated pieces in a complex puzzle that never revealed the full story.

Perhaps the full story was too much for their viewers and readers.

I crossed the black, white and gold tiles in the main reception and took a seat under the parasol in the far corner of the outdoor bar built on a platform over the Little Zab. I ordered a pint of cider and watched the river flow by the hotel on its journey to or from the Tigris, I wasn't sure which. It was 11.50. I sent Natty a couple of shots of the Citadel on WhatsApp. I had half a mind to call Hassan to ask him how he had got on delivering Sophian and Diana in Kasnazan, but decided it was better to wait for a debrief face to face.

MI6 arrived in a double-breasted blazer and a white straw hat. The muezzin's voice sang out from the mosque, calling the faithful to noon prayers. He was right on time.

Oliver recognized me, of course, and I recognized him. He had my head shot in a dossier, and I recalled him sitting behind me with another man the day I asked Cornelius Visser for top cover when we went into Mosul. He had enjoyed the joke.

'John Carney, so pleased to meet you,' he said.

'Finally,' I replied, and he raised his eyebrows in what passed for a smile.

He glanced from side to side, checking the location for cameras, listening devices, I'm not sure what, then took the seat opposite me at the small table. He dropped his hat on another chair and his eyes ran over me like a security scan, my clothes, hair, expression, every tic and tell. Gamblers do the same, probing for weaknesses.

I studied him, too, across the table. Oliver had a semblance of a movie spy, perhaps that's what he cultivated – blue eyes, neat hair, a strong nose, handsome, but as ruthless as someone who had a licence to kill, or at least thought he should have.

'So, Oliver, what can I do for you?' I began.

'Diana Abbasi?'

'What about her?'

'You tell me.'

He ordered coffee, local style. He would have received the intel on the two girls from Asayish ten minutes after Hassan had reported in and would already have a file he was anxious to complete. It was a commonly held myth that we in Britain punched above our weight on the battlefield. I didn't think this was true, not after our undistinguished campaign in Iraq. But, in security circles, there was none better than MI6.

I rolled my shoulders. 'Nice girl,' I said. 'British as you and me. Ran away from an arranged marriage. Raped by maniacs. If you're as smart as you look, you'll have her working for us.'

'So, no doubts on your part?'

'She's not a jihadi. She's a girl who doesn't feel as if she belongs, and she wants to belong. Make her one of ours.'

His coffee came, thick and black with a layer of foam on top. He stirred it slowly and I watched a dhow pass by on the river, the big sail snapping in the breeze. He drummed his fingers silently on the table top.

'When you were working in close protection for Aegis, you were on the right side. Now, it's no longer clear on whose side you are on.'

'Is that a question?'

'It's a question you need to answer.'

'I'm surprised you would ask me that, Ollie,' I said. 'Do you mind if I call you Ollie?'

'Actually, yes, I do. The name is Oliver.'

'Well, as I say, I'm surprised you'd ask me such a dumb question.' I shrugged. 'You know as well as me, we've been sharing intel on ISIS tunnels, escape routes, arms dumps...'

'You, on the other hand, Mr Carney, are indeed smarter than you look. You could be a sleeper...'

I laughed.

I called the waiter to order another drink.

Oliver sipped his coffee, then placed the glass with its shiny chrome handle precisely back in the saucer.

'You could be bringing women out of the Caliphate who are themselves sleepers. They will settle back into English society, French society, and wait for orders to do more mischief.'

'Why the fuck would I do that?'

'Money, my dear. Money. Don't they say it's the root of all evil?'

'I'm sure you know a lot more about evil than I do,' I said.

I wondered about that 'dear' he'd slipped into the conversation. Was it an affectation? Did it mean anything? Was it a code? My pint came. There was a faint breeze kicking up a swell on the grey surface of the river and the palms seemed to whisper *Allah, Allah, Allah.*

'I've got a question for you,' I continued. 'What do you think of Margaret Thatcher?'

He sat back and did the finger drumming thing. 'What has that got to do with anything?'

'Come on, Oliver, humour me.'

His eyes were as cold as the cider glass.

'She was the right person in the right place at the right time.' He finished his coffee. 'Money,' he repeated. 'How are you surviving?'

'On a bloody shoestring, if you must know. I'm using up savings that should be going to pay for my daughter's education.'

'Ntileini is a bright girl. She'll do just fine. Didn't she just get the Duke of Edinburgh Award?'

This was the standard stratagem: by mentioning your child he lets you know he has you by the balls. Or imagines he does.

I ignored the question and watched two Gulf Arabs in white *dishdashas* join two waiting Europeans in dark suits – bankers, lawyers, accountants? Erbil was booming still, in spite of the war across the border. Perhaps because of it.

'I just brought out two girls from Islamic State. They are not enemies, or sleepers, or double agents. They're just girls who need our help. They hate Islamic State. You play them right, you've got allies, not enemies.'

'You don't know that.'

'Look, no one knows anything, right? You go on what you feel in your gut. Have some bloody compassion and do the decent thing.'

He smiled and tapped his fingers.

'What do you know about EMNI, John? Do you mind if I call you John?'

'Call me anything you like, mate. Do I have a code name?'

'I'm not going to tell you that.'

'No, not the name, just if I've got one or not.'

'You imagine you're so important?'

'Not at all. You called me this morning. I didn't call you.'

'What about EMNI?'

'Scum of the earth,' I replied.

EMNI was Islamic State's External Action Command, their equivalent of MI6. It had been set up to smuggle commanders to safety and loyal jihadis back to Europe to recruit 'clean men' and plan terror attacks.

'They're the people we should be going after,' I added. 'Not girls with babies who've been raped and turned into slaves.'

His expression changed. Lines opened on his brow as he reached into his blazer pocket and removed a sheet of pink A4 paper folded in three. He held it up like a summons, then slid it across the table.

'What's this?' I asked as I unfolded the sheet.

'It is a list of attacks by Islamists that have occurred in Europe and the United States in the last year or so. When you get back to your safe house, go online and you'll see that this is just the tip of the iceberg. There were scores more in Europe. Hundreds more across the world.'

This is his list, as he gave it to me:

1.   14 February 2015. Gunman opens fire at the Krudttoenden café and later at the Great Synagogue in Copenhagen, killing two and injuring five.

2. 3 May. One person injured, two terrorists shot dead after attacking an art exhibit including cartoons of Muhammad in Garland, Texas.
3. 26 June. A decapitated head marked with Arabic writing and Islamist flags found in a factory near Lyon. Fire caused from booby-trapped gas canisters, one dead, 11 injured.
4. 13 November. Paris. 137 dead and 368 wounded in a series of coordinated attacks consisting of mass shootings and suicide bombings.
5. 2 December. Married couple Rizwan Farook and Tashfeen Malik kill 14 and injure 22 in a killing spree in San Bernardino, California.
6. 22 March 2016. Two suicide bombings at Brussels Airport and metro resulting in 35 deaths and more than 300 wounded.
7. 12 June. Nightclub, Orlando, Florida. Omar Mateen kills 49 and injures 53 during a mass shooting. He called the police during the attack to pledge loyalty to ISIS.
8. 14 July, Bastille Day. Mohamed Lahouaiej-Bouhlel drives a 19-tonne truck along the promenade in Nice; 87 dead, hundreds injured. It was a sign of the terrorists diversifying their weaponry.
9. 8 July. A teenage Afghan asylum seeker injures five people, two critically, with a knife and an axe on a train outside Wurzburg, Germany. He was shot dead by police.
10. 26 July. Terrorists cut the throat of an 85-year-old priest and take four nuns hostage in a church in Rouen, France.

I looked up from the list.

'We are at war. Somewhere, every day, every single day, innocent lives are lost to Islamic terrorism.'

'You think I don't know that?' I picked up his straw hat and dropped it back on the chair. 'I've taken my fair share of incoming and I've slotted a few who were trying to slot me.'

'I know your record.' He drummed his fingers. He was working me and wasn't sure of the best approach. 'My job, your job, when it comes down to it, is to prevent terrorism and catch terrorists. You should be working for us.'

'I am working for you. Everything we get we report to Asayish. They pass it on to all the agencies.'

'Chinese whispers. Things get lost in translation,' he said. 'Sometimes, they just get lost. You have a reliable network. We know that. You should be using it so we can stop future attacks before they happen. I want to know what EMNI is up to…'

'Are you offering me a job?'

'Indirectly.'

'With pay?'

'There is a contingency for that possibility.'

I shook my head. 'I don't have the right tie, mate.' I took a sip from my pint. 'I've got a daughter, as you know. When I think she could be out there in Islamic State, it makes my heart pound twice as fast. There are young women who made a mistake going to the Caliphate. I want to help them get home.'

'And there is nothing in it for you?'

'Yeah, a couple of ounces of hot lead if I don't keep my head down.'

'Do your Kurds have the same motivations?'

'You won't find better people. They've got an agenda, course they have. Long term, they want the United States to back a Kurdish state…'

'That's not very likely.'

'Well, you fight for what you believe in. If not, what's the point? In the meantime, if there are jihadi brides we can help, then that's what we're going to do.'

His cold eyes did another scan and it struck me that, like Cornelius Visser, Oliver couldn't work out why a man like me was doing what I was doing. He was unable to see beyond his own prejudices – a fault in him, I thought. He had been too long in the intelligence game. Spies put everyone in boxes and dossiers. They forget we are individuals, all unique.

I leaned across the table. 'You know they can get married online, just drop into muslima.com. All official. Blessed by an imam,' I said. 'They call girls jihadi brides even if they're not brides. They think it gives them status.'

'Not that it does.'

'Well, we both know that, don't we Oliver.'

It was nearly half past twelve, hot under the parasol. I loosened my tie, slipped my jacket off and hung it on the back of the chair. Oliver remained cool in his Union Jack colours, crisp white shirt, blue blazer with the red handkerchief like a bloody gash.

'We come back to the same impasse,' he went on. 'The government would rather that these jihadi brides do not return to the United Kingdom.'

'But they're British. They've got British passports, at least they did have…'

'They lost their British rights when they joined a terrorist organization intent on destroying our way of life. One hundred and thirty-seven people slaughtered on the streets of Paris. Another eighty-seven in Nice. I will tell you this, and I trust it will go no further, there are attacks being planned right now in London. We stop them, most of them, but some will get through. They always do. We have to hunt these people down,

John. We have to hunt them down and kill them.'

'I don't disagree. But we've also got to decide who is a terrorist and who is a victim of terrorism. I told your Dutch mate the same thing.'

'That's woolly thinking, a platitude.'

'No it's not. The girls I've seen are all victims, every one of them.' He went to speak and I held up my hand. 'Yes, we need de-radicalization programmes. Yes, there will be people who have to be monitored. But if we're a so-called civilized society, we have to behave in a civilized way.'

'Very passionate. Very holistic. But EMNI also has programmes. They are becoming more skilled at brainwashing techniques that allow terrorists to appear de-radicalized while they remain loyal to the murder and mayhem of terrorism.'

He held up his hand, copying my gesture.

'You remember Laura Angela Hansen?'

'Very well. Safe at home with her two kids in Amsterdam.'

'That day you tried to bring them across the border, her Palestinian husband was shot in the legs by his own jihadi comrades. He was nursed by a team led by a German-trained Muslim doctor and re-educated.' He raised his hand a few inches from the table and brought his fingertips down one at a time. 'Two days ago, he drove a VBIED – a vehicle-borne IED – into a Humvee carrying a group of American advisers. Four died in the explosion, one lost his eyesight and both legs.'

'Bastard.'

'The kind of bastard you would have tried to smuggle back to Europe?'

'You know that is not what I'm doing. People we bring out, we deliver straight to the Kurdish authorities. No exceptions.'

'The officer who lost his legs and eyes was stationed in London for two years. He happens to be a friend of mine,' he said. He indicated the sheet of notepaper on the table between us. 'A priest with his throat slit in his own church, a decapitated head, mass killings at a Florida nightclub. As I have already made it clear, we are at war and you, sir, must climb down off your high horse and serve where you are most needed.'

We sat back in our seats. The palms murmured and the river raced by. I had disliked Oliver the moment he sat down, with his shiny buttons and double-barrelled surname. He was similar to Matt Lambert, certainly in looks and tailoring, but Matt had lost his certainties, wrenched out of him by tragedy. Oliver retained that deep, unwavering belief that being English of a certain class made you omniscient, chosen, that there was only one way to look at the world and that was through his own precise vision of service and patriotism. He wasn't a bad bloke. He was what he was.

'Listen, mate,' I said. 'I'm not going to stop doing what I'm doing. But I'll tell you what I can do. Anything important comes up, I'll be on the blower.' I mimed the telephone.

'It would be more useful if you got on the blower *before* it comes up.'

'Good point.'

I paused before I continued. I hadn't really told him anything. That's the way to play it, the less you tell the less likely you are to get tripped up. But I thought it best to leave the meeting on good terms and decided to throw him a titbit.

'Two things you probably already know more about than me, but anyway, EMNI is smuggling commanders and important people out of Mosul to North Africa. That's where the next Caliphate is going to spring up. The seeds are being planted as we speak. We're winning the military battle and losing the ideological war. They blame the West for their poverty and, one way or another, they're probably not far off the mark.'

He nodded carefully. 'And the other?'

'The bastards weren't training women to be suicide bombers. They've changed their minds. Now they are. Some woman grabbed a sword, apparently, to defend Muhammad in battle…'

'Nusaybah bint Ka'ab.'

'That's the one. So that's something else to look forward to. Women coming at us with suicide belts under their dresses.'

'And this comes from the two women you drove out of Mosul?'

'Them and other sources. You put all the bits and pieces together.' I finished my pint. 'When you see Diana Abbasi, as I know you will, put her through as many tests as you like, but I tell you, she is ripe for turning. Don't mess her about. Bring her in from the cold.'

'Now you sound like John le Carré.'

'My daughter's favourite author. But then, you know that.'

He smiled. 'I will add it to the file.'

He clicked his fingers and the waiter came. He glanced back at me. 'They do a very good single malt here, will you join me?'

'Never say no to a free drink.'

He turned back to the waiter and ordered in flawless Arabic.

CHAPTER 14
Free Kurdistan

When I got back to the house, I typed out a summary of the meeting. An old habit. If you don't do it straight away, the memory grows hazy and the mind invents fictions.

Hassan and Dozan had reported the extraction of two foreign nationals from Mosul to the Kurdish refugee authorities before delivering Sophian and Diana Abbasi to the Danish Community Centre; the usual procedure. The two women had learned nothing about their long-term futures. That would be decided by security officers, quotas, the quirks of chance. Some women were returned within weeks to their own countries with their children. Others remained in internment camps for months, even years, growing ever more desperate and broken. I never understood the process or the logic, and no one could explain it when I asked.

What exactly went on behind the fences at those camps was something I would learn several months later, and it broke my heart.

*

Dozan made mint tea. I glanced at the notes on my laptop as I outlined my conversation with Oliver from MI6.

'If we get heads up on any attacks planned in Europe, I told him I'd pass it directly to him.'

Hassan paused from counting his beads. 'You had to give him something?' he observed.

'Give and take, mate. That's how it works.'

'We must continue to inform Iraqi intelligence and the Peshmerga,' he added. 'Our freedom to operate relies on what we can provide.'

'I'm well aware of that…'

'If I may, John, I will repeat something I said before. At all times, we must be…' He paused and turned to Dozan with a phrase in Kurdish.

'On our guard,' Dozan translated.

'Yes, we must be on our guard,' Hassan continued. 'With our people. More with your people. Arabs are cunning. Turks are treacherous. They are easy to understand. The English?' He unfurled his big hands and formed a shape from the air. 'I remember a statue in Nineveh. It had a head with two faces looking in opposite directions. A man on one side, a jackal on the other.'

'Very subtle,' I remarked.

'There is much to learn from Nineveh. That is why the Islamists want to destroy it.'

'And that's why they don't want girls to go to school,' Dozan said. 'When you keep people in ignorance, they are easy to manipulate. There is nothing the clerics hate more than an educated woman.'

'Or an educated man who doesn't agree with them,' Hassan suggested. He wrapped his beads around his wrist as he stood. 'Enough now. I should go. It is my cousin's wedding. I will give him a Kalashnikov as a present.'

'I'm sure his bride will love that.'

He couldn't resist a smile. 'His bride is YPJ' – the Women's Protection Units – 'a sergeant, very solid. She has four days' leave, then she will join her unit in Kirkuk.'

'The female battalion,' Dozan explained.

'Yeah, I got that. What's happening in Kirkuk?'

'ISIS is amassing forces in the villages outside the city.'

'That's the first I've heard of it.'

'That's because you spend too much time with MI6,' Hassan said, and I noticed the wings of Dozan's moustache bob in amusement.

'This is unconfirmed intel,' he added, and I shook my head.

'ISIS is under siege in Mosul. Why would they open a new front in Kirkuk? It doesn't make sense.'

Hassan shrugged his big shoulders. 'You are right. It doesn't make sense. It is ISIS thinking. They are not trying to capture the Earth.' He pointed at the low ceiling. 'They are seeking a way into Heaven.'

'Someone ought to tell them, the door's locked for those fuckers.'

Dozan grabbed the car keys. 'Do you need a ride somewhere, John?'

'No, I'm going to take a shower. Say hello to your wife for me.'

He smiled. 'That is the last thing she wants to hear.'

I opened the gates for the car to pull out and watched the dogs along the lane rise from their pools of shade. They had grown so used to being kicked and having stones thrown at them, the first few times when I appeared with bags of offcuts, they cowered away. Not any more. They gathered around, yapping and brushing against my legs. People passing stopped to watch, then wandered off shaking their heads and muttering to themselves.

Foreigners with their funny ways were a part of the new Erbil, a sign of transformation, a seismic shift in customs and attitudes. Cano was spending the afternoon with his wife and four girls in Shanadar Park with its pleasure rides, tables for picnics and a cable car that looped down to the main square. The park was designed for men and women to spend time together with their children. This was audacious new thinking in the Middle East, where men and women are kept apart at prayer, at school, where girls go to school, even at meal times, when the women serve the men and eat alone. These strictures, amplified by the teachings of Islam at the heart of Islamic State, lead to a society far from at ease with itself, but constantly anxious and paranoid.

Muslim communities in Europe find it difficult to reconcile the traditions of their home nations with the western way of life, a schizophrenia that creates feelings of alienation and rejection, the malaise that drove Diana Abbasi into the arms of the Caliphate. During the Middle Ages, Christians burned women as witches and tortured enemies as devil worshippers. Islam is going through a similar stage in its evolution. The Kurds, as far as I could see, were trying to avoid this trap. They were more concerned with carving out their own state than imprisoning women in the kitchen and covering their faces. The 30,000 volunteers in the YPJ weren't just liberated, they were on the battlefield liberating other women from the jihadi imams.

I took a kip for an hour, then made some calls. First to Kali – I could hear the relief in her voice when she saw on Skype that I was in the big kitchen back in the safe house. We chatted without saying very much. She didn't ask when I was coming home. Which was just as well. I had no idea. I was caught up in something and would see it through, whatever the cost, however long it took.

We kissed screens and I sat back with the afternoon light falling through the barred windows thinking about my life, my other life, my daughter, the clutter of cats, the olive trees heavy with fruit, ready for gathering. I liked to be there for the annual harvest, the pressing in an old mill outside Heraklion, that first slice of warm bread with virgin oil and a pinch of salt. I was going to miss it, and missed it even more just thinking about it.

Matt Lambert was next on my list. He had 'potentially good news', as he put it: a meeting with an American Christian charity that was considering donating funds to our operation. We needed it. I could get by on my savings, but we had run through the $5,000 Matt had banked in Erbil. My companions never complained but I knew they were squeezed.

'How's your investment in Erbil going?' I asked.

'Up six per cent. Not brilliant but steady.'

'Sounds a bit like my life,' I said, and he chuckled.

'Steady is what we must aim for,' he replied, and changed tone. 'I read your notes on Diana Abbasi. You think she can be turned?'

'That's what I told Oliver. She wants to find her place, a purpose. Play her right and we'll have her running profiles at Vauxhall Cross.'

'That's just what MI6 needs, more girls in headscarves.'

'Girls who've burned their headscarves, you mean.'

'You're completely right. Converts are the most fanatical. It works both ways. I'll get in touch with an old school chum of mine,' he said. I was about to click off when he added: 'That reminds me, how's Ntileini getting on?'

'You know, working hard, playing hard. I miss her…'

'I can imagine. I was most impressed. Her knowledge of Ancient

Greek history is exceptional, quite exceptional,' he said. 'How's her school, by the way?'

'How do you mean?'

'In another year, you may be thinking of sending her to board in England. If you do, John, if I can give you any advice, any help, it would be a pleasure to do so.'

'I may just take you up on it.'

'You said that about investing.'

'I've spent all my money since then. Seriously, though, it is something we're thinking about, you know, schools and that.'

'The thing is with schools these days, they're oversubscribed. The sooner one makes a decision the better. I'd be happy to send you some links. You can take a look for yourself.'

'Thanks. I will.'

'I don't want to be pushy, John.'

'That's what mates are for, innit?'

'That's exactly what they're for. Stay safe.'

We clicked off. I fancied a cigarette, that snap of the flame, the first drag when the smoke touches the back of the throat and the grey matter opens to new possibilities. Natty was coming up to 13. It was true what I'd told Matt. Kali and I had talked about sending her to school in England. But I had this obsessive little insect gnawing away at the back of my mind. I was afraid she'd turn out so posh and sophisticated she would feel ashamed of who I am, what I lack. Of course, that was unfair to my daughter. She was proud of me. Deep down, I knew that. The past is like a tattoo. Your life changes, but the tattoo is still there to remind you who you were and you forget who you are.

Under different circumstances, it would have been a bit weird having

Matt Lambert taking such a keen interest in Ntileini's schooling, but for obvious reasons it wasn't and I was pleased for them both. If anything happened to me, I was sure my family would have a friend.

Finally, I called Jack Fieldhouse. We arranged to meet at the usual place. I showered, ordered a cab and watched the city lights gush towards me as we headed downtown with the early evening traffic.

A whining zither played on the radio and the beads hanging from the rear-view mirror swayed back and forth to the rhythm. The driver was an old guy in grey *salwars*, a military jacket and a pale pink *shemagh*. He assumed I was a tourist and drove slowly, pointing out sites and gabbling on in a mishmash of English and Arabic.

A new poster of a freedom fighter breaking his chains against a backdrop of the Kurdish colours decorated the sides of buildings, and the distinctive flag – red, green and white with a yellow sun – danced on the breeze from every pole and rooftop. I thought the driver was going to have a heart attack as we passed the new Salahaddin University with its towering entrance lighting the sky. He waved a clenched fist as he jumped up and down in his seat and told me what every Kurd I have ever met has told me the first moment they got the chance: the Great Sultan Salahaddin, who united the Muslim world and seized Jerusalem from the Crusaders, was a Kurd – of the best type. By the time he died in 1193 in Damascus, he had given all his money away to the poor and there was nothing left to pay for his funeral.

It was well known in the streets of Erbil – as well as the corridors of the Pentagon – that Kurdish forces in 2003 played a vital role in the capture of Saddam Hussein, who was executed after being convicted of crimes against humanity. His videotaped end was sweet revenge for the Halabja Massacre, or Bloody Friday. On 16 March 1988, in reprisal against Kurdish rebels, a gas attack by Saddam's war planes on the Kurdish city of Halabja killed close to 5,000 people in what has been described as the worst chemical bombardment against a civilian population in history.

In 2011, after a decade in which the world had been scoured for Osama bin Laden, it was Kurdish intelligence officers who spotted and tracked the courier who took messages to the al-Qaeda leader's hideaway in Abbottabad, Pakistan. It resulted in the raid by US Navy Seals ordered by President Obama that brought an end the bin Laden myth.

With its treasury filled thanks to the steady rise in oil prices, the new regional government in Erbil had visions of turning the city into a trade, banking and tourist hub, a cross between Dubai, with its glass towers and marble shopping malls, and Paris, with its boutiques and bistros. New laws brushed Sharia aside and gave women protection and independence. I had seen girls wearing hijabs and mini-skirts – a fusion, or confusion, of the traditional and contemporary. Young guys were clean shaven in T-shirts, or hipster style in tight suits with pointy shoes. The changes were arbitrary, inconsistent, but you could feel the blast of fresh air sweeping through the ancient streets.

Kurdish tribes have inhabited the same fertile plateau between the Zagros and Taurus Mountains for 5,000 years – the time of the Old Testament, 3,000 years before Christ. Following the defeat of the Turkish Ottoman Empire at the end of the First World War, Kurds were promised an 'official' homeland in the Treaty of Sèvres in 1920. Before they had time to unite the clans and write a constitution, the Treaty of Lausanne three years later – drawn up by Britain, France and Italy – set the boundaries of modern Turkey with no provision for a Kurdish state.

The Kurds since then had been brutalized, exiled, even gassed, but the embers of Kurdish nationalism were never extinguished. They quietly burned on until they burst into flames again in 2013 when Islamic State seized three Kurdish enclaves in northern Syria. The YPG, the armed wing of the Syrian Kurdish Democratic Union Party, went on the offensive. They fought against the odds with inferior equipment for nine months until, in June 2014, they drove out ISIS fighters and led the displaced Kurds back to their villages.

Hassan Ghazi disagreed with Oliver's assessment that the Kurds were still a long way from establishing a homeland. He was following the US presidential race. He saw Donald Trump as the most likely victor and a force for political realignment across the world.

'He will be a dictator, and nothing annoys dictators more than the mirror image of other dictators.'

'Erdogan?'

He nodded his large head. 'Mr Erdogan is too self-assured, too pleased with himself. He will trip up. You wait and see.'

As we neared Jack's 'local', my driver made a detour to take me down a street named for the historic leader of the Kurdish independence movement, Mustafa Barzani, father of the current president, Masoud Barzani.

'Barzani good,' he cried.

'Long live Barzani,' I yelled back.

He pulled up with a grin on his face.

'Happy holiday,' he said, shaking my hand. I gave him a good tip and he zoomed off with folk music pouring from the window.

Jack Fieldhouse occupied his usual seat, a rock in the shifting sands, a pint and a plate of nuts before him. I was dressed as myself, cargo pants and a khaki shirt. I was still thinking about my conversation with Matt Lambert and had decided to take his advice. I had to stop dwelling on my past and consider my daughter's future.

'Still alive then?' Jack said.

'I wouldn't have made the bloody phone call if I weren't.'

He laughed and glanced at his watch. 'You look like a man who needs a pint.'

The bar owner with the burned face limped up. He touched his hand to his heart and bowed. Since he'd seen us with Hassan Ghazi, we were treated as honoured guests. He snapped his fingers and a pint appeared, frothy and cold, better looking than tasting. The bar was buzzing. When there's a war, people want to be out chatting, enjoying life today in case the battle moves across the border tomorrow. Two local expats I knew were chin-wagging with Rob Dyson, the freelance, who was sweating like a geyser in spite of the evening cool. There was something odd about war correspondents, the women were all blonde and the men were always sweaty. There was a couple of undercover agents like cuckoos in swallows' nests. You could spot them a mile off with their brogues and neat hair.

Jack pointed out a couple of EOD – Explosive Ordnance Disposal – guys looking grim at another table.

'Americans,' he said. 'They arrived before the advance. Been out in the field seventy-two hours straight through.'

'Lucky they're still in one piece.'

'You're not joking.'

'You know them?' I asked.

'Well enough.'

'Let's go buy 'em a drink.'

Jack called the waiter as we crossed to their table. We shook hands and sized each other up, the way you do. It takes about two seconds to know who's real, who's full of shit. These guys were old school, ex-forces, working with the Halo Trust, a charity set up to clear and teach locals how to clear land mines. Good people. Serge was in his forties, Mexican-American, smooth tanned skin and dark hair brushed back with wax. The Special Forces tattoo on his right arm featured a skull in a red beret, and it occurred to me that it was no different from the death cult symbols of ISIS and Iraqi commandos, that war is about death first and those virtues we extol – courage, grace, pride, honour, patriotism – are shallow and meaningless in comparison to the crude reality of human annihilation. Joe must have been well into his fifties, with cropped iron-grey hair, grey eyes in a fixed stare, his lean face dappled with shrapnel scars and three fingers missing from his left hand.

The beers came. We clinked glasses. I looked Joe in the eye.

'How is it out there?' I asked. He sat back, staring at me.

'Who wants to know?' he said.

Jack tapped his glass. 'He's working with a team of Kurds bringing out women and their kids from Daesh,' he explained for me. 'He's out there as well.'

'After the mines have been cleared,' I pointed out.

Joe took another long look at me, faintly nodded his head and leaned forward again.

'Some places there's more mines than fucking sand to cover them. And they're getting smarter,' he said, forming a circle with his thumb and surviving finger on his left hand. 'You defuse the mother load, take out the booby trap and there's a wire thin as a hair connecting to a third device.'

'Is there a pattern? Anything that makes them easy to spot?'

He shook his head as he gazed back across the table.

'They conceal them in mosques, madrassas, lost shoes, refrigerators, heaters, televisions. Dead fucking dogs. Some are primed to explode just by opening a door. A kid can set them off. Kids are setting them off. Out in the desert, they plant them on an industrial scale. Fuck knows where they get the manpower from. There's mile after mile of active devices powerful enough to shred a battle tank.'

He paused, and cleared his throat with a swig of beer.

'I read a report from the UN Mines Action Service. It says we've lost one hundred people in the few days since the siege on Mosul began. Mostly Iraqis and Kurds. They're keen, but they don't always know what they're doing.'

'That's why we're here, to teach them,' Serge put in.

He took a cheroot from a red tin, lit up and blew two smoke rings that curled into the pomegranate trees. I noticed there weren't any parrots and wondered if they'd found another resting place, or if they were all locked up in bamboo cages.

Joe glanced back at me. 'The bomb makers put them in kids' toys, can you believe that? Rubber dolls, plastic cars,' he said. 'Just enough to blow off their hands or their feet. They're building surgically implanted devices without metal to dodge the X-ray machines, and women are going to be able to travel undetected with breast implants that can be exploded by a chemical trigger.'

'Fat bastards as well,' Serge added.

We necked our watery pints of Roj and sat back with our own thoughts. I needed to remember all this. I logged every scrap of information and Hassan fed it to Asayish. We brought in real-time intelligence that was often more up to date than the intel gathered by multi-million-dollar CIA stations miles behind the action. I was an asset. MI6 called me. Asayish gave me a free pass. Why the fuck was I weighing up the pros and cons of sending Natty to school in England when that was the only choice for a smart girl who happened to be my daughter?

I spoke to Serge. 'You haven't got a spare smoke?' I asked.

'Sure, buddy,' he said, and he flipped open the tin.

He rolled his Zippo across his palm and I sucked the sweet smoke down into my lungs.

'Nice one,' I said.

Jack placed his empty glass down on the wet table and glanced at his watch. That same moment, a petite woman in a long dress with her hair free and a babe in her arms appeared at the end of the narrow corridor leading to the bar. Jack gave us a thumbs up as he stood, six foot six of ex-Para with an apologetic curl about his lips.

'Got to go,' he said, and left the table.

He put his arm around the woman – she was at least a foot shorter than Jack – and they vanished from view.

'Talk about fucking henpecked,' Joe said.

'Same every night. You can set your watch by it. Here at six, five pints and his old lady turns up at eight to take him home for dinner.'

'Horses for courses,' Joe noted, and Serge blew another smoke ring.

'Excuse me,' I said.

I noticed Rob Dyson was leaving and followed him down the passage and out through the restaurant. He was about to cross the road to a waiting taxi.

'Hello, mate,' he said when I caught up with him.

'You remember the Dutch girl, the first jihadi bride who came out.'

'Sure. What's her name, Laura something?'

'Laura Angela Hansen. She had a Palestinian husband. He took her into the Caliphate. Anyway…' I passed my finger across my throat. 'He's brown bread. Drove a VBIED into a bunch of Americans in a Humvee. Observers, high placed. Three dead, one almost.'

'Hey, that could be good…'

I leaned closer. 'You did not hear it from me.'

'I wouldn't dream of it…'

'It won't be a dream, mate. It'll be a nightmare. Your mum and dad will get a box delivered with your head in it.'

The colour drained from his wet face.

'I swear…'

'She talks a lot. Good English. Get a quote and you'll get your name in the paper.'

'Listen, thanks, John.'

'Don't thank me. I haven't told you nothing.'

I went back and had another pint with the EOD boys, then walked home, 90 minutes at a good pace. I felt happy. I wasn't sure why.

CHAPTER 15
Triangulation

As dawn broke on 21 October 2016, ISIS guerrillas entered Kirkuk and spread out on foot in units of three to five fighters. In numerous coordinated attacks, they overwhelmed police stations and government buildings, killed the occupants and hunkered down for the final shootout.

It appeared at first light to be a daring raid to capture the oil-rich city, but was soon recognized as a suicide mission to spread terror and divert attention from Mosul. By nightfall, except for an isolated death squad clinging on in one district, the jihadis had been wiped out by Iraqi and YPG forces.

We learned later that same day, from sources inside Mosul, that while the attack was taking place, a number of highly placed ISIS bureaucrats had slipped by boat across the Tigris to a village still controlled by the Caliphate. It was the first leg of their journey on a safe route across the border to Antakya, in Turkey.

We followed the YPG as they went to the defence of Kirkuk. Hassan had family in the city and we were able to drop in on an 'uncle' for lamb kebabs and fast internet access. The whispers we heard over the wires had little significance on their own, but every rumour and anecdote added to the overall picture. Through the course of the day, we passed on what we had to Asayish – they, in turn, to the CIA and MI6. The major agencies had legions of operatives feeding intel into some subterranean mainframe where all the fragments were processed and interpreted. Being a spy seems glamorous and although informers are usually paid or manipulated into sharing information, they like to feel as if they are taking part in history.

Espionage networks operate on a system called triangulation, that is the assembly of intelligence from a number of assets without them knowing other members of the group. For example, you may call a fixer with an unconfirmed piece of data and see if he can confirm or expand on it. You then go back to the original informant and other contacts with the additional material to add detail and nuance. You may extract what appears to be useful information from a jihadi bride or a penitent fighter, but that will then need to be verified across the network. Through triangulation, you can influence the relationship between rival parties by controlling communication between them.

The intel we gathered came largely from Kurdish and Arab circles, but I had my own connections in Jack Fieldhouse, Roy Underhill, expats working for charities, and various Iraqis from my old days running close protection. I could not have organized the network without Hassan Ghazi, but my history in Iraq was the thread that linked it all together. This explained the continual interest MI6 had in me, as well as the loyalty of Hassan, Dozan and Cano Ali. We were friends, yes; we would die for each other, absolutely. But they could have been serving the Kurdish cause in many different ways. They had chosen to work with me because my concern with rescuing rebel brides brought a new dimension to their struggle. I never knew how close Hassan was to Asayish, and had to assume that he was Asayish.

Rajan, Hassan's 'uncle' – a generic term for older members of the tribe – was an engineer who had trained in Cairo and knew the oil business better than the lines on his own palms. He opened his two big hands to show me and explained that what distinguished ISIS from al-Qaeda could be summed up in one word. He leaned forward and lowered his voice.

'Oil,' he said.

Islamic State's control of extensive areas of territory in Iraq and Syria allowed the terrorists to earn up to $2 million a day selling crude on the international black market. Even while Mosul was under attack, the jihadis continued to operate refineries in the eastern province of Deir ez-Zor and deliver oil at night in caravans of up to 60 vehicles to Syrian government officials across the border.

'That's unbelievable,' I said, and Rajan shrugged.

'Business is business. Money is power,' he replied in excellent English. 'When the land is lost, the influence remains until the money is gone.'

'The same as an old man with a young wife,' Hassan remarked, and we laughed.

Cano didn't seem amused after Dozan's translation and left to check on the vehicles parked outside in the compound.

Rajan nonchalantly continued: 'Every whale that crosses the desert carries more than two hundred barrels of crude in its belly.'

'Worth up to twenty thousand dollars on a good day,' Hassan added.

They called trucks *whales* for some reason, perhaps because the deserts at night were like shifting seas.

213

The fact that Syria's President Assad was fighting ISIS by day and buying ISIS oil at night was perfectly coherent to my companions. Everything that I found bizarre or confusing was part of the palette of Middle East life – and always had been.

Coalition air hampered the oil convoys and targeted the oil fields, but the production in Syria's two most productive refineries at al-Tanak and al-Omar never stopped.

'They love petroleum so much, Deir ez-Zor will be the last stronghold of their Caliphate,' Rajan Ghazi predicted, and laughed. He was a big man, like Hassan, with a big laugh and wore a European suit with a long collarless shirt over his trousers.

Rajan had been in the piracy business in the dark days of Saddam, and I got the feeling that he would not have been averse to handling a few whales of petroleum if it fell into his hands tomorrow. His plan was to join the exodus to Erbil and build a low-rise, five or six floors, he said, live in the penthouse with a view of the mountains and rent out the rest.

The people of the region, Kurds, Arabs, Turks, had never lived through an agricultural or industrial revolution. It explained the nomad mentality and why the Kurds only discovered that they did not have a recognized state when Europeans imposed borders that had divided tribes and brought misery and conflict until this very day.

When they talked about the past, Kurds became melancholic and resolute. They clenched their fists and tightened their jaws. They lit cigarettes and blew out streams of smoke. We had been on the phones and Skype most of the day. It was late afternoon, the sky streaked in silky clouds tinted with pinks and greens. We sat cross-legged on a carpet with hexagon patterns in blue and red. Rajan's wife, a chubby, cheerful woman with a braid of dark hair down to the base of her spine, poured

214

coffee flavoured with cardamom from a brass *dallah* and the conversation turned to ISIS money, its extent and implications common knowledge among the oil men of Kirkuk, although much that I heard that day was new to me.

The majority of Islamic State's wealth came from the clandestine sale of oil, gas and chemicals on the international market using smuggling routes set up during the years of embargoes against Saddam Hussein. Unlike al-Qaeda, its predecessor, ISIS had created an efficient bureaucracy that collected taxes from the eight million people obliged to live under the Caliphate.

ISIS accountants also managed the income from farms, factories, power stations and dams; bank robbery, extortion, kidnapping for ransom, the sale of plundered antiquities and fundraising in the West. The terrorists received secret donations from Sunni organizations in Saudi Arabia and Qatar, where the government of the tiny oil state had been accused by the US Treasury Department of actively funnelling cash to ISIS.

The icing on the cake was Afghan heroin trafficked over the ancient silk routes through Islamic State to the West, a business worth up to $1 billion a year, according to anti-drug agencies. It was drug money that bankrolled Boko Haram, brother jihadists based in north-eastern Nigeria and active in Cameroon, Chad and Niger.

With money flooding non-stop into the treasury, ISIS had risen in three years from a gang of killers and petty criminals to a multi-billion-dollar nation state with its own flag, hierarchy, clergy, effective bureaucracy and fanatical supporters. It was clear, even to jihadi brides, that the Caliphate would end as a territorial entity, but the jihadi ideology would live on as long as there was finance to entice new recruits to the promise written in the Hadiths that Islam would win the war only after losing every battle.

To stay at the top of the news agenda, the Islamists would continue their crusade of mayhem and bloodshed. Every atrocity created more fear and divided the Muslim community from the rest of society – the objective of radical Islam. Muslims who felt under threat, despised, second-class citizens, would become more sympathetic to jihad and more likely to pick up arms or wait to take their skills to the next Caliphate.

Now that Mosul was under siege, while its commanders dispatched loyal troops on suicide missions, the bankers and bureaucrats were quietly slipping across the border to Antakya in southern Turkey, a two-hour journey on the highway, six on the backroads.

Antakya was known in ancient times as Antioch, for centuries one of the largest cities in the Roman Empire. Today, it is a maze of congested narrow streets – not unlike the City of London, likewise built by the Romans – with a population of 250,000 and batteries of faceless accountants well versed in investing the ISIS billions in complexes of shell companies based in financial havens on island paradises across the world.

There was nothing odd or unusual about this. It is what the South American drug cartels and the Italian, Russian and Albanian mafias do. It is what the international corporations and internet giants do. It is what the rich, the famous, the titled and our own politicians do. It is the same rationale as Bashar al-Assad buying oil from ISIS. The United States and Western governments did not want Islamic State to conceal its ill-gotten gains in the black holes of the universal financial system, but the system was set up in such a way that it was impossible to stop.

Money is power, as Rajan Ghazi had said. As long as ISIS had its portfolio of hidden assets, far worse terrorist attacks would kill and maim innocent people in London, Paris, Berlin and Barcelona, in cities across the United States and in every Muslim country in the world.

ISIS money would find its way into legitimate businesses, hedge funds and pension funds, digital accounts, crypto-currencies and traditional criminal outlets, drugs, human slavery, prostitution, people smuggling. The jihadis could justify the corruption and perversion of the Quran as a holy enterprise. The corruption and perversion of the banking and tax system in Britain and the rest of the western world was harder for me to accept.

It was depressing.

'We can find out where the bankers meet and bomb the whole fucking lot of them,' I suggested. Hassan sat back, his beads silent.

'I don't think bombing undefended cities is practical, John,' he said. 'You bombed Baghdad and ISIS rose from the ashes.'

'And the United States and Turkey are NATO allies,' added Dozan.

'For now,' I said.

They liked that. They raised their fists. Rajan called his wife and she poked her head around the door. He spoke in Kurdish and, hands on her broad hips, she replied in English so that I would understand.

'You know where it is. Get it yourself,' she said.

He struggled to his feet, shrugging and complaining. He left the room and returned with a bottle of arak on a tray with glasses.

'From Lebanon,' he said, holding up the bottle.

Cano Ali returned, his smile still absent. We toasted Kurdish independence and set off back to Erbil with the sun going down over the mountains in the west.

We hadn't done very much in Kirkuk, but it had been an interesting day and I wondered if Hassan had taken me to see Uncle Rajan so that

I would have something new to report back to London. It was likely that MI6 already had copies of ISIS bank accounts – nothing was safe, a teenage student had just hacked into the Pentagon. And Oliver had probably gone to school with the City asset managers and lawyers who liaised with the money men in Antakya to set up shell companies in the Cayman Islands, the British Virgin Islands, the Bahamas, Panama.

CHAPTER 16
A Place without God

From October until Christmas, the television news across the Western world showed a day-by-day slow-motion film of Mosul being bombed to desolation, long tracking shots of shattered apartment buildings, street after street of smoking ruins, entire districts laid waste.

But it's only people who touch our emotions, and the cameramen in soft focus jerked tears into our eyes capturing the same scene over and over again: women in black fleeing across the debris with children in bright T-shirts, the splashes of colour rendering the sight incongruous and absurd.

What they didn't show the viewing public were old men and women with their children being shot in the back by their jihadi husbands and keepers as they scaled the cliffs of rubble, trying to get away.

The siege of Mosul was not a battle in any normal sense. Before fighting to the death, the two sides in any conflict normally have the humanity to first allow the vulnerable to leave the field of battle. Not Islamic State. The women and children were human shields. Pawns. Irrelevant. The jihadi martyrs were ascending to meet the 72 virgins promised to them in paradise over the backs of 72 dead women and children.

This is what the Islamists had planned. Two million people were trapped inside Mosul and they were living through the apocalypse. There are shots of Dresden after the thousand-bomber raids in 1945, and of Hiroshima turned to a nuclear desert. This was Mosul in the dying months of 2016.

Our network had gaping holes. Our fixers had fled or were crushed below collapsed walls and iron girders. Their phones played a mournful silence. For those we could reach, we had one message: keep your heads down and wait until Peshmerga and Iraqi troops overrun the area.

But it was hard to wait. After being traded like cattle, beaten and raped, women watched the bombs falling and buildings turning to empty shells all around them. Their instinct was to cast off their *abayas* and run with their children. They were baby factories and they didn't want their babies to be fed back into the treadmill of holy war.

In the eyes of those young women fleeing from the ruins I saw the glassy look of supreme terror. They were damaged. They carried scars that would never heal. Children had seen things children should never see. Life under the Caliphate was not worse than we imagine. It was worse than we can imagine.

Hassan Ghazi's hand gripped my arm, holding me back as we watched people vaporized into mists of red spray as their toes touched off explosives. Buildings vanished as bombs fell from great heights and the ghosts of those buildings hung over us in clouds of shimmering dust. The death smell layered the landscape like a shroud. You could taste the dead in your mouth. The dead, the chemicals, the tar-black smoke.

We got info on IED placements from Roy Underhill, still fighting his lone war against ISIS from inside the city. But everything was moving so fast, by the time we passed it on, the YPG had advanced and the people who had waited to escape from their tormentors were caught in the crossfire.

The conflict was what has come to be known as asymmetric – meaning unequal, typically a professional army against less well equipped insurgents. It also describes warfare employing unconventional methods: non-combatants as human shields, suicide bombers, VBIED drivers; the deliberate targeting of humanitarian field workers, ambulances, hospitals and the buses brought in by charities to take the evacuees to refugee camps where many would remain for years in a political vacuum, unclaimed and belonging to no one.

It is hard to imagine anything more distressing than seeing people crowd around a bus with their babies and bundles, that moment of optimism, until a stray round picks one of them off. The others scatter, women sheltering the bright T-shirts, leaving one lifeless body beneath the blue sky in a spreading pool of blood, a pointless killing at the edge of freedom.

We watched a family cower inside a disintegrating building while a marksman took pot shots around the entrance. The area was supposed to have been cleared. It wasn't cleared. Our orders from the Kurdish militia were to remain passive. That was impossible. We were soldiers. We were men. We were angry. I felt the tension cross my chest and had a moment of déjà vu.

I remembered extracting Marie-Claire and her son from an outlying village and taking them to the UN camp on the Kurdish border, the flags biting at the wind, lines of empty tents surrounded by red sand. It was earlier that same month, but seemed long ago in a life lived by another person. Time in combat is out of sync. Every second is short, like a gunshot, and stretched like the long descent of an airman parachuting into enemy territory.

We had taken cover in the carcass of the building opposite, the family caught halfway between us and the sniper. While we returned fire, Cano Ali ran up the remnants of the stairway to get a line on the sniper from above. Cano was a patient man. He waited. He waited. He let the sniper go back on the offensive and the instant he saw muzzle flash, he let off one shot that sent the jihadi on his way to *jannah*, the land of milk and honey.

Hassan shouted instructions in Arabic and six people set off, skirting the twisted remains of a set of traffic lights, a bus on its side. They were hidden for a few seconds between high slabs of smashed concrete, then reappeared, shunting their way across the last 30 metres of open space to safety.

The family consisted of a skinny man, maybe 40, with a thin beard in a floor-length grey shirt, an ancient man with rheumy eyes, a woman with her face hidden behind a veil and three girls in dusty black like deflated balloons. They seemed more dead than alive. But they were alive. The man fell to his knees and kissed the ground in front of Hassan's boots.

'Allahu Akbar,' he gasped. 'Allahu Akbar,' God is Great. I couldn't help thinking that if there is a God he had abandoned Mosul that day.

I glanced back at the crossroads and saw a woman standing in the same entranceway with two boys wearing striped Barcelona football shirts. She must have heard Hassan and observed the family's flight. I raised my arms and motioned for her to come towards us. It was all that she had needed, consent from a stranger. She ran, holding the hands of her children, around the bus, into the concrete gully, and I heard myself calling out: Come on. Come on. You're nearly there. You're going to make it…

A memory came into my mind, a flashback. I was driving in from Baghdad airport when I was with Aegis. It was hot. Midday. We stopped at the side of the road where an old farmer stood beside a pile of watermelons. We bought the entire stock and set the fruit up on a target range.

As the woman emerged from the slabs of concrete, the head of one of the boys burst in an eruption of blood and brains and it seemed suddenly as if everything is connected, that life has a pattern stitched together with invisible thread, that our feet find a pathway that is already marked for us to follow. I was there that day on the shooting range watching melons explode, as I was destined to be in the ruins of Mosul as a boy's head was targeted in the same way.

I bolted towards the woman and her surviving son. Hassan, Dozan and Cano emptied their weapons in the direction of the sniper and the noise was like a helicopter crashing inside my head. Either Cano had only winged the shooter or there was more than one out there. You never know the answer to these questions and have to force yourself to stop asking them.

The woman struggled in my arms as I dragged her to safety. There was no way back. The child was dead. She would never get over it. The other boy was about seven, thin as a stick, with the same lost look as the old man with watery eyes. When he turned away, I saw on the back of his shirt the name MESSI, the world's best footballer, and it reminded me of what these children had been denied by ISIS: the chance to play and be children.

The unexpected good fortune of reaching us unharmed appeared to have given the veiled woman and her daughters new life. They comforted the mother and the little boy. I walked with them to the end of the block where the cars were parked. Dozan escorted them back through the security corridor to the support troops coming up behind us.

*

Every distressing scene you can imagine, and many you can't imagine, flickered by in the horror film of those long days in Mosul – the old woman stumbling towards us with a limp naked baby in her outstretched arms; lost children blinded from chemical attacks; bodies in torched bonfires; vultures pecking out the eyes of the injured and the dead; gagged prisoners slung from rafters in hoods as if from some bondage game gone wrong; blackened corpses in blackened beds in a firebombed hospital. The waste, the smell and the banality of war is not a sealed unit you can hide in the back of your head. It leaks into your dreams, your conversation, the saliva in your mouth that churns your food to ash.

The YPG unit we followed captured four ISIS deserters wearing women's clothing. They looked pathetic, moronic. They were crying.

'What's going to become of them?' I said, and Hassan shook his head. 'Don't ask,' he replied.

As he spoke, the pink of his tongue was so vibrant in his mouth it seemed unnatural. We had just chased through the cascade of a toppling building and he was covered from boots to helmet in grey cement dust. He coughed and spat. You couldn't talk. It was too noisy. There was nothing to say. A bomb went off a block away and a dome of choking smoke mushroomed into the sky.

I watched a jihadi, small and fast, dart over a surviving rooftop. My brain picked out a solitary shot from the lead storm and he stopped, freeze-framed, then dropped from view.

My heart went out to the YPG volunteers. They were a decent lot, more like college kids than fighters, clean shaven, neat haircuts. They were facing boys as young as ten in combat uniforms and black headbands. The children of Islamic State had seen and suffered it all –

hunger, poverty, separation from family, the dark arts of the jihadi imams with the Quran in one hand and a Kalashnikov in the other.

The girls from the villages had gone to ISIS commanders in one-day rape marriages. The boys were trucked off to training camps to learn about life in 7th-century Arabia. They were taught how to hate the Infidel, and how to add and subtract using live bullets as counters. Now the 'Caliphate Cubs', as they were called, were on the front line, spotters, runners, suicide bombers. Some 30,000 babies had been born in Mosul in the 30 months of the Caliphate. They had not been vaccinated against diseases – polio, smallpox, measles – and lacked birth certificates to show they had been born or had ever existed.

What made me furious was that while children served as concubines and cannon fodder, their spiritual guides slipped away on the night winds down the river on dhows, across the camel trails and through the disused tunnels from the railway built when Mosul was under British rule. One tunnel on the south side stretched nearly two miles underground to the hills beyond the city. By the time the exit was discovered, unknown numbers of high-profile terrorists catalogued in CIA files had vanished to safe houses in Raqqa, Beirut, Antakya.

As I said to Oliver when I reported in: follow the money.

The phones worked sporadically. We pushed out intel on escape routes, arms caches, potential strongholds – details that confirmed or added to the collage of intelligence analysed ultimately by algorithms that took the pain from human decision-making, the responsibility as well as the intuition. War was digital. Drones were guided from secret bunkers in the United States, and Islamic State ran its PR campaign on internet platforms too narcissistic to take them down.

I was in contact with several European-born jihadi brides and it was no surprise to get a text from one called Karima. I called her back immediately.

She was trapped in the garage below a building that had been bombed, and the two exits were blocked. She was one of 30 people, including ten children and two other foreign girls, both German. I got her exact location on Google Maps. It wasn't far. Nowhere in Mosul is that far from anywhere else. I showed Hassan.

'This is what we're here for,' I shouted, and his pink mouth opened in a rare smile.

He had a sardonic look about him as he replied. 'I knew there had to be a reason,' he said.

He called the YPG. The area had been 'cleared', and we set off. Left and right, back again, right and left, our two vehicles, weighed down with metal plating, lurched and skidded over the piles of masonry to a six-storey building derelict in a sea of rubble. When the building imploded, the beams and support columns had fallen into a concrete cat's cradle, impossible to budge. It wasn't hard to find the two exits. Hassan got back on the phone.

Twenty minutes later, an American-built M88 recovery vehicle ground its way down the street on metal tracks. It carried a gigantic mechanical spade for shifting debris and a winch capable of lifting up to 30 tons. The crew jumped out. Everyone touched cheeks and shared cigarettes. I was waiting for someone to put the kettle on when Dozan introduced me to the vehicle commander. The man stroked his moustache as he gave me a quick scan. I must have looked like a dung beetle that had just crawled from the dust. He touched his chest then stretched out his hand.

'I am very happy to meet you, sir,' he said.

'Not as happy as I am to meet you,' I replied, and he bowed his head in a knowing way, although knowing what I wasn't sure.

'*Inshallah*,' he added, the polite end to the conversation.

Another few minutes passed. They nipped out their fags and we took shelter as the M88 began shovelling the cement slabs to one side. I got on the phone to Karima and told her to keep the people well back. I didn't have my computer with me, but as far as I could recall, she was from Canterbury, the cathedral city, small, safe, south of England. Her father was a university professor. What the hell was she doing trapped under an apartment block in Mosul?

What was I doing standing in the wreckage of an apartment block in Mosul?

Our cars were parked in the shade of a half-demolished mosque. I went back to grab a bottle of water. We had risen three or four metres as we drew closer to the old part of Mosul – built, as was the tradition, on a hill with long views over the desert. Looking back from that point, the panorama of gutted buildings was reminiscent of Nineveh, except the ancient ruins had an ascetic quality, and modern ruins are a monument to our quick-fix throwaway society that I had tried to escape by moving to Heraklion. I thought about calling Kali and was terrified I might break down in tears.

It was quiet except for the wind. I felt a strange emptiness as if I were alone on an abandoned planet. But there was life. A pair of vultures dropped from the sky like auguries and watched me from the top of a hollowed-out building. I thought about shooting them. But why? They couldn't avoid their own natures and had no less right to survive than me or any other creature. I slapped the dust from my clothes and took bottles of water back to the guys.

The work was slow. The iron struts inside the girders were snarled up and every time a chunk of concrete was removed, loose fragments tumbled down into the hole. After hauling out a girder with the winch, the spade went into action, scooping up the detritus, reversing and unloading it in dusty pyramids. I was sure I could smell asbestos. It was hardly surprising that soldiers, quite aside from battlefield mortality, have the shortest lifespan of any profession.

We stood around, drinking water, the smokers smoking, the quiet in this quarter more ominous than a relief. My guts were twisted up. I had lost the four kilos Kali had told me I ought to lose and had moved the pin back one hole on my belt. At least action was good for something.

The digger was like a mechanical ballet dancer, the spade spooning the rubble into piles, the winch slow and steady as it lifted beams to one side. It was not necessary to take out every obstruction from the vehicle exit, just enough to construct a clear passageway. That took the best part of two hours, and Cano Ali grabbed a flashlight to make sure there was a safe way in with enough space to bring the people out.

'How come Cano always goes in first?' I said to Dozan. He shrugged.

'He is a brave man.'

'I know that. That's not the point.'

He shrugged again. 'It is the tradition.'

'Really! No one told me that,' I replied, and thought for a moment. 'He's not himself lately. You don't see him laugh any more.'

'There is not much here to laugh about.'

'No, but you know what I mean.'

'He is a private man. I believe he has problems at home which have not been resolved.'

I stared back, waiting for him to continue, and Dozan explained that it is the role of women in Kurdistan to arrange marriages. Cano's wife had made a good match for Pelin, their eldest daughter, but Pelin was against it and Cano supported her. The girl was 17 and wanted to study interior design at college. Her suitor was 40, an engineer, well respected, and his mother happened to be a good friend of Cano Ali's wife.

'Cano should put his foot down and say no way,' I said. Dozan held up his two palms.

'No, no, no, no, no. We are making a modern Kurdistan. Women have equal rights.'

'What about Pelin's rights?'

'Pelin must obey her mother.'

'It's not modern marrying your daughter off at seventeen to an old man of forty. Trust me,' I replied. 'You remember Diana Abbasi? That's exactly what happened to her.'

'In England,' he said emphatically. 'While we become modern, like you, in Europe, we do not want to lose our traditions.'

'You know something, traditions have got a lot to answer for. They lose their meaning and we cling on to something that does more harm than good.'

'An interesting viewpoint, John.'

'What do you know about this bloke? A forty-year-old marrying a teenager. It's not right.'

'I know nothing about him.'

'Then we should find out, don't you think?'

He nodded his head slowly up and down. 'A good point. I will tell Hassan,' he said, then he pointed. 'There, he's back.'

Cano had emerged from the tunnel. He had found a suitable passage and we followed the cone of his flashlight as he led us over beams and under fallen pillars, an assault course that got darker the further we penetrated.

The first thing that caught my eye as we entered the garage was a couple of tasty vehicles, a silver Toyota Crown Royal and a white Alphard people carrier, which would have been useful if we could have got it out. Beyond them was a row of pick-ups with rocket launchers bolted onto the back and graffiti spelling out how great God is.

The light from an iPhone flashed from beyond the pick-ups and we found the people huddled in the far corner.

'Karima. It's John Carney,' I called. 'We've come to take you out.'

A tall girl stepped forward carrying a baby, head beneath a black shawl, her face uncovered.

'We thought we were going to die in here,' she said.

'Well, you're not. You're going to be just fine.'

The two German girls joined us, with two children apiece. The rest of the women and children were Iraqi. There was an elderly woman who couldn't walk. Her leg was swollen, probably broken, and she had lost a lot of blood from a gash that went from her knee to her ankle. Hassan applied a field dressing. She was shaking with fear and panic. He stroked her cheek and whatever he said calmed her. She nodded her head, and again I admired Cano Ali as he bent and gently lifted her over his shoulder in a fireman's carry.

Dozan led the way back through the warren of jagged masonry. Cano Ali passed me the injured woman before climbing each beam blocking the way; she was as light as a five-year-old. The women passed their small children in the same way. No one spoke. It was eerily silent until I heard the sirens of screeching car alarms. Hassan, I later discovered, had smashed his way into the locked vehicles to see if any files or intel had been left behind.

The M88 waited until we emerged back into the daylight and the team waved clenched fists as the recovery machine rolled on to its next tasking.

A bus had already arrived, from where I had no idea. For a volunteer force with minimal training, the YPG was incredibly efficient.

Cano Ali lowered the injured woman down on the front row of seats and the rest of the Iraqi women and children climbed into the bus. There were no smiling faces, no thanks, just blank looks from traumatized people still unable to believe they had been saved. If the building from which they had escaped was their home, they had lost everything.

We climbed into our vehicles with the foreign girls. We were not giving them priority over local women. They had to go through different procedures and protocols.

The bus was on the road. We followed at a distance. Women and children deserting the Caliphate were a regular target for jihadi mortars.

The German girls were in the Previa with Hassan and Cano Ali. Dozan drove the trusty old Pathfinder and I sat in the back with Karima. It was two hours to Erbil, enough time for a nominal debriefing. We had some water, dates, some biscuits. She held her baby wrapped in a blue blanket tight to her and seemed relieved to talk, her story a version of many stories we got from the jihadi brides we had spoken to.

Karima had fallen in love online and fallen out of love in person the day she was driven across the border from Turkey to meet Mohammed, her Iraqi husband. She was a feminist who had rejected the idea of Western feminism, 'dressing like a man and acting like a man', for the spiritual empowerment Islamic State seemed to promise.

'It was a chance to be a part of something different, special. I thought they were building a new world where greed and privilege would not exist, where everyone was equal.' She paused. 'My life was okay, it was safe. But I couldn't see that anything interesting was ever going to happen to me.'

'You would have got married in England, Karima, had a family?'

231

'Call me Karen. That's what I was called at school. I'm not Karima any more.' She opened the blanket so that I could see the face of the baby. 'This is Johnny. I used to be crazy about Johnny Depp.' She shrugged and her expression changed. 'I still am.'

'Did you feel empowered when you got to Mosul?'

She shook her head. 'No, not for one second. I realized immediately, most of the girls do, that it was a stupid terrible mistake. A disaster. They just want us to make babies so there would be a new generation of fighters to carry on the war. It's never going to stop, you know. Never.'

'How do you know that?'

'That's what they talk about. Holy war goes on until God returns. It will be in the lifetime of our children. That's what they say. Our job is to make them ready.'

'You believe that.'

She smiled for the first time. 'I don't believe anything. We are just here. We are born and we live and we die. It doesn't mean anything. The fact that it doesn't mean anything means we have to invent something to give it meaning. Does that make sense?'

'It does to me.'

'I went to a Catholic school. I used to feel sorry for my friends because they wouldn't be going to heaven. Only me. I was chosen. There was a place waiting for me up there,' she said, pointing. 'The Jews are told they are chosen, so are the Christians, the Buddhists as well, I suppose. You can see how stupid it is. How divisive.'

'Still, you must have believed. You were radicalized enough to travel to Iraq?'

'Yes, it was like an escape from being who I was. I never felt excluded, but I always felt different. I hate the burqa, they're ugly and horrible and

232

they make women miserable wearing them. But I hate it when they ban them. Women go out half naked and the authorities attack women who cover themselves up. It's stupid.'

'What will you do when you get home?'

She shook her head. 'I don't know. I have a baby. No husband. No one will want me. Certainly not in my own community. I thought I was going to die here and I haven't died. I will survive.' She raised her shoulders. 'I want to go to teacher's training college, become a teacher, take Johnny somewhere where nobody knows who we are.'

I did not disagree with anything Oliver had said that day at the Divan Hotel. He was right. We were at war.

We are at war.

Islamic State is inspired by the extreme, ultra-orthodox Salafist doctrine recognized as the state religion of Saudi Arabia. The core belief is that the original teachings of the Prophet must be restored in order to defeat the 'soldiers of Rome' in preparation for the Day of Judgment, which is near. Beheadings, crucifixion, genocide and child suicide bombers are acceptable tactics to fulfil the prophecy that a Muslim kingdom will rise from the chaos to rule the world.

For young Muslims who felt disillusioned or marginalized, the ideology had an internal logic that made perfect sense in the wake of the invasions of Afghanistan and Iraq; the drone campaign in Yemen, Somalia and Pakistan; the unwavering US support for Israel in the Palestinian conflict. The War on Terror, rendition, water-boarding, Guantánamo and drone attacks on wedding parties had allowed Islamic State to show through relentless propaganda that the West was at war with Islam. The call to arms to expel the 'crusaders' from Muslim holy lands was the duty of every believer.

Abu Bakr al-Baghdadi and the founders of Islamic State never assumed that they could defeat the United States and its Western allies – not for the time being, that is – but bloody conflict and theatrical displays of terror with its consequent mass-media coverage were effective techniques to recruit combatants for international jihad. Terrorism had not changed the politics of the West, but it had spread fear and remained permanently on the agenda.

In the battle against ISIS, the endgame for all participants was broadly the same: defeat the terrorists, then settle the civil war in Syria. The United States and its allies had their view on how this should be achieved. Russia, Iran and Turkey had a different view. The Kurds had their own agenda, and there was one more player in this new Great Game that rarely got a mention in the news: Saudi Arabia, which to my mind played a far greater role behind the scenes than any other nation.

Evidence that Saudi Arabia supports ISIS terrorism was first uncovered in the emails leaked from the office of Hillary Clinton, US presidential candidate and Secretary of State from 2009 to 2013. Wikileaks published the following message from Clinton's campaign chairman, John Podesta:

We need to use our diplomatic and more traditional intelligence assets to bring pressure on the governments of Qatar and Saudi Arabia, which are providing clandestine financial and logistic support to ISIL and other radical Sunni groups in the region.

In 2009, Wikileaks published diplomatic cables from the State Department with similar concerns:

Donors in Saudi Arabia constitute the most significant source of funding to Sunni terrorist groups worldwide. While the Kingdom of Saudi Arabia takes seriously the threat of terrorism within Saudi Arabia, it has been an ongoing challenge to persuade Saudi officials to treat terrorist financing emanating from Saudi Arabia as a strategic priority. More needs to be done since Saudi Arabia remains a critical financial support base for al-Qaeda, the Taliban, and other terrorist groups, including Hamas, which probably raises millions of dollars annually from Saudi sources.

A third Wikileaks file revealed in 2013 a speech in which Hillary Clinton said: 'The Saudis and others are shipping large amounts of weapons – and pretty indiscriminately – not at all targeted toward the people that we think would be the more moderate, least likely, to cause problems in the future.'

Fifteen of the 19 al-Qaeda terrorists inspired by Osama bin Laden to fly planes into the World Trade Center in New York on 11 September 2001 were Saudis – plus a Lebanese, an Egyptian, and two men from the United Arab Emirates.

What made me angry was that while I was standing in the ruins of Mosul trying to save blameless women and children – me, Hassan Ghazi, Dozan Rostami, Cano Ali, Roy Underhill, Kurdish volunteers, charities, humanitarian organizations – the evidence may not be conclusive but it raises the prospect that Saudi Arabia provides weaponry to the killers of ISIS and to any Sunni terrorist group seeking finance. Saudi Arabia wears a veil, and we in the West turn a blind eye to protect arms sales and the flow and price of oil.

Business is business.

CHAPTER 17
Small Successes

Cano Ali removed the batteries from the weapons and put them on charge. He would normally have cleaned and oiled the rifles straight away, but left them till morning and started chopping vegetables to make bean stew. He pureed fruit for the children.

I poked my head around the door. 'Listen, mate, you need a hand?' I asked. I repeated the question in Arabic.

He held up his two hands and vigorously waved them about.

'Two, Englishman,' he replied.

'You want a beer?' I asked.

He paused to think about that, then looked back, rubbing the flat of his palm over his bald head. 'No,' he said, and held up two fingers. 'Two.'

I unsnapped a couple of Ava Zer black label beers cold from the electric cooler Hassan had borrowed 'from a contact'. It had saved my life. I plonked them down on the counter beside Cano.

'Greedy bastard,' I said.

'*Shukran*,' he replied. Thank you.

'*Ahlan wa sahlan*.' You are welcome.

In his room, Cano had a collection of baskets full of dresses, underwear, shoes and baby clothes scrounged from his extended family. When I showed the three young mothers, they acted as if they were at a shop sale and sifted through every item. They took turns in the shower, dumped their *abayas* and appeared downstairs in embroidered costumes, smart enough to my eyes, but behind the times for the hip city girls of Erbil. As we had witnessed with Diana Abbasi and Sophian, the odd normality of sitting at a table with fresh food and a pot of mint tea gave them a sense of well-being that would last a couple of days before the decline into PTSD.

From the moment we arrived back, Hassan had remained in the entrance, jaw set, his cell phone glued to his ear. When he left with Cano, I latched the gates and remembered the conversation I'd had with Dozan about Cano's daughter. I made a mental note to remind him to mention it to Hassan. The horrors of Mosul were made a little lighter with Cano's smile. I missed it. We had the connections to find out everything there was to know about the girl's 40-year-old suitor and I felt an obligation to put the wheels in motion – for my sake as much as Cano's.

After our guests had eaten, Dozan opened a couple of beers and Karima – Karen now, she insisted – gave me a sideways look across the table. 'I love that sound,' she said.

'There's plenty more where these came from,' I replied, and she pushed her cup of mint tea to one side.

The girls all had a beer. It was good. They relaxed. It wasn't easy to talk about their lives in the Caliphate. Karen slowly opened up and her long dark hair swayed freely about her face as she spoke.

'Every day, they rewrote Sharia to make it harsher,' she said. 'It was like a disease. First you had to cover your face, then gloves to cover your hands, socks for your feet. I saw one woman beaten by the moral police because she had a hole in her sock…'

'Then we had to cover our eyes so we couldn't see.'

It was Miray who had spoken. Her parents were *Gastarbeiter*, Turkish guest workers in Germany. She was petite, with green eyes and reddish-brown hair the colour of polished leather. The remaining girl, Emilia, was a convert from Munich with a solemn expression and apologetic dark brown eyes. She didn't say very much, but one phrase stuck in my mind. Later, I wrote it down.

'They passed us around like sweets,' she said, and lowered her sad eyes. 'It says in the Quran, women should be honoured. We were dishonoured and abused.'

Karen continued. 'Cover your face and open your legs. It's disgusting,' she said. 'They put up posters of a woman correctly dressed in a black *abaya* from head to foot, everything covered, a mesh flap over the eyes. It was called the *new* look. The outfits arrived in the shops with a label saying that a woman's gown should not draw attention or reveal what is beneath.'

'What happened if you did not obey the dress code?' Dozan asked. Karen took a sip from her beer before she replied.

'If Al Khansaa saw you, they took your husband's ID card and he had to go before a judge. Depending on how serious it was, he either had to pay a fine, or he or his wife or both were whipped in public. If you had a mobile phone, they caned the soles of your feet. If you were caught more than once, the sentence was death by stoning.' She shuddered. 'They made us watch.'

I'm not sure what expression I was wearing, but Karen suddenly became annoyed.

'You don't believe me, do you?'

'I do believe you,' I said, softly, with patience. 'You aren't the first one to tell us this.'

She glanced at Dozan, then back at me.

'We stood in a circle. We picked up stones and threw them at this poor French girl. I joined in. You have to be a part of it. You are not a person, just a robot. The girl was proud. She didn't budge. Then a man got hold of a big rock in two hands and crashed it down on her skull. Everyone went forward and threw stones from close up. She bled to death.'

We were quiet, imagining this scene.

'No one will believe what we've seen, what we had to do,' Karen added. 'We were locked up most of the time. The only distraction was stonings, or crucifixions, or seeing someone's head being cut off. It was like living in the Bible. You don't know what was going on in the outside world. You are hungry all the time.'

'If a man has food and comes to our building, all the girls will offer to sleep with him,' Miray said.

'We are prostitutes for food,' Emilia added – words I would hear again a year later in the refugee camps run by the Turks on the Syrian border.

'What about your husbands?' I asked, and Emilia shook her head.

'Your husband is the man you sleep with. It is the law,' she replied.

'Islamic State is about money and sex,' Karen continued. 'That's the hypocrisy. All the truths in the Quran tell one big lie.'

We were quiet again. The children were sleeping in Dozan's room. One of them woke. Miray went to check on them. Karen had another beer.

'I met Mohammed on the internet,' she said. 'He was killed three weeks after I arrived in Mosul. The women came to our apartment.

We had a party to rejoice. They were smiling and said how lucky I was because Mohammed was a martyr on his way to paradise.'

She paused. Her features grew tense.

'Mohammed didn't speak English. I don't speak Arabic. Someone else was writing to me in his name. I'm certain it was another woman, like me, from England. Women know what women want to hear. She recruited dozens of girls.'

'How do you know that?'

'Gossip. All we can do is talk and talk and talk.'

'What happened after Mohammed died?'

'I was sold to another jihadi. He was my second husband. When he went to Raqqa, he sold me again. I'm like a second-hand car, not too many miles on the clock, a really good runner,' she said, and shrugged at her own irony.

'*Vergewaltigen*,' Emilia said. 'That is the German word for rape. They have a lot of pretty words, but it is just *vergewaltigen*. One boy told me he had had thirty-six wives.' She broke off. 'I have two babies and I do not know for sure who their fathers are.'

Karen nodded. 'They all seem a bit mad. They're hyped up on drugs. They're like boys in a street gang. Sex is the only outlet and it's sanctioned by the imams as an Act of God.'

Miray returned. The children were sleeping.

It was not easy for the three women to discuss the subject of rape with two men, two strangers. They had been bought and sold, mated like animals, mentally and physically abused, for so long it had become normal. And what's normal hurts less until you realize it isn't normal.

'They're building paradise on earth by rape and murder. What kind of paradise is that?' Karen said.

241

Emilia had tears running down her cheeks. 'It was all a lie,' she said. 'We have lost everything. Even the future.'

We were quiet for a moment, then Karen stood. It was late.

'Do you have a pair of scissors?' she asked.

'Scissors?'

She made a cutting motion with her fingers.

'I want to trim my hair,' she explained. 'They like us to keep our hair long and remove every trace of body hair. In the same shops selling the new-look *abayas*, they have the sexiest underwear in the world. Seriously. It's not a joke. When they peel away our clothes they want to find children dressed as porn stars.'

Hassan did not return for breakfast, but Cano Ali came scuttling in with a box of pastries. He ground beans for coffee, then took the babies one at a time to feed them pureed fruit. Karen, Emilia and Miray discarded their black robes and wrapped their children in blankets. While Cano remained at the safe house prepping for the journey back to Mosul, Dozan and I drove the girls to the Danish Community Centre in Kasnazan. In the coming months, as the trickle of refugees became a flood, the centre would fill and overflow with evacuees living in tents in the car park.

The reception area was packed. It smelled of floor cleaner and unwashed clothing. A Kurd official in a yellow tie and yellow *taqiyah*, a rounded skullcap, sat at a desk heaped with files. He had a chubby face, a moustache shaped in a chevron, and a tic in his left eye that made me wonder if his mind had wandered and he was unable to pay full attention to the people screaming at him in Arabic, Kurdish, Turkish, English, French, Indonesian and Russian.

'This reminds me of the Tower of Babel,' I said to Dozan.

'I wouldn't know, *mate*. I haven't been.'

He grinned. Dozan Rostami was learning my bad habits.

At the edge of the turmoil were stressed Europeans in charity-logoed T-shirts, men with round John Lennon glasses, women wearing ethnic jewellery. They were representatives of humanitarian organizations there to defend the rights of the jihadi brides, most of whom squatted on the floor in *abayas* like rows of small black pyramids. The children were either crying or staring wide eyed at the chaos.

The process was in Kurdish, a task Dozan had taken on. I shook hands with Miray and Emilia. Karen then moved to one side. She took a firm grip on my two arms.

'You saved our lives. I will never forget it,' she said.

'I'm going to speak to an intelligence officer I know, try and put him on the case. It's going to be a long process, but we'll get you out.'

'Thank you,' she replied, and boldly kissed my cheeks. 'After what we've lived through, I can face anything.' She threw out her hands. 'I feel like I'm back in my old skin.'

Karen had returned to Cano's clothes store and dressed in jeans, a long-sleeved blouse and a short jacket. She hadn't trimmed her hair, she had cut it short and brushed it up, punk style. She turned and walked away with a confident stride, Johnny in her arms. I called her.

'Hey, Karen. You're going to do fine.'

'You betcha,' she replied, and smiled.

Queuing, as in forming an orderly line, had yet to come to contemporary Erbil. Dozan, with his aviator bearing, strode through the crowd, leaned over the desk and engaged the distracted official in his own language.

The girls vanished into the press of people waving ID cards and shabby sheets of paper. They didn't use bar codes in Erbil, but old-fashioned rubber seals. Every document had to be countersigned before you could move on in a game of snakes and ladders to the next official to secure another printed stamp. There was no way to avoid the bureaucracy, except bribery, of course, and we didn't have the money for that.

I strolled back up the corridor asking myself if I were satisfied with what we had achieved in the last 24 hours. Never being entirely contented chimes with my nature, I suppose, but it wasn't bad. We just had to do better.

As I pulled open the door to leave the building, I bumped straight into Cornelius Visser. He glanced past me at the madness around the reception desk.

'More managed returns?' he asked.

'Wouldn't you like to know,' I replied.

He laughed. We shook hands and he stood back. 'You look well, John. Have you lost weight?'

'Can't afford to eat, mate. Still waiting to get funding from you people.'

'All you English ever talk about is money. You are worse than the Americans.'

I thought of Roy Underhill for some reason. 'American foreign policy's got a lot to answer for, but there's nothing wrong with Americans.'

'Is that so?' He swept back his hair. 'There's a new club open, just behind the clock tower in the main square. I must take you there one evening.' He lowered his voice to a whisper. 'They have the most beautiful dancers.'

'Not my cup of tea, mate. Saw all the girlie shows I want to see when I lived in Manchester.'

'I never said the dancers were girls.'

'Bloody hell, you spooks really know how to live.'

He laughed and turned on his heels. I listened to the beat of his leather shoes on the stone floor as he entered Babel.

Those three months, October to Christmas 2016, were the most distressing, but also the most constructive that we had spent since my arrival in Erbil in June. I had stayed in regular contact with numerous young women who had been deceived into travelling to the Caliphate and wanted to return home. On my computer, I had their profiles and photographs with their children, usually in pyjamas.

Most days, we found one, sometimes two or three foreign girls, most with babies, and took them to the authorities in Erbil. We also brought out large numbers of Iraqi and Syrian women and delivered them to the overflowing refugee camps, not the best place in the world to be, but better than inside the Caliphate. Our network continued to shrink, but we still gathered high-quality intel on EMNI, which gave Oliver a head start building profiles of European jihadis fleeing with orders to create new terror cells in Europe.

When I was stationed in Crossmaglen, an Irish corporal who had done 12 years in the Yorks told me that if a young IRA lad was on the run in the Republic, he could knock on any farm door and they would give him a bowl of soup and a hayloft to sleep in. No questions asked. It would be naïve to think that returning jihadis do not have similar safe havens across Europe at mosques and with families sharing their extremist beliefs.

The British government's position regarding jihadi brides was much like Pontius Pilate washing his hands. The unspoken, or better said, unwritten policy was 'Leave them there. Let them die.' Once the girls were out of Mosul and in the system, registered by the Kurds and in the orbit of the NGOs, then British diplomats were obliged to acknowledge them. They visited the refugee camps and offered weeping mothers their clean white handkerchiefs, as if this were a sign that they were doing everything they could to get them home.

Were they? I doubted it.

There were thousands of young people, mainly women, some men and lots of children who would die if they remained with Islamic State. I believed they deserved a second chance. I was likewise aware that the more girls we rescued, the bigger the headache in European capitals and the greater the odds of unreformed radicals slipping through the net.

This was the conflict between my work and government policy. But it was their moral dilemma, not mine.

The same impasse existed with refugees. People living in poverty with terrorism and no future in failed states in the Middle East and North Africa see on their mobile phones the way we live, heave their bundles on their backs and set out to face the razor-wire fences and machine-gun posts going up around Europe.

What are we going to do for and about these millions of people?

The idealists would say let everyone in. The populists say keep everyone out. This is the difficulty governments must solve, and the predicament will grow worse through the coming decades.

I made my opinions clear to Oliver, not that he showed much interest. What he did like was the intelligence we brought in, which in turn gave me some wriggle room to plead individual cases. It was this process that led to my first small success: Diana Abbasi had been returned to her family in London and was taking part in Prevent, a de-radicalization programme.

To maintain credibility with MI6, only when I was convinced that someone had abandoned their faith or was ready to be de-radicalized did I say so. If I had the smallest doubt, I said nothing at all.

Our focus moving through the ruins of Mosul was on finding Europeans. That didn't mean we ignored the exodus of Iraqi families deserting the Caliphate as Iraqi forces pressed forward. The people had not been citizens of Islamic State, but hostages. They fled the moment they got the chance, often being shot at as they ran.

We laid down fields of fire against jihadi assassins and ten-year-old boys in black headbands and suicide vests. Yellow-edged smoke reeking of toxins billowed into the air. Coalition bombers turned apartment blocks into pillars of flame. When people froze in fear, pinned down in the no-man's land between tumbling buildings and our position, one of us would race rashly into the lead storm to drag them out of the danger zone.

If Hassan didn't take a grip on my arm, holding me back, I found myself in competition with Cano. Not that I wanted to show I was braver than him, I wasn't, but I couldn't bear to see him taking all the risks. I was unsure why Hassan was so protective of me until I brought the subject up with Matt Lambert. I would not have put it this way, but he described me as 'the key to the Chinese puzzle' that bound the network together. Most of our contacts were Iraqis and Kurds known by my companions. But I was the connection to the jihadi brides. It was this combination, providing intel and confirmation of that intel, that we passed on to Asayish, the Iraqi military and MI6.

Although our network was smaller, it was not difficult getting information from informers still in the Caliphate. They ran the risk of being caught by ISIS, but did so to accrue good will with the Iraqi authorities. There were cases of Iraqi security officers torturing suspected jihadis captured during the advance and several times we had been called upon to vouch for our assets.

After bringing families out of danger, we led them through safe corridors to the white government buses parked a mile or so behind the action. They climbed aboard in various states of shock, and we watched the convoy of vehicles shunt its way over the rubble towards another sort of hell in the vast tent cities holding hundreds of thousands of displaced people.

Government buses did not run at night; it's when Coalition smart bombs find the wrong targets. If there were stragglers left behind, we took them to the Khazer refugee camp, a little over 40 miles north of Mosul. When there were too many people for our two vehicles, I called Jack Fieldhouse. He had acquired a minibus and was always willing to pick up the slack.

The camps had always been unfenced. For some reason, they had started rolling out the barbed wire and people were camped outside, as well as inside, waiting to see if family members they had lost touch with during the battle for Mosul were among the survivors. We were funnelled into the gate to debus the refugees and I watched emotional reunions as families touched fingers through the fence. They held up new babies. Old men cried. For a moment, they were joyful.

The balmy autumn passed and the thermometer dropped below freezing. Frost gathered on the tents at sunset. The refugees were Iraqi. The guards were Iraqi. But for some reason I never understood, there was a reluctance to open the gates, and families on the outside who brought food and other items had to throw them over the fence to their relatives inside. Blankets caught on the fence unfurled like black flags and lifted on the night winds.

Traumatized children in rags without shoes or hope or documents begged for food. Across the many refugee camps, there were thousands of stateless orphans with blank stares and no futures. They were abused, physically and sexually. Those who survived, the strongest, the meanest, would grow into psychopaths or jihadis, perpetuating the cycle ISIS had begun. Every child I saw made me think of Ntileini. Christmas was coming. I was going home. I had a home to go to, and I would remember every day those young boys and girls with nothing and no one.

After dropping refugees at the camp, we went back to the dust and death of the battlefield, following leads, making phone calls, waiting for the cry for help that would take us deeper into the labyrinth. Sometimes we stayed in a derelict house or an empty apartment in Mosul. Most nights, we managed to get home to our own beds. Cano cooked. Hassan hissed down the telephone. I made notes that often made little sense when I read them back. We drank beer and never talked about the people we saw killed.

We were up at dawn after sleepless nights, prepped for another day. Now the roads were clear of IEDs and ISIS patrols, it was barely a 90-minute drive from Erbil to Mosul. We started to see civilian traffic, convoys of whales filled with crude, and I wondered if Rajan Ghazi was back in business.

On the morning of 6 December, airstrikes knocked out the last bridge held by ISIS. The river crossings were closed down, and the blackened pyres of wooden boats littered the west bank of the Tigris. Jihadi fighters recaptured the al-Salam hospital, taken after the bombing, and routed the advancing Iraqi troops.

As the street battles expanded from the east side of the Tigris to the more populated west bank, the United Nations warned that the Mosul offensive would trigger a humanitarian crisis, with up to one million people fleeing the city. The end game was close, but not that close.

Mosul would never be rebuilt. The suburbs were a wasteland of mortar-and-pestled cement blocks. The wind never chased the dust from the air. It scratched your throat and eyes, it changed the tone and texture of your skin. You wash, but the dirt and dust of war leaves a stubborn stain. I was a changed man. I knew that.

We had another small success – perhaps that is too modest, it was actually a grand success. We identified three separate factories making car bombs in Mosul and a larger underground warehouse stacked with weaponry. They were destroyed by airstrikes. How my name was linked to this I still don't know, but when I reported in Oliver was pleased to tell me that my name was now on the ISIS death list.

'Is there a bounty?' I asked him.

'Interesting question. I don't think the fundamentalists have thought about that. Good work, my man, I'm proud of you.'

'I didn't think I'd ever hear you say that.'

'I didn't think I'd ever say it.'

We chuckled. We hung up, and the killing went on.

CHAPTER 18

That Green and Pleasant Land

The immigration officer at Heathrow sat on a high stool behind a computer. He opened my passport and tapped on his keyboard. He took a long look at my photo, back at the screen, then back at me.

'Would you mind standing to one side, please sir?'

'I will. But why?'

'Just do it.'

His tone had hardened. Before I spoke again, two Border Force officials in suits approached with two armed police in stab-proof vests, a man my height with a beard, and a young blonde woman weighed down with handcuffs, a radio, taser, baton, pepper spray, a sidearm in a holster and a Heckler & Koch MP5 submachine gun almost as big as her.

Kali and Ntileini had gone through before me. They stood watching the drama with nervous expressions.

'What's happening?' Kali asked.

'Nothing to worry about. Happens all the time. I won't be long.'

I was taken to an examination room where our three pieces of luggage, two suitcases and a duffel, were standing on the desk. They went through every item: clothes needing to be ironed, my wife and daughter's underwear, Christmas presents. They seemed quickly bored with the exercise and pushed everything to one side. They gave me a token body search. At least I didn't have to spread my arse cheeks.

The two cops guarded the door while the two suits sat before me at a metal desk. They wanted to know what I'd been doing in Iraq and I told them the truth, all of it. Well, most of it.

'I run a private security service in Baghdad. I've been there since 2003, right after the war. I was six years in the Yorks.'

'The Yorkshire Regiment?'

'That's the one. Fortune Favours the Brave,' I said, quoting what must be the most unoriginal motto in military history. 'In June, I was asked to bring a girl out of Mosul. She had married a jihadi from Palestine and changed her mind about the Caliphate. All that shit. She wanted to get home to Holland.'

'Did you have authority to do this?' one of the officers asked. He was tall and thin, with brown curly hair and round, green-framed glasses that made his eyes look cartoon-like in his long narrow face.

'I don't know that you need permission to save someone's life, but, yes, more or less. I work with three Kurds, ex-soldiers, like me. They feed intel to Asayish…'

'Asayish?'

'The Kurd secret service. They're the ones who found Osama bin Laden.'

'Is that a fact?'

I shrugged my shoulders and didn't answer.

It was the other officer who had spoken. I thought they may have been playing good cop/bad cop. He had taken off his jacket and wore a gold tie on a white shirt with wide blue stripes. He was two stone overweight and, out of his suit, his shaved head would have made him look more like a villain than a copper. It also struck me that the four people with me in the room had the sickly white pallor of the English winter, while I had retained some tan from months in the desert sun.

The fat guy flicked through the pages of my passport. 'You go in and out of Iraq a lot?' he remarked.

'Yeah, well, like I said, that's where my business is.'

'But you live in Greece?'

'In Crete.'

'And what is the purpose of your visit to England?'

'It's Christmas. I'm going to visit my mum and we're going to look at some schools for my daughter...'

'Private schools?' the fat one asked, and glanced at his colleague.

'As it happens.'

'You're doing all right then,' added the thin guy, and I thought, that's the one thing the English can't stand: someone getting above themselves.

'When you drive oil men through Baghdad with kamikaze drivers coming at you from all directions and a bomb on every exit, they pay to be safe.'

As I glanced towards the policewoman, for some reason, I broke the cardinal rule and spoke out of turn. She was holding her weapon low slung, parallel to the ground.

'You should hold your piece slantwise across your chest, that way you can keep your trigger finger poised as you shoulder your rifle...'

'And you should mind your own fucking business,' she replied.

I looked back at the fat official as he rapped his knuckles on the desk. He leaned forward and slid his glasses over the shiny dome of his head.

'How do you explain, Mr Carney, that your name appears on the UK Terrorist Watch List?'

'Fucked if I know. And I'm fucked if I know why your departments aren't integrated. I provide intel on terrorists. Call MI6, we're the best of mates.'

'Don't use that language in here…'

'Excuse me, but it's the fucking irony of it,' I said. 'I'm on the ISIS death list and you've got your knickers twisted up in your own algorithms. I go in and out of Iraq, Syria, Turkey, same as the jihadis. It's computers that track us. It's the computers that have put me on the list.'

'You know this for a fact?'

'It's obvious, innit. Same as Amazon sending you offers for books you've already bought from Amazon. There's no human hand running the internet. Even the terrorists know that.' I took a breath and lowered my voice. 'Look, we're on the same side. While you're in here giving me a grilling, jihadis are out there slipping through on false passports they've picked up in Istanbul.'

'You have evidence of this?'

'Evidence! It's on Facebook, mate. There are dozens of sites where you can apply for a passport, real as well as forged, European residency IDs, refugee travel documents. Do a quick search, it's all there. If you've got a grand, you can buy passports for Malta or Croatia or Bulgaria.'

'A thousand euros?'

'Euros, dollars, it's all the same now.'

'Why those countries?'

'Well, you know, they're not like us, all pasty and pink. They're a bit swarthy, like the Arabs. You can get on a train with a Maltese passport in Istanbul and pull into Paris two days later, no questions asked,' I replied.

'Course, if they want to come over here, it's a bit more difficult.'

'How do you mean?'

'Schengen helps, we're not in the area. If your heart's set on getting the dole and good schools for your kids, a hip replacement on the NHS, it's going to cost fifteen thousand dollars a pop.'

There was a hint of national pride in their expressions as they exchanged looks.

'For a British passport?'

'You have to pay for the best,' I replied.

I found it hard to believe the fat one was making notes. It only occurred to me at that moment that the two border agency officials were no more than 30. They'd been teenagers at school when we went gunning for Saddam in 2003. I felt old and patient all of a sudden.

'You need to get your heads round all this stuff,' I told them. 'We know where the print shops are, the tea shops where the deals are done. I've told MI6. Not that they don't already know. Course they do. To be honest, I can't understand why we don't just blow the fuckers up with a few laser-guided Hellfires. Blame the Russians.'

They thought about that for a moment. Then the thin officer stood and went to the clothes they'd emptied out of my duffel. He sorted through and, like a conjuror, whipped out a black and white *shemagh* still in its plastic wrapping. He unwrapped it and held it up like he was selling a tablecloth in the bazaar.

I laughed. 'Present for a mate of mine. A reminder that while I'm out in the desert eating dust, he's sitting in an office in polished brogues,' I said. 'Think about it, terrorists on their way to England will shave off their beards. They'll have nice haircuts, books to show they're studying to be doctors. They won't be carrying a Quran or a headscarf.'

He put the *shemagh* back on the pile and left the room. His colleague took another look at my passport. I noticed the female officer was holding her rifle correctly.

'That's better,' I said. 'If there's an accidental discharge and your weapon is pointing up, it's only going to make a hole in the ceiling.'

'You've got quite a mouth on you, you know that?' she remarked.

'You're not wrong. It's a problem,' I replied, and felt my expression tense up. 'I've been in Mosul for the last ten weeks seeing women and children shot in the back running from terrorists. It puts everything in perspective.'

The thin guy returned, eyes bulging behind his glasses. The faint nod he gave his companion must have been the all clear. The fat guy stood, hoisted up his trousers by the waistband, and gave me back my passport.

'Happy Christmas,' he said.

'And you, mate.'

We spent two hours with my mum. That was enough. She still thought of me as the petrified little boy hiding in the chicken coop from my father. He was dead now. I didn't miss him and I didn't go to the funeral.

Kali and Natty sat next to each other on the couch, dark and exotic with lively eyes, so obviously not English that Mum kept studying them as if they were from another planet.

My mother had voted for Brexit. She wanted her country back. She was born in 1950, after the war, but carried that feeling that we were still fighting the Battle of Britain. We were at war with Brussels, the traffic, the climate, the alien hordes taking our jobs and abusing the NHS. It's what made her happy, having so much to moan about.

Kali had brought a *Christopsomo*, a round loaf decorated with a cross and spiced with cinnamon, cloves and orange. Mum studied it and looked back at her with a confused expression.

'What do you do with it?' she asked.

'Eat it. It's sweet bread.'

'Sweet bread. Never heard of it.'

'We call it Christ's bread.'

'Oh, I see.'

She put it on the kitchen table next to the bunch of flowers, ready for the dustbin. She made a pot of tea and brought out a plate of Bournville biscuits, her favourite. The curtains were half drawn and we sat in the gloom while she talked about my brother. I hadn't seen him for a decade. He had run for Parliament in the last election. She didn't say for which party, but it had to be UKIP, where all the nutters ended up.

Ntileini told her gran that she might be going to school in England and I knew what went through Mum's mind: another bloody foreigner.

'That's nice, dear,' she said, and Ntileini gave her a hug.

Mum stood on the doorstep as we made our way up the path. The door shut before I closed the gate and it felt as if I were walking away from a part of myself that I was glad to leave behind. Coming home always felt as if I had moved back in time, and my mother and most people I met seemed nostalgic for some better, more hopeful past.

A taxi was waiting to drive us to the station. Kali took my hand.

'You all right?' she asked, and I immediately felt the tension slip from my face muscles.

'You know something, I think I am. Yes, why not?'

She laughed. 'First they won't let you in. Then your mum's not exactly the friendliest person in the world. It's not easy going home.'

'My home's in Heraklion. I love going home.'

We were in the back of the taxi, Natty in the front seat beside the driver. Kali leaned close and whispered. 'I love you, you big lump,' she said, and bit my earlobe.

'Ouch!'

Natty turned, shaking her head. 'You two!' she said.

The train to Oxford was two hours over familiar tracks. Trowbridge, Bath, Chippenham, Swindon, Didcot. The trees had shed their leaves and stood like scarecrows at the edges of empty fields. The sky was dark, overcast, swirling greys like dirty water. Matt Lambert was waiting at the station in an old Land Rover. He leaped out and hoisted the bags in the back. He kissed Kali and Natty on the cheeks, then pumped my hand firmly.

'Merry Christmas, John. So glad you're here.'

He seemed strangely content to have this sudden glimpse of Greek light in the midwinter dusk. He and I spoke often on Skype. Since that night when he told me about his daughter's riding accident, we had become good friends, something I would never have imagined when we first met. We shed and regrow new cells every day. If life's circumstances change, we change. We become a different person and sometimes when you are reminded of who you were, you forget for a moment who you are.

The shadows deepened as he drove west through the green and pleasant land to his farm in the Cotswold hills. Raynott Manor was 16th century, Matt said, but it had gone through some modernizations in the last four hundred years. Over three floors were parlours and bedrooms with four-poster beds, a long kitchen with a slate floor and exposed beams. It was what I thought of as officer chic, everything discreet and tasteful.

Outside, two dozen Aberdeen Angus stood pressed together with glum faces behind a three-bar fence. There were stables, but no horses, and two black Labradors that had bounded up to me the moment I stepped from the vehicle. They licked my face, and I missed my dogs, the troop of cats, Nikko, the big tabby, squatting among the dog-eared papers and empty beer bottles that littered my work space, the very opposite of Matt's kidney-shaped glass desk with nothing on it but a new Apple iMac.

We had two days before the holidays and Matt had planned visits to four boarding schools within an hour of London. They were all very similar in that they were housed in fine old mansions with ivy-clad walls, small dorms, well-equipped classrooms and libraries that smelled of leather books and learning. I was grateful to Matt. It was dead right for Ntileini. I could see it in her eyes as we walked the shiny corridors and peeked into rooms containing small groups of thin healthy girls with their lives in front of them.

We had lunch in country pubs – log fires, roast beef, bar staff in Father Christmas hats, trees with winking lights. In his oilskin jacket, cords and yellow cashmere sweater, Matt played the gentleman farmer. I couldn't help wondering if the people around us supping ale would ever have guessed he was a former intelligence officer, still in the game, as intelligence officers never entirely leave it.

It was odd everyone speaking English, understanding them. The streets were clean, cars polished, the houses neat, freshly painted. Of course, this was Oxford, not Newcastle or south London, and perhaps I would have felt more in my own skin with a bit of dirt and poverty around me. I tried to tune into Natty evaluating the schools we had seen, but all the while my head remained somewhere else.

CHAPTER 19
The Battle for Raqqa

Raqqa is a small Syrian city straddling the banks of the Euphrates, 400 miles west of Erbil, an eight-hour drive. Greeks, Romans and Christians had all in their time erected their shrines and basilicas. When I read that it was the capital of the Abbasid Caliphate for 13 years between 796 and 809, I thought that was a good sign; caliphates don't last too long.

Two years after the outbreak of the Syrian civil war in 2011, troops loyal to President Bashar al-Assad in Raqqa were overwhelmed by Syrian opposition forces, in an uncomfortable alliance with the al-Nusra Front, affiliates of al-Qaeda. Islamic State – better organized and thirsty for oil – seized control of Raqqa in January 2014.

The jihadis introduced Sharia law and sent bulldozers into every religious structure not built by Sunnis, including the revered Shi'ite mosque of Uwais al-Qarni. The fact that Sunni fundamentalists reviled their Shia co-religionists more than Christians, Jews and Americans perfectly describes the meaning of the word 'extremism'. ISIS assassins executed Alawites – followers of the Shia-related sect to which Assad belonged – while Christians fled through the minefields into the desert.

By January 2017, when I arrived on the outskirts of Raqqa, what Islamic State had left standing had largely been destroyed in airstrikes by the Syrian government, Russia, the United States and France – the latter payback for the massacre of 129 people in coordinated attacks in the heart of Paris, the plot conceived in Syria and nurtured by an ISIS cell in Belgium.

The civilian infrastructure in Raqqa was totally wrecked. People lived like rats in the ruins. And, yet, in spite of the bombing, shortages and turmoil, the city had become known as 'the hotel of the revolution', the population rising from 220,000 to 500,000 as Sunnis escaped rebellions against Assad's rule in Aleppo, Idlib and Homs.

The assault on Mosul had been well planned: Iraqi and Kurdish forces, backed by American advisers, were methodically clearing the suburbs and looping a noose around the city. The Battle for Raqqa was a free-for-all.

Elind and Usef were waiting at the airport chewing sunflower seeds and spitting the husks out the window. Blondie blasted from the speakers for my benefit. Elind opened the door. I spoke to Usef as I climbed in the back.

'How's that moustache coming along, sunshine?' I asked, and he grinned.

'Thank you very much,' he replied.

Erbil was cold and bright, with heavy traffic. They were constructing a two-and-a half-mile stretch of new highway between Shaqlawa Road and Koya Road. It had slowed circulation to a standstill. Debbie Harry sang 'I sit by and watch the traffic go' – and I thought, I wish.

The sky was criss-crossed with the arms of cranes, perched over the shells of new office blocks and apartment buildings. I noticed when we finally got moving that a lot of modern shops had New Year sales signs in English on the windows, a ploy imported from the west. *Nawroz*, the Kurdistan new year, arrived with the spring equinox and was the most important celebration on the calendar. People dressed in traditional clothes and lit bonfires to mark the passing of the dark season.

'How's the studies going?' I asked Elind.

'Very good, sir.'

'John,' I told him. 'You studying every day?'

'Every day, John. But I have spare time when you need good driver.'

'I'll bear it in mind. You don't want end up useless like Usef.'

Usef looked back at me in the rear-view mirror. 'Fucking English,' he said with a straight face, and I laughed until my gut ached.

'Nice to see you're learning the lingo,' I told him, and he grinned again.

'Thank you very much.'

He blasted the horn as he swerved around a donkey cart. The driver, an old man in a red checked *shemagh*, waved his fist as we passed, ancient and contemporary Erbil captured in a snapshot.

I had left Kali and Natty with Matt Lambert and cut short Christmas to set up the extraction of Layla Adlani, a French girl trapped in Raqqa. Matt had received €50,000 from a French charity to finance the operation and believed further funding would follow. It's the way it works, he said, once one charity takes a liking to you, others jump on the bandwagon.

It was confirmation that our work was being recognized by humanitarian organizations, even if governments across Europe neither agreed on strategy nor had firm policies on how to deal with their own nationals returning from the Caliphate. The numbers of returnees remained modest that winter, but I was sure come summer the innumerable land and sea routes leading out of Turkey were going to flood with jihadi travellers.

The road cleared and Usef put his foot down. When he turned on to the potholed track and the safe house came into view, I felt glad to be back, and ashamed for feeling that way. I had enjoyed those days in Oxford, fine food, clean sheets, long walks in the hills, but my mind kept wandering and, every time I closed my eyes, what I saw was a vision of spectral wraiths stumbling over the ruins of Mosul.

One evening, when Kali and Natty had gone to bed, I mentioned to Matt the irony of being on both the Islamic State death list and the Home Office warnings index. He pulled up a file: 20,000 people were listed as 'extremists' in the UK – mostly Muslim, some right-wing radicals and neo-Nazis. Among them were 3,000 people 'considered dangerous'. They were under regular, though rarely 24/7 surveillance. The US had its own list, as did every country in Europe, and they shared intel to cross-reference and seek out networks.

'With all that manpower, I can't see why we can't get our hands on the bad guys,' I remarked.

'On the contrary. It's manpower we don't have. You need a minimum of ten agents, the French say twenty, to track one suspect twenty-four hours a day,' he explained. 'Another problem, governments make mistakes. When they do, the usual reaction is to double down.'

'Meaning what?'

'Persistence in error, they call it. You know when you have a coffee after dinner it's going to keep you awake at night. Still we do it.' He paused and thought for a moment. 'I don't know that it's a question of

264

leave them there, let them die, as you said, more a case of wishing the entire problem would just go away.'

'No chance of that, Matt.'

'We know that. The government knows that. They just don't want to let the public know.'

Elind opened the gates. The moment I stepped from the car, Cano Ali emerged with his arms spread. He took me in a bear hug and lifted me off the ground.

'Fuck me, what are you up to now?'

'You home, Johnny.'

'You should be in a bloody asylum, mate.'

'Practice,' he yelled and took me in another hug.

The marriage was off.

Pelin's suitor had twice been arrested for 'indecency' with another man. The charges had been dropped – bribery or contacts, or both – but it was enough for Cano's wife to stop matchmaking and let Pelin go to college.

Dozan took six beers from the cooler and peeled off the tabs. Hassan stood from where he had been studying a map on the table. He lowered his head and touched his hand to his heart.

'My friend. I am happy to see you.'

'Thanks, mate, appreciate it.'

'How is your wife and daughter?'

'Two happy bunnies. They stayed on for a while.'

'With Mr Lambert?' he said, and I nodded. 'How is Mr Lambert?'

'He got hold of a decent bit of cash for us.'

'That he did. I shall write him to say thank you.'

'You know, I didn't like him much when we first met. Now I do. He's a decent bloke.'

'We all have light and darkness inside us. First you saw the darkness.'

Dozan passed us each a beer and we rattled the cans together.

'Is a Merry Christmas,' Usef announced in his newly learned English.

I asked after Hassan's family, the same with Dozan and Cano. I couldn't be sure in the half light, but Cano's cheeks seemed to redden and he changed the subject by producing one of his surprises. With a recipe from the internet, he had foraged through the souk for figs, dates, almonds, dried cherries, flour and, with a cup of Lebanese brandy, made a traditional fruit cake.

We scoffed it down with a few cans of Ava Zer and the boys went home to their mums. We got an early night. Not that I was tired. I had tensed up with a swirl of muddled emotions and lay in my iron cot thinking about Kali and Natty, and feeling oddly content with the mini-Christmas I had shared with my team of Kurds. Muslims, Christians and Jews had always respected the 'community of faith' among monotheistic religions. Why in modern times it had disintegrated I had no idea.

We were wheels up at sunrise and watched the day awaken as we headed west towards the Syrian border. We ascended mountain passes below snow-capped peaks and plunged into primal valleys. The countryside as we left Iraq grew more verdant but desolate, with neglected walnut and almond groves, rogue olive trees and grapevines, the fields steaming with melting frost in the early morning sun.

We flew the Kurdish colours and passed through checkpoints manned by Kurds with just a nod. Hassan had been shaping a new network with assets still embedded in Raqqa and officers in the Kurdish militia. As in Mosul, the YPG, the People's Protection Units, were key to everything we set out to do.

Military vehicles raced by in both directions. There was no civilian traffic except a few carts carrying tools little changed since the time of the Romans. The only people we did see were Bedouin nomads wandering from nowhere to nowhere, and a few gnarled shepherds standing in fields, wearing blank stares that imitated the long dark faces of the goats they watched over. We entered liberated villages without dogs to chase us or children to wave their hands. The thick-walled adobe houses stood in their habitual state of windswept decay, amid fresh rubble from neighbouring houses arbitrarily demolished by bombs and field guns.

Tall grain silos stood like wounded chessmen on the horizon. Much of the canal network pieced together over hundreds of years had been dismantled. Before the war, Syria had enjoyed a brief financial upturn, inspiring the desire for more democracy and planting the seeds of discontent that had brought the dictator's wrath down upon them. Half the population had worked the land before the war. Now, five million Syrians were displaced within Syria. The same number had fled across the border to desperate camps across the Middle East. A million people, the best educated, the most qualified, had marched across Europe to seek asylum.

Since early January, Syrian Democratic Forces (SDF) backed by the Kurd militia had seized Ayuj, Abu Suseh and Mashrafa, strategic villages north of the irrigation canal running from Lake Assad to Tal Saman. It was a modest start. Surrounding Raqqa was a web of hundreds of rural communities with populations ranging from a few hundred to several thousand, each controlled by well-supplied ISIS fanatics primed to make a last stand.

We were aware of what we were getting into. My companions knew Iraq, they were Iraqis. Syria was fragmented, with more factions and more foreign government interests. Russia, America, Iran, Saudi Arabia and Turkey all had an oar in the turmoil. Another factor to consider is that advancing on villages is not as straightforward as defending them. ISIS fighters didn't care who got slaughtered. Syrian forces wanted to minimize the bloodshed as they freed their own nationals.

The United States supported the operation with air cover and bankrolled the Kurdish militia, knowing that the Raqqa siege was complicated by Turkish-backed Syrian rebels advancing on the ISIS-held city of al-Bab, a manoeuvre that would end Kurdish hopes of uniting their two separated areas of self-rule in north-west Syria. As we had seen in Iraq, Turkey's first concern was not the defeat of Islamic State but the prevention of Kurdish expansion.

It was messy and asymmetric, and still unwise to underestimate ISIS. With Russian air support, the Syrian army had driven the jihadis from Palmyra. After holding the city for nine months, Assad's professional troops had been routed in a surprise attack in December 2016, shortly before my return to Iraq. The jihadi black flags had been raised and the looting and destruction of Palmyra had begun again.

The fact that Islamic State diverted fighters to a city of no strategic value, while under attack on numerous fronts, seems extraordinary, even reckless. But holy war is abstract, a battle of doctrines and symbols. To western eyes, the desert oasis settlement was a masterpiece of Roman style and European progress, a vibrant meeting of cultures on the Silk Road. For Muslim fundamentalists, Palmyra was a constant reminder of the imperial presence of the West in the sacred lands of Muhammad.

When Islamic State was first driven from Palmyra, President Putin had sent the Mariinsky Theatre Orchestra to play to a largely Russian audience in the remains of the ancient amphitheatre, a cultural gesture with powerful political undertones. The jihadis would be driven out again, and the orchestra would no doubt be back for a repeat performance.

The civil war in Syria was in its seventh year and it was shameful that Europe and the United States had done so little towards bringing about a negotiated peace. Worse, we had allowed Russia, Turkey and Iran – and to a lesser extent Israel and Saudi Arabia – to drive the agenda and plant their forces in bases that would almost certainly become permanent. A combination of the separatist core of Brexit, the rise of nationalist, anti-immigration parties across Europe, and the 'America First' tendencies of President Donald Trump, sworn in on 20 January 2017, were dividing the western alliance and allowing the world's power balance to change in ways that could only be detrimental.

The day was bright and clear, 12 degrees according to my iPhone. Dozan was humming along to the radio. He was in a good mood and hadn't mentioned his wife all morning. I lowered the window and tasted the clean dry air.

Cano Ali, driving the lead vehicle, had kept to a leisurely pace. He now put his foot down.

Dozan glanced at his big aviator watch as he accelerated.

'Fasten your safety belt. Ten minutes to landing,' he said.

We had been on a gradual incline between low hills. As we descended into a wide plain, the rush of air from the open window was drowned out by the whistle and boom of shelling; mortars, 60mm, I guessed, with a range of a little over two miles. I heard the sound of a cobbler hammering nails into a boot, machine guns, *rat-a-tat tat, rat-a-tat tat*. My hand went instinctively for the AK tucked down beside the door. I ran my fingers over the cold metal of the trigger guard and felt my war face slip onto my features.

We were entering the combat area to bring out a French national of Moroccan origin, a girl aged 22 with an infant and pregnant with her second child. I had sent Layla Adlani's profile to Hassan while in Oxford. He had found a Kurd fixer who wanted $1,000 in US currency to coordinate the extraction. Money we now had, and money well spent.

Dozan had limited French, but with the help of Google Translate, enough to communicate on WhatsApp with Layla's father. According to intelligence from Asayish, shared no doubt by DGSE, the French secret service, Dr Adlani was a surgeon at a hospital in Perpignan, highly respected in the community and shocked that his daughter had run off to the Caliphate.

Layla had married a Syrian jihadi who had been killed in the opening days of the assault on Mosul. She had joined the exodus fleeing the city and found herself in Jazrah, a rural suburb surrounded by untended fields three miles west of Raqqa. There she had taken shelter in a 'women's guesthouse' with several women and children. They had little food or water. The fixer reckoned the babies would be dead in three days.

We followed the satnav to the YPG. The unit was dug in below a gully next to the remains of a grain silo. We got out of the vehicles and did the rounds of kissing and hand-shaking. Smoke blossomed like grey roses in the air above us. The guns boomed. In the brief silences between explosions, Hassan introduced me to the unit commander, Agrin Kemal.

'So, you are the John Carney,' he said, and glanced back at Hassan. 'I hope you are taking care of my friend.'

'He's taking care of me, as it happens.'

'And us all.' Kemal smiled, large, brilliant white teeth. 'I love your country. I study one year in London. You have beautiful girls.'

'There's a few.'

'Good times.'

'They will come again,' Hassan interjected, and Kemal slapped him on the back.

'The eternal politician.'

Agrin Kemal was a history professor at Istanbul's Koc University, a short, solid man, stocky as a pillar box, with a toothbrush moustache and streaks of gun oil on his cheeks. Always a good sign: an officer who led from the front.

I pointed behind us towards the gunfire. 'We need to reach a house about three miles that way.'

He glanced again at Hassan as he nodded his head. 'This is a battle of attrition, my friend. We must wear down the enemy.'

I suppose it was naïve of me, but I had thought we would be able to nip in under the cover of dark, grab the women and babies and get home in time 'for tea and medals', as we used to say in the Yorks. What I now learned was that the three miles that separated us from our target was the snail trail of war – trashed vehicles, IEDs, the wasteland of crumpled buildings. If by some miracle we could cross this death trap, we would reach a ring of heavy armour, sharpshooters and Caliphate Cubs wired with explosives.

'So, how long before you wear them down?' I asked, and Kemal shrugged.

'It is not possible to say.'

'Give me a rough estimate.'

'The siege of Troy lasted ten years, and would have been longer without the wooden horse.'

'Ten years! We've only got three days.'

'These young jihadis are not like the Trojans. They take so many drugs, they don't feel the bullets. You must shoot them in the head to be done with them.' He scratched his cheek thoughtfully. 'It is not easy to fight men who are already dead.'

I threw up my hands. 'Now what?' I said.

'We wait,' Hassan answered.

There was another round of back-slapping before we climbed into the vehicles and drove a few miles further behind the lines to the nearest village. We set up camp in an unoccupied villa. It had been stripped clean. Across the northern zone, houses were systematically pillaged by gangs that crossed the Turkish border in empty trucks and returned laden with TV sets, refrigerators, motorcycles, carpets, wrought-iron gates, window frames, cooking pots, tools, even babies' prams.

The YPG had provided us with rice and beans. Cano Ali, ever the gourmet, decided to go out in search of vegetables, spices, mint for tea. I went with him. Dozan unloaded the vehicles while Hassan made his calls.

We descended on a steep track towards the village, weapons ready, one in the box. The buildings we passed appeared to be empty – literally – but this was obviously an upmarket quarter, houses set in walled compounds with stunning views over the Euphrates. We reached a square with a dry fountain and looted shops in an avenue of date palms.

At the far end, in the courtyard outside a destroyed mosque, a family of Bedouins was building a fire, the grey tendrils of smoke rising into the cold air. The instant they saw us, they stood, hands held in surrender, something they must have rehearsed and performed many times. Cano dropped his rifle back over his shoulder and displayed his hands in the same gesture. I copied him as we entered the camp.

The family consisted of a man, ageless as the desert in a white turban and grubby *dishdasha*. His wife was a wiry woman with faded tattoos around her chin and green eyes of a shade and brilliance I had never seen before. They had six children aged from about three to fifteen, two boys and four girls in bright clothes, hair wild, their faces lit by their mother's mesmeric eyes.

Cano and the man spoke formally for a few moments, establishing some context I didn't understand. They then touched their hearts and bowed their heads in a way that was strangely moving, and I felt like Lawrence of Arabia transported back in time. Empires come and go. The Bedouins are still there. They know how to survive in the wilderness. They know every stone and well, the secrets of nature. They had nothing and wanted for very little. Their way of life had barely changed since the time of the Prophet, something the jihadis respected and had enabled them to endure the years of war.

I tried to follow the conversation. Cano and the man laughed and gesticulated, threw up their hands, agreed then disagreed, on what I wasn't sure. The two boys observed, taking mental notes. Finally, Cano handed over two AK-47 magazines and a wad of Iraqi dinars for a few packets of spices and a bag of mint. The woman made tea, which we drank from metal cups cleaned with sand, while her green-eyed daughters watched me with the fascination of cats stalking prey.

As far as I could see, Cano had swapped the equivalent of a Rolls-Royce for a donkey cart; a prize cow for a handful of beans. Only later did I learn from Dozan that barter among Arabs is not the exchange of goods of equal value, but equal consequence.

'Poverty comes to those who need a lot,' Dozan quoted. 'The Bedouins only want the respect of those whose paths they cross in the desert.'

Cano had at least been able to confirm that the looting of Syrian houses – the Arabs called it 'refurnishing' – was controlled by Turkish soldiers on near-zero wages obliged to 'keep their women contented'. More important, Fahed, the Bedouin patriarch, turned out to be central to our mission in Jazrah.

The YPG was making progress clearing mines planted around Jazrah. Two volunteers had died in their work. Shelling had destroyed several jihadi gun emplacements – and with them, more buildings. One of those buildings was the women's guesthouse. According to Hassan's fixer, Layla Adlani and company were now sheltering in the cellars without food, water or milk for the babies.

It felt to me as if the whole mission was slipping away, another failure. I am impatient by nature and reluctantly passed the time following Cano as he unearthed objects people had discarded as they abandoned their homes: cooking pots, cutlery, a box of flower-patterned Limoges plates that we ate from when he cooked stews with game birds shot on the wing. Dozan had knocked up two trestles from odd bits of wood and used a door as a table. These were men who could put their hand to anything, and did so without overthinking everything. It didn't have to be a work of art. It had to work.

On the morning of the third day, when we had finished drinking mint tea and eating potato pancakes, Hassan wrapped his amber beads around his wrist and took a breath. We knew what that meant.

'My friends, I think we have two options,' he began in English; Dozan translated for Cano. 'We should return to Erbil, find something more useful to do with our time.'

He took a long pause and looked at each of us in turn.

'Option two?' I asked him.

'There are six women and seven babies in Jazrah. They have little time left.' He held up his hand before anyone spoke. 'I would be prepared to try and extract them.'

'Fuck, yes,' I said.

'I'm in,' Dozan added, and again translated.

Cano lit a cigarette. 'Very good, Johnny,' he said, and Hassan tapped his knuckles on the table.

'Before daybreak tomorrow. We have less than twenty-four hours.'

Hassan stood and made a call as he left the room.

This wasn't just dangerous, it was stupid. We knew that. We had to cross almost three miles of no man's land on foot with nothing to light the way but the moon in its first quarter. We had to find the building, not so difficult with Google Maps and a satnav. Then lead six women and their children back over the mine-studded wilderness to the YPG lines. I would have thought nothing of it once upon a time. I was a mad bastard back then. I was somebody else now.

I followed Cano back to the Bedouins' encampment. Cano and Fahed chatted intensely for several minutes. With my limited Arabic, what I thought I heard was Cano sharing information on our plan to enter Jazrah, the most basic of all errors before a mission. I was about to jump in and say something, when Fahed stood, shaded his eyes and looked up

275

at the sky. He touched his hand to his heart and spoke solemnly.

Cano grinned and looked at me.

'Good Englishman.'

'What the fuck?' I said, and he threw his arm around my shoulder.

'Good. Good. *Linadhhab*,' let's go, he said.

Fahed returned with us to the villa. Hassan was with the YPG and Dozan joined us on a long-winded journey over old camel tracks towards Jazrah. We stopped on a narrow river tributary, climbed out of the vehicle and scrambled down the overgrown bank to a dry water culvert. Fahed pointed down the tube.

'Jazrah,' he said.

The pipe was a little over four feet high. Cano dropped his rifle, doubled over and went straight in. I followed with a flashlight until we saw a patch of light around an outlet. I scraped the dirt and cement dust from around the drain cover and poked my head out. The buildings were closer and we were clearly going in the right direction. We had penetrated far enough and made our way back again.

'Jazrah,' the man repeated.

I am not sure if Fahed was rewarded for his information, those things are complicated, but we now had a way in.

Later in the day, Cano drove Hassan to see the entry point, while Dozan and I converted our canvas sacks into sledges we could drag behind us with our rifles, Kevlar vests, ammo, rope and tools.

We ate our evening meal early, caught a couple of hours of shuteye and dressed for the coming performance as jihadi warriors in black trousers, shirts and balaclavas from the YPG wardrobe department. All four of us were over six feet tall, but the costumes helped us get into character. Two minutes after midnight, we were on the road, lights turned off, terrified that a drone guided by a pilot in Texas might swoop down and take out our two-car package.

Cano led the way into the tunnel. You can walk a mile at a steady pace in 15 minutes. Bent over at an odd angle, we reached a blockage after an hour. We backed up. Cano dug through the sandy earth and rubble, pushing it back for the three of us to distribute further down the tunnel.

We kept this up for the best part of an hour. I had started to worry that we would never break through when I saw Cano's torso vanish with Hassan behind him. Hassan turned, zipping his lips. We took shallow breaths for what seemed like for ever. Cano then lowered his head back down the hole and motioned for us to pass up the equipment.

The mouth of the tunnel was inside a derelict water pumping station on the outskirts of Jazrah, half a mile from the women's guesthouse; better than we'd hoped. Hassan called his contact. He was with the women. They were waiting, ready to go.

I rubbed my palms over a greasy patch on the wall, camouflaged my red face and pulled the balaclava over my head. We slapped hands like basketball players. The sky as Cano led the way into the dark deserted streets was lit by explosions. The unit of YPG based on the east side of Jazrah was shelling the suburbs, drawing defences from the west, where we had infiltrated. Hassan had set up the barrage with Agrin Kemal.

We reached the pile of debris where the women's guesthouse had once stood. Hassan sent a text. Within seconds, the fixer appeared. He held up a clenched fist. Hassan returned the gesture. The man looked left and right. He then moved cautiously through the rubble. A raggedy line of ghostly shapes followed, some of the women with babes in arms, others holding the hands of small children. They were as quiet as moths, even their footfall hushed in the brick dust.

Hassan lifted his balaclava. He touched his finger to his lips to remind them to remain silent. Not that it was necessary. The women and children had lost the will to use their voices. They were starving, traumatized. I had seen jihadi brides throwing off their *abayas*. These women wanted to remain unseen in their black veils. Cano Ali led the way back to the water pumping station. The sky was pinpricked with stars. A sickle moon, like an Arab sword, hung high above us, washing the rooftops in a silvery glow.

CHAPTER 20

The Long Game

With his coat draped about his shoulders and his eyes shiny in the moonlight, Agrin Kemal was waiting at the end of the tunnel with an empty minibus and three men from his unit. They threw out their hands to help as we scrambled up the bank to the road. The Syrian women with their children never spoke; faceless and nameless, they climbed into the vehicle to vanish among millions like them – literally millions – flooding into the refugee camps along the 500-mile frontier between Syria and Turkey.

The fixer had come out with us. He was promptly arrested, as he knew he would be. Informers always keep back some intelligence to barter with and, being a Kurd among Kurds, he expected to be on his way to Erbil in a few days. With $1,000, he had enough to find his way into some new enterprise.

We had no authority to separate Layla Adlani from the others, but Kemal always assumed the position of a junior officer around Hassan. He kissed his cheeks, then turned to me, waving a stubby finger.

'Take care of my friend,' he said.

'With my life,' I replied.

'I can ask no more.' He shook my hand warmly and lowered his voice. 'I will never forget those pretty girls,' he waxed nostalgically, and I thought, that's the burden of the historian, you must always be clinging to the past.

We now set out on the long haul back to Erbil. It was a cold, black, windy night with dust grating against the windscreen. We crossed the border into Iraq without having to show our papers – which was just as well, the jihadis had long since burnt Layla's passport and Yaffa, her little boy of six months, had never been registered. We delivered her to the French consular officials, who were waiting for us. Layla was one of the lucky ones. Three days later, she was on a plane back to Paris.

After our shambolic attempt to extract Laura Hansen in June, I had collated from various sources 140 emails from people desperate to get loved ones out of the Caliphate. We had delivered on half that number. There were women in camps tied up in red tape. Some had disappeared, probably dead. Others were still out there.

The moment we arrived back at the safe house, I kicked off my boots and cranked up the shower. The guys had families to see. Dozan had told me he had made the fatal error of telling his wife he didn't like jazz. Naturally, sod's law, that's where they were going that night, to the jazz restaurant at Park View, upmarket Erbil with its new apartment blocks and city gardens.

After a siesta, I scoffed some toenail bread with cheese and then called Kali with an update on Dozan's music tastes and emotional life. I fed the dogs and passed an enjoyable five minutes watching Usef working on the Previa eight-seater. A sheet of armour plating had dropped off in the desert, and he broke out in a sweat using a hand drill to bolt a new strip along the driver's side.

'You're not so useless after all,' I said, and he grinned as he looked back at me.

'Practice,' he responded, just like Cano. He then sang some words from Blondie. It came out something like this: *Onza hava hearta glass.*

'Not bad, mate.'

'Thank you very much.'

My muscles were tense from sitting in a vehicle for eight hours and I decided to walk into town. I thought I'd surprise Jack Fieldhouse, and ended up being the one getting a surprise. As I entered Jack's local, a tall, broad, bearded man in a spotless white tunic and turban stood with open arms like a prophet.

'Holy Roller, if it ain't my man.'

'Still keeping a low profile, I see.'

'Brother, you would not believe my laundry bills.'

'My laundry bills!' Jack corrected.

The people at the other tables went back to their own conversations. We ordered pints of Roj and chinked the glasses together. Roy Underhill had driven out of Mosul with his woman and two kids, flying the Stars and Stripes from the roof of a white Cadillac 'pirated' from an ISIS commander who had long since hightailed it to Turkey. Roy was a known asset working in the shadows – the regiment of the dead, as he put it. He had been debriefed over several days without spending a night in a cell. He was now lodged with Jack and his family.

We drank a few beers. Then a few more. I'm not quite sure what we discussed – time flies when you're talking bullshit – but something about the treasure hidden in Mosul and why British Paras were smarter than US Navy SEALs because it was quicker by air than by sea. The beer is piss weak, but you drink enough and it does the job. A taxi had to be called to take me home, and I had a thick head sitting down with a pot of coffee in the Divan Hotel the following morning with Oliver from MI6. He was wearing a blinding white shirt and I wondered if it was the UK taxpayers who paid his laundry bills.

What did I have? Not much. Background info on Layla Adlani, the fact that we'd got her out without a firing a shot, some money from an NGO based in Paris.

'France is a rich country,' Oliver remarked.

'Like we're so poor?'

'We have different priorities.'

'Yeah, take the money from the poor and give it to the bankers.'

'My dear boy, there is something you just don't seem able to grasp. You have crossed over. You are not poor. You are a businessman, large house, a child about to attend an exclusive school.'

'Been poking about in my private life again, have you?' I swigged back my coffee. 'What you're saying is you're either one of them or one of us.'

'I'm not saying anything. The problem is, John, neither are you.'

'Listen, poverty comes to those who need a lot,' I said, quoting Dozan. 'I'll tell you what my priority is, getting my name off the terrorist list. I don't want to be dragged off planes and interrogated every time I arrive home.'

'We'll see what we can do,' he said, and called the waiter back to our table. 'Brandy?' he asked. I thought, why the hell not.

'Make it a big one.'

He ordered.

The hotel was buzzing. People hurried by, shoes drumming on the marble floor, their reflections multiplied in the mirrors; Arab princes, arms dealers, oil men, bankers and spooks, news anchors with camera crews, the all-night girls in heels and silk – the money circus that follows war. The drinks came. I took two sips and began to feel like my old self again.

'Were you about to tell me something?' Oliver asked.

'Nothing you don't already know,' I said, and leaned forward. 'There are factions inside ISIS,' I began, and he nodded. 'The British battalion hates the French, the French don't get on with the Germans. We get bits of gossip from one faction, and pass it on to another, stir them up a bit. We send what we've got up the ladder to Asayish and Uncle Sam has taken out some high-level targets. You must know all this?'

He shrugged. 'Carry on.'

'It cuts both ways, like a Swiss Army knife. When the bad guys get eliminated, our informants rise up the ranks.'

'At this rate we'll end up running ISIS.' He glanced away as a tall Arab in a European suit passed the table, then straightened his tie, black with a pale blue stripe. 'Names, profiles, photographs?'

'I'm working on that.'

'You'll be pleased to know, we have dismantled a number of networks in the last two months. You made a contribution to at least one of them.'

I raised my glass. 'I wondered what the drink was all about.'

'There's something in the air. You can smell ISIS all over London. We need to stop these people.'

'And I need my name off that watch list.'

'I'll see what I can do, John,' he said, and I took that to mean that he'd do nothing at all.

What I didn't tell MI6 – it had no bearing on national security – was that Matt Lambert had, as he had predicted, received an additional tranche of cash, this time from a UK charity based in Birmingham. The money was not explicitly linked to a new tasking – but a British Pakistani family was anxious to bring their daughter out of Raqqa. It was the same old story. Sonia Roy had a baby and a jihadi husband, and had called home after 12 months of silence.

The way it had worked out, extracting Layla Adlani, plus the new shot of cash from the UK, had given the team a renewed feeling of confidence – of respect – and we were wheels up back to Raqqa through a glorious sunrise the following morning.

We would have left earlier, after my rendezvous with Oliver at the Divan, but at the last moment, Hassan had been invited to a meeting of the officials who planned to greet UN Secretary-General António Guterres during his trip to Iraq in March. Guterres would spend a few days in Baghdad, then journey on to Erbil to confer with Masoud Barzani, president of the Kurdistan regional government. Guterres had referred to the 'Kurdistan question' on a number of occasions, and local luminaries had deciphered his visit as being supportive of their independence claims.

The YPG was again on the frontline, taking Raqqa street by street in close-quarters battle (CBQ). We followed two blocks behind in helmets and body armour, our senses overwhelmed by the familiar smell of blood and cordite, burnt oil, the constant banter of the big guns, the taste of brick dust on your tongue. It's funny how you forget when you're away from it; the mind blocks out the horror. One whiff of explosives and it all comes flooding back.

I watched jihadis shot by marksmen crying a last prayer to Allah as they dropped like sacks from rooftops. Boys of 12 in suicide belts sprinted at the YPG lines. Kurdish militiamen lost limbs and lives stepping on IEDs and were cut to shreds in bursts of crossfire. You stand in the wreckage of an entire district and three blocks away, life continues in an eerie sort of virtual reality. Islamic State propaganda had painted a utopian portrait of Caliphate life with its social programmes, schooling, free medicine, land management, bird conservation. Those people attracted by the hype now made themselves believe the crusaders at the door were being annihilated.

We adopted the same ploy we had used when Roy Underhill helped us liberate Sophian and Diana Abbasi from Mosul. I instructed Sonia to take the baby to the nearest hospital – which was miraculously still standing – and wait for a fixer engaged by Hassan to make contact. He would escort her one block in our direction on foot, while we dashed through the firefight in our jihadi costumes to collect them. I wasn't sure that Hassan supported this strategy, but it was all we had. There is a maxim in combat: don't criticize a plan unless you can come up with a better one.

Our contact went to the hospital – we had no reason to doubt him – waited for an hour, and the girl failed to turn up.

When I spoke to her the following day, I got the feeling that Sonia was playing for time. Sure, she wanted to get out of Raqqa, it was crumbling all around her, but I sensed that she still believed in the dream of an Islamic paradise. Not all the young women recruited to holy war had their feet caned by the moral police. There were those who held the canes.

Next time I tried to contact Sonia, the line was dead. Our fixer was unable to locate her. We learned from him that as heavy artillery enfiladed central Raqqa, women and children were herded into underground bunkers. Rather than allow them to be freed by advancing forces, they would be used as human shields if ISIS decided to withdraw, or eliminated by explosives if the city was lost – the true face of jihadi paradise.

We passed on this information, not that it made any difference. The big guns kept barking and the street combat was worse than anything I had ever seen. It was a bloodbath. As night began to fall, we retreated through street after street of ruined buildings, an apocalyptic landscape hard to describe. And hard to imagine that it would ever be cleared and rebuilt.

Cano Ali was leading, Dozan in the rear, covering our backs.

'Wait,' he called, and we went to ground.

He removed his helmet and laid down his gun. Dozan had seen a woman in the window of a half-demolished building. She looked back at him for two minutes, three minutes, then removed her veil. The sun had gone down like a diver leaping into a pool. The shadows had thickened. It was dark, just flares of luminescence from the nocturnal gunners.

We picked our way back through the rubble and cleared the debris from around the main entrance. We found clustered inside, behind the door, silent and petrified, two women, one Spanish, the other Syrian, and nine children in rags, flotsam from the outgoing tide of war. We stuffed them into the vehicles and ferried them back to the Kurdish authorities.

Having assumed Sonia was dead, I received a text from her two days later. She had survived the bombing and fled to Deir ez-Zor with her husband and baby on a motorbike. The city, 90 miles south-east of Raqqa, was the temporary refuge of ISIS commanders who had abandoned their men and disappeared along escape routes that had remained open and remarkably efficient in the midst of the advance by Syrian and YPG forces. Dealing with jihadis was like handling a bag of wet eels. You grab one and the rest slip away.

We left immediately for Deir ez-Zor. Military trucks blasted their horns as they approached from the opposite direction and the drivers leaned out from their cabs with clenched fists when they saw our Kurdish flags. The day was cold and dry, with wreaths of grey cloud ringing the mountain tops. I reread Sonia's text and was struck by a flash of déjà vu. Her husband had obviously had it with life in Shangri-la. He was lightly injured and was coming out with her.

En route, Hassan had set up a meeting with the Kurd militia. I joined him in the Pathfinder and we motored a few miles south of Deir ez-Zor through a valley lined with olive groves. We entered tall iron gates and crunched over a pebble drive to a Romanesque villa with white marble pillars and a swimming pool – a reminder that Syria had a wealthy elite before the war. The villa had been commandeered by Kurd General Rekan Qadir. He greeted Hassan with a kiss on both cheeks, then came to attention and nodded formally.

'I am happy to meet you, sir,' he said, and shook my hand.

We sat around a glass-topped table on gilt chairs. Tea with a plate of baklava was served by a flunky in a white jacket with brass buttons. It all seemed terribly English and I felt the sugar rush as I gobbled down the pastries.

When Hassan and the general reverted to Kurdish, I watched their body language. It brought to mind that time when Cano and I met Fahed, the Bedouin patriarch. They weren't chatting, they were negotiating – over what, exactly, I didn't learn until we arrived at the smashed apartment block where Dozan and Cano had set up camp. We had driven through the twilight in a strange silence and I understood why when Hassan summarized the two-part agreement he had reached with General Qadir.

I will start with part two: a group of Assyrian Christians – six women, their children, a priest and several elderly men – were being held hostage in Altun Kupri, a market town 30 miles from Kirkuk. We were going in alone, the four of us, a small commando squad, to take on their ISIS guards and bring them out.

Hassan had always been cautious, particularly with my safety, but had accepted the assignment in order to 'recruit' the general, a high-placed asset he believed would lead to a rich new source of intel. This would include ISIS troop movements as well as the location of jihadi brides and foreign fighters ready to betray Islamic State. Hassan was playing the long game. That was good enough for the rest of us.

Part one was a walk in the park. I had made a provisional arrangement for Sonia Roy to leave at dawn on the motorbike with her family and drive north out of Deir ez-Zor to the YPG lines ten miles distant in the desert, a journey of twenty minutes at 30 mph. The general's militia would be looking out for the lone motorbike and would lend assistance if it was followed.

I confirmed the details with Sonia. We ate rice and beans and shared the bottle of arak the flunky in the brass-buttoned jacket had handed to Hassan as we left the villa. The night had turned icy. I crawled under my blanket on the dusty floor, with the alcohol drumming in my brain and sleep as distant as the stars beyond the frame of the empty window. The mission to Altun Kupri ran through my mind on a loop and I remembered promising Kali that I would never put myself in danger. Then, I thought, closing my eyes, serving men always tell their loved ones what they want to hear.

We joined the YPG unit 30 minutes before sunrise and stood about in the cold mist, blowing warm air into our cupped palms. Cano Ali managed to get through half a packet of cigarettes before I finally got the call from Sonia to say they were leaving. The mist had worked in our favour and we heard the grating sound of the motorcycle long before it came into view.

I was given a few minutes to speak to Sonia before she was taken with her baby to an internment camp. Her husband would be interrogated in jail – then what, I had no idea. We had completed the task. I sent a text to Matt Lambert. He would inform the family Sonia was out.

After the usual round of kissing, we mounted up and motored out of Deir ez-Zor on an empty road with the sun burning off the haze. In the back of the Previa, stored in a foam-lined case, were four M15 white phosphorus smoke grenades made in America, General Qadir's last disquieting gift.

I called Jack Fieldhouse.

'Fancy a day out? Best lamb kebabs you've ever eaten.'

'What's it going to cost me?'

'A minibus and a drive down to Kirkuk.'

'When?'

I glanced at my watch. It was just after eight.

'Four o'clock this afternoon.'

'Text me the coordinates. Do I need to be tooled up?'

'It wouldn't hurt.'

'I may have company.'

'Sounds good. Appreciate it.'

Dozan smiled and turned the radio on low.

'You don't mind?' he said.

'No, mate. I'm beginning to like the sound of zithers. Puts me to sleep.'

I lowered the back of my seat and closed my eyes. Fuck it, we can do this, I thought.

When Jack had said he might have company, I had anticipated Roy Underhill going along for the ride. When we drove into Rajan Ghazi's compound in Kirkuk, the minibus was already parked up and, to my amazement, Jack was there with his wife.

Of course, it made perfect sense. If he needed to be tooled up, it meant someone might get hurt, and Tamara was a nurse. She had left the baby with the Underhills and had dressed with purpose in camouflage pants and a combat jacket. I'd seen Tamara plenty of times standing in the doorway ready to take Jack home from his bar, but it was the first time we had been introduced. She was a small, finely drawn woman with her hair pulled back in a ponytail, good English and watchful eyes that missed nothing.

We squatted in a circle on leather cushions. Rajan was nagged by his wife to help with dinner and he scampered in and out of the kitchen with plates of lamb kebabs on beds of rice. I drank a beer, and remembered our last visit to Kirkuk in October when ISIS guerrillas had made a surprise attack. The jihadis were being pushed back on all fronts and life in Kirkuk, at least, was getting back to normal.

It's not easy to socialize before a mission. The last thing you want to do is talk. It was a relief when the sun slipped behind the hills. It was time to go. We spilled out into the compound. Cano Ali took me in a bear hug.

'Fucking English,' he said.

'Fucking Kurdish,' I replied, and banged the door shut as he climbed into the lead vehicle.

Hassan was expressionless at his side, head wrapped in his *shemagh*. He nodded and allowed a faint smile to cross his lips. The minibus started up. I joined Dozan and the small convoy set off on an empty road.

Darkness came quickly. Dozan hummed. It sounded like air being blown through paper and a comb, irritating, but his way of trying not to think. The landscape was flat, low-build houses, the occasional tree like a lost soul. Kali and Natty slipped through my mind like figures on a screen, or a photograph on a shelf. The adrenaline gushed through me like a wave of broken glass. You are alert, but muddled. Did I check the spare mags? Should I retie my boots? Take a leak? Was the tape secure on the phosphorus grenades? I was nervous, that's a good thing, but unafraid. You become brave when you find something more important than fear.

I opened the window and enjoyed the cold air on my face.

'Are you ready for this?' I said.

'Yes and no,' Dozan replied cryptically.

'Right.'

Incredibly, road signs in English and Arabic stood at junctions. We had arrived. Altun Kupri was a rural town on the banks of the Little Zab. It had a population of 10,000, a mixture of Turkmen, Christians, Kurds and Arabs. Until ISIS came along, they had rubbed along together pretty well for centuries.

The market square and main streets were in ruins. Stretching out into the countryside beyond the centre in all directions was a network of smallholdings crammed with chicken coops, animal sheds, stables and modest houses with corrugated iron roofs. We concealed the vehicles in an untended olive grove. Jack's jaw tightened when we left him behind with Tamara to guard them. Once a Para always a Para.

'Just fucking call if you need me,' he whispered, and we slapped palms.

We set out, evenly spaced, heads covered by *shemaghs* that hid earbuds, a microphone and sensors, devices supplied by the Kurdish militia. We carried AKs, eight spare mags apiece, one phosphate bomb each and, between us, knives, wire cutters and pliers. The track was made up of compacted desert sand with stones laid on the edges, just wide enough for a vehicle. Cano Ali led the way. If there were IEDs, he wasn't going to see them. Dogs picked up our scent and barked, the sound like an old saw on hard wood.

We were three miles from our destination. I hit the same footprints as Hassan in front of me, pounding boots and pounding heart. I felt a heightened level of consciousness. My nose picked out the smell of goats, wood smoke, the ice in the cool air. The shape of the night was vibrant, a black and white photograph, the outlines solid, the stars above speckles of wan ghostly light. My weapon weighed nothing. It was a part of me. When you have trained for combat, your mind and body are in harmony when you go into action. The fear subsides. Death is close and it makes you feel so utterly alive it's addictive. You miss it when you hang up your boots for the last time.

We knew from General Qadir's intel that the Assyrians were being held in a farmhouse with a white water tank on the roof. Outside we would see a half-stripped-out Toyota Camry and a Nissan Navara. When the water tank came into view, we knew we had found the right place. What we did not know was the deployment of their jihadi guards, or how many there were.

It was coming up to midnight. The farmhouse was quiet, without a glimpse of light from inside. Beyond was a smaller house, a dim luminescence around the windows and doors. I took the buds from my ears. I could just make out the murmur of talking, the occasional burst of laughter. The hostages were hungry, beaten down, silent. Their jailers were fed, armed, contented. Why the group of Christians was being held was unclear. The most likely answer was that they would be used as human shields when the jihadis retreated.

We circled the farmhouse seeking booby traps, obstacles, tunnel exits. We covered Hassan as he approached the building. He ran his fingertips over the surface of the door and inspected the site for several minutes before backing away. We withdrew to a low thorn hedge with good sightlines to the two buildings. There was no hurry. People are at their lowest ebb after 2am. The guards would be in deep sleep.

Cano passed me his canteen and I swigged down some water. His eyes were bright and there was a smile on his full lips.

'Jack?' he whispered, and shrugged.

I sent Jack a text. No movement at his end. I stretched out, finger hooked around the trigger on my weapon, my head resting on a flat stone. I watched the constellations on their journeys across the firmament and wondered when I would next take my boat out. The dogs had shut up. We had become a part of the environment.

Hassan roused himself a few minutes before two. He pointed at himself, then at the farmhouse. He led the way. Dozan followed. When they were in position, Cano Ali and I moved to cover the door of the second building. It was the same design as the farmhouse, probably built for a son who had brought a wife into the extended family.

There was a sheet of tin across the front window with a gap big enough for me to see a fan spinning inside. This was odd; it certainly wasn't warm enough to need ventilation. Perhaps it was for the smell? I could make out sleeping bodies – men in black jihadi gear. I reached for the phos grenade. We had taken the precaution of taping the safety pins. I now removed the tape, kept watching through the gap in the tin sheet and waited.

The night was silent, even the wind had dropped. The sound of Hassan breaking through the door of the farmhouse was like a bomb exploding and the jihadis woke with a start. I pulled the pin and posted the grenade through the gap. Cano Ali was watching me. He nodded and we retreated together to the farmhouse. The white light from the phosphorus lit the night and I heard the sound of men screaming in agony.

We continued to cover the second building. One guy, half-dressed, came running out. Cano put him out of his misery with a single shot. It was hard to imagine that anyone had survived the phos grenade, but the explosion and the shot would have roused other sleeping jihadis across the whole of Altun Kupri.

I backed into the farmhouse. Cano Ali remained outside, eyes peeled to his gun sights.

'Call Jack. We need the bus,' Hassan said.

As I did so, he turned back to the people cowering against the far wall, the women and children, half a dozen elderly men with white beards, the priest, another old man wearing a skull cap, a white dog collar on his grey shirt.

Jack answered the phone. 'Follow the track to the farmhouse. Over,' I said.

'Roger that,' he answered and I heard the bus engine start before he hung up.

I spoke to the priest. 'Do you speak English?'

He looked back at me with a quizzical expression. His mouth dropped open. Then he spoke.

'Not very well,' he said.

'Tell them we've come to take them out of here. We are not ISIS.'

It took several seconds for him to compute this. Then he spoke to his flock and appeared to convince them they were safe. They followed Hassan out of the building with their children, their bundles. Dozan now led the way back towards the track we had taken. I remained at the rear with Cano Ali, watching our backs. It was a stroke of luck that the

Assyrians had been kept imprisoned in one building while the militants were bedded down in another.

Our luck didn't last. I could already hear the minibus hammering towards us when shots rang out.

Rounds zipped through the undergrowth and bit into the dirt around our feet. It seemed to be coming from our left flank. Cano Ali went down on one knee and sprayed lead into the darkness. I copied him. Hassan and Dozan remained with the escape party. They had left the track and hurried along the side, not that the scrub gave them much protection.

Three figures in black like ninjas with heads wrapped appeared from the undergrowth and Cano emptied his mag on them.

'Out,' he called, and reloaded.

We withdrew towards the rest of our party. The minibus had arrived and Jack was awkwardly trying to turn it about. Talk about a three-point turn. He had to make a 73-point turn, the rear wheels skidding and sliding in the soft sand outside the track.

Sporadic bursts of gunfire came in from the right. The people scrambled onto the bus and Hassan made them stretch out on the floor. One of the babies started screaming. It was like a chorus as the others joined in. Vehicles are bullet magnets. Jack had taken the precaution of covering the engine area with a Hesco blanket, but the sound of rounds chinking into the metal sides was a warning signal. Time to go.

Hassan and Dozan were on board. They had smashed out a right-side window and were pouring rounds into the darkness. Cano Ali was down on one knee again, taking single shots in the direction of the muzzle flash. The bus was going.

'Come on you fat bastard, time to go,' I yelled.

'Go, go,' Cano yelled back.

I jumped on board and remained in the open door as the bus gathered speed. Cano emptied every shell from his mag, then ran to catch up.

'Faster, faster. Come on.'

He was grinning. His *shemagh* had fallen off. His head was shiny in the moonlight. He reached out and I grabbed his hand. I felt a wave of relief and heard a burst of gunshots at the same time. Rounds zipped up his right leg and drilled into his bulletproof vest. One shot found its way into the back of his neck.

I dragged him inside. Jack put his foot down.

'Tamara,' I called.

She was already picking her way over the prone bodies with her medical bag. She unsnapped Cano's vest. It was already too late. There was blood everywhere. I gripped his hand.

'Hold on, mate, hold on,' I repeated.

His eyes came into focus. Cano Ali smiled for the last time.

'Good Englishman,' he said, and his eyes closed.

Postscript

Dressed in a black turban and robes, Abu Bakr al-Baghdadi declared the birth of the Islamic Caliphate from the marble pulpit at the Great Mosque of al-Nuri in Mosul on 5 July 2014. It was the first and only time the self-anointed 'Caliph Ibrahim' appeared in public. His call to 'make jihad for Allah' resonated across the Muslim world.

Three years later, on 21 June 2017, after nine months fighting street by street, the Iraqi army surrounded the mosque, an iconic landmark built in the 12th century and famous for its leaning minaret, where the black flag of Islamic State was still flying. The general leading the assault had the good sense not to let his troops enter. ISIS had laid hundreds of kilos of explosives. They were ignited moments before the last fighters fled and the building was destroyed beyond all repair. The battle for Mosul was over.

Abu Bakr al-Baghdadi had long since escaped. His whereabouts remains unknown. Two recordings – believed to be of Baghdadi but not confirmed – have since been released urging the jihadi faithful to continue the struggle. The last message was delivered on 23 August 2018.

The fighting continued in Raqqa until Tuesday 17 October, when Kurdish YPG forces drove ISIS out of their last strongholds – a sports stadium and a hospital turned into a fortress. The Caliphate had fallen. Like the phoenix, or a disease, I have no doubt it will rise again – not in one hundred years, it is rising now in North Africa, sub-Saharan Africa, Afghanistan and Asia.

After our mission to Altun Kupri, we made several more sorties into Raqqa and extracted numerous Syrian refugees and several European women and their children.

Those last months were the most bloody. ISIS recruits knew the end was near. They were ready for martyrdom. I read an account of the speech by General Raymond Thomas at the Aspen Security Forum when he quoted the number of jihadi fighters eradicated. The head of US Special Operations Command told delegates: 'We have killed, in conservative estimates, sixty thousand to seventy thousand. They declared an army, they put it on the battlefield, and we went to war with it.'

My daughter started at her new boarding school close to Oxford. We stayed with Matt Lambert while she was settling in. Thanks to Matt, the work we do has been recognized and supported by charities and NGOs.

In January 2018, we were invited to Brussels to attend a conference of non-governmental organizations. We were asked to assist in bringing out the many hundreds of young European women and their children still caught up in the sprawling, dangerous, rat-infested refugee camps stretching for miles along the Turkish-Syrian border.

De-radicalization programmes are in place. My job now is to find those women and bring them to the attention of the European authorities. Visiting the camps is heart-breaking. Food provisions supplied by the United Nations are managed by Turkish guards who demand sex from the young women in exchange for their rations – 'prostitutes for food', as one of the German jihadi brides once said. There was a time when I would have broken a few jaws, and sometimes I regret that time has passed.

I meet up with Hassan Ghazi and Dozan Rostami whenever I am in Erbil. We go to bistros, listen to folk music – truth be told, I still prefer Blondie and Fleetwood Mac. We raise a glass or two of arak. We will never get over the death of Cano Ali.

Hassan, after the visit of UN Secretary-General António Guterres to Erbil, gave up his AK-47 for the world of diplomacy and works on the security team for President Barzani. Dozan Rostami is doing something he said he would never do. He completed retraining and is now a commercial airline pilot. His wife is happy.

Oliver at MI6 was as good as his word. I am no longer stopped when I arrive in Britain.

In January 2018, I also met up with Diana Abbasi in London. She had undertaken the government Prevent course and now works as a counsellor for the programme. She wasn't wearing a headscarf and she did not marry her cousin from the Hunza Valley. She was free. The same applied to Laura Angela Hansen. After nine months of court cases, she was finally found not guilty of terrorist offences and has begun a new life.

*

It was Matt Lambert who suggested turning my notes into a book. I sent an email to the literary agent Andrew Lownie. He recommended that Clifford Thurlow write it with me. This is my story. Some of the names have been changed to protect the innocent. The guilty are dead or have fled to make jihad in Africa. It will never end.

ACKNOWLEDGEMENTS

We are extremely grateful to the masterful literary agent Andrew Lownie for putting us together. Writing *Operation Jihadi Bride* has been a meeting of the minds and the beginning of what will be a lifetime friendship.

Many thanks to Jake Lingwood and his team at Monoray – Sophie Elletson, Karen Baker, Hazel O'Brien. And finally to Iris Gioia for her keen eye for errors and repeats in the manuscript.

There are many others who have contributed in all manner of ways to the writing of this book. They know who they are and we appreciate their desire for anonymity.

RESOURCES

The resource list below is for those who are lost or in need of protection, for those who have changed their minds and want to come home.

It is to those people that the book is dedicated.

Let's Talk About It – What is Prevent?
Prevent – also known as Let's Talk About It – is an integral part of the UK Government's Counter Terrorism Strategy known as CONTEST. Prevent provides practical help and guidance to the public in order to stop people becoming terrorists or supporting terrorism. It also aims to identify vulnerable people and intervene in their lives before they become terrorists. In 2018, 7,318 people were referred to the programme.

Another essential part of Prevent is Desistance and Disengagement, that is the de-radicalization and rehabilitation of people already convicted of terror offences and those returning from conflict zones. Its principal approach is learning why someone was drawn to violent extremism, then redirecting these motivations to create a more positive future. The website provides a wide range of resources.

Police Hotline: 0800 789 321
https://www.ltai.info

Lost Now
Supported by John Carney, this UK charity is dedicated to bringing

missing children and adults back together with their families.
Email: info@lostnow.org / volunteer@lostnow.org
www.lostnow.org

Government E-Learning Training on Prevent

Government-sponsored introductory site on deradicalization for Islamist and far-right extremism.
https://www.elearning.prevent.homeoffice.gov.uk/edu/screen1.html

ACT – Action Counter Terrorism

Report suspicious activity by contacting the police in confidence on 0800 789 321 or dial 999.
https://act.campaign.gov.uk

Counterextremism.org

Managed for the Home Office by the Institute for Strategic Dialogue, counterextremism.org – in collaboration with local authorities, the police and statutory partners, such as the education sector, social services, offender management services and children's and youth services – supports those at risk of being drawn into violent extremism. It has three objectives: to identify individuals at risk; to assess the nature and extent of that risk; and to develop the most appropriate support for the individuals concerned.
https://www.counterextremism.org/resources/details/id/115/channel-process

BOOKS

Deradicalization Programmes: Introductory Guide, Centre for Research and Evidence on Security Threats, 2019

Sarah Marsden's introduction to deradicalization programmes sets out the types of interventions in operation, the methods they use, and how to evaluate their effects. Free to download at: https://crestresearch.ac.uk/resources/deradicalisation-programmes-introductory-guide/

Deradicalization in the UK Prevent Strategy: Security, Identity and Religion,
M. S. Elshimi, Routledge 2017

The Age of Jihad: Islamic State and the Great War for the Middle East,
Patrick Cockburn, Verso 2016
Patrick Cockburn's acclaimed eyewitness to history.